Routledge Revivals

The Collective Spirit

The Collective Spirit (1925) lays down a rough outline of what science can tell us as to the progress of evolution, and criticises the various interpretations, before endeavouring to formulate an idealist theory of evolution.

The Collective Spirit
An Idealistic Theory of Evolution

Viggo Cavling

First published in 1925
by Methuen & Co. Ltd.

This edition first published in 2025 by Routledge
4 Park Square, Milton Park, Abingdon, Oxon, OX14 4RN

and by Routledge
605 Third Avenue, New York, NY 10017

Routledge is an imprint of the Taylor & Francis Group, an informa business

All rights reserved. No part of this book may be reprinted or reproduced or utilised in any form or by any electronic, mechanical, or other means, now known or hereafter invented, including photocopying and recording, or in any information storage or retrieval system, without permission in writing from the publishers.

Publisher's Note
The publisher has gone to great lengths to ensure the quality of this reprint but points out that some imperfections in the original copies may be apparent.

Disclaimer
The publisher has made every effort to trace copyright holders and welcomes correspondence from those they have been unable to contact.

A Library of Congress record exists under LCCN 26013947

ISBN: 978-1-032-93766-3 (hbk)
ISBN: 978-1-003-56756-1 (ebk)
ISBN: 978-1-032-93769-4 (pbk)

Book DOI 10.4324/9781003567561

THE
COLLECTIVE SPIRIT

AN IDEALISTIC THEORY OF EVOLUTION

BY

VIGGO CAVLING

TRANSLATED FROM THE DANISH BY

W. WORSTER, M.A.

METHUEN & CO. LTD.
36 ESSEX STREET W.C.
LONDON

First Published in 1925

PRINTED IN GREAT BRITAIN

NOTE TO THE ENGLISH EDITION

The Collective Spirit (Fællesaanden) was first published in Danish in 1924. The present translation has been approved by the author.

CONTENTS

	PAGE
RELIGION, SCIENCE AND EVOLUTION	1
THE PROGRESS OF EVOLUTION	10
THE MECHANISTIC THEORY OF EVOLUTION (DARWINISM)	22
THE VITALISTIC THEORY OF EVOLUTION	33
THE IDEALISTIC THEORY OF EVOLUTION	47
THE CREATIVE POWER	67
NATURE'S AIM	102
THE COLLECTIVE SPIRIT	116
IDEALISING OR REFINING ACTIVITY	160
ETHICS, ART AND SCIENCE	193
CRITICAL OBSERVATIONS ON THE IDEALISTIC THEORY OF EVOLUTION	220
INDEX	239

THE COLLECTIVE SPIRIT

RELIGION, SCIENCE AND EVOLUTION

> Man finds it as easy to cease from existence as to cease from philosophising.
> *Posidonius.*

READER, have you never chanced to wake in the night and suddenly, in the silence, fall to wondering, wondering at the great mystery of yourself, a thinking being, lying there in bed like a little world all to yourself? Why are you there at all; to what end were you born? What is the sense of it all, the house you live in, the people sleeping there, the city, the country surrounding you, the whole of this mighty planet where millions of similar beings breathe and think and work? Your thought turns from your own little world out over the earth, seeks back into the past, and tries to penetrate into the future. What can be the meaning of it all, this gigantic struggle, in which you are permitted to take part for a moment, only to be wiped out and forgotten directly after? What is it that keeps the whole together—where have you come from, and whither are you bound?

It is in such a moment that philosophical reflection is born. Surely there must be some meaning in existence, some plan uniting all these milliards of apparently chaotic and conflicting units? This question, which in the light of day is often set aside, may suddenly thrust itself upon us with a painful, merciless insistence. And if you have not, then, the faith of your childhood to hold by and content you—what then?

Many will say it is futile to occupy oneself with metaphysics. Is it possible to find any explanation of the universe at all? Have we not sufficient proof that it is impossible, in the collapse of the great philosophical systems of the past? From time to time some great thinker appears, offering some " system " that claims to solve all riddles, so that the sphinx can fling itself into the abyss for lack of further mysteries to brood over. All such, however, have met with a sorry fate. Critical examination soon makes an end of all fair dreams. Has not philosophical science realised this, and long since given up such foolishness? One thing at least is certain; no philosophy will ever be able to solve the profoundest mystery of existence; the question, why this universe of ours, with its myriads of suns and spheres, its mechanical and living forces, should exist rather than not exist. What then is the good of philosophy? Is it not best to follow the agnostic, and plant cabbages in one's garden? And, as regards the profoundest problems of life, to adopt the attitude of an onlooker, aloof, unmoved, leaving religion to serve the needs of the masses? This is the attitude of science—it is the scepticism of Hume, Kant and Voltaire, applied to life itself.

Goethe's question: *ob die Natur zuletzt sich doch ergründe* must be answered in the negative. If the great poet and philosopher of Weimar, gifted with the deepest insight into all things human, sought in vain to fuse the results of science and art into one by his crystal-clear reflection and ardent feeling, what can we hope to attain?

And yet . . . ! The spirit of man will never be content to give up the attempt. There will always be some who call on us to open our eyes and seek for clarity, unity, coherence, for a self-consistent view of life and the universe.

There are some who now consider that we cannot in the long run make do with two views of life; a scientific scepticism for the educated and a primitive religion based on myth and revelation for the uneducated souls. Would it not be worth while to subject both these views to a revision?

But has religion, then, no vitality? Undoubtedly it has, despite its conception of the universe, contrary to the results of science, despite its own contradictions and plainly irrational features.

This vitality is due to the fact that religion answers to one particular side of our nature which science up to now has disregarded, that of feeling. Science aims at being impartial, weighing and measuring, observing from without; seeks as far as possible to express all phenomena in terms of quantity, and only endeavours to bring about a purely external coherence by means of the law of causality.

Human feeling, however, protests against this chilly attitude. We *feel* that life is more than this. There are instincts at work within us, which in their higher stages reveal themselves as ideals. Phenomena such as love, conscience, remorse, the joy of liberty, artistic enthusiasm and the longing for immortality are altogether unscientific; yet they are nevertheless the most far-reaching and deep-rooted forces we know, the forces that urge us on.

In regard to all this vitally important side of our being, science and empirical philosophy have nothing to say. Consequently, science has not up to now been able to offer mankind any substitute for religion. All it did was to make vague attempts at filling the void that would arise if men should relinquish faith.

With the spread of enlightenment, more and more have come to realise that the religions of the world are mythical, largely interwoven with ancient mysticism and naïve mediæval ideas. The comparative history of religion, working on an enormous mass of material from different sources, has shown that there exists a close connection between widely different religions, each claiming to be sole bearer of truth based on revelation. The Bible in particular has been thus dealt with, and it has now been demonstrated beyond question that great parts, and these, moreover, the most important, both of the Old and the New Testament, are not of Jewish or Christian origin at all, but can be traced back to the culture of earlier peoples, who in turn may possibly have had them from older sources still. Religions have undergone a process of evolution, like languages and culture generally and everything else on earth. And on closer examination, we find that their character has been greatly influenced by the changing fortunes of their devotees; so much so indeed, that the more we study them, the more distinctly "human" they appear, as regards their origins, and the splendour of the "revelations" on which they are said to be founded dwindles disquietingly under our scrutiny.

The whole natural science of modern times: physics and chemistry, astronomy, biology and the theory of evolution itself have ranged themselves against the teaching of the Church. Men like Copernicus, Galilei, Giordano Bruno, Bacon, Hume, Spinoza, Kant, Goethe, Darwin, Karl Marx and Nietzsche have been forward in the assault upon revealed religions; and have, with other independent spirits, encountered the most violent opposition accordingly, on the part of the Church. All were declared heretics, some forced to renounce their teaching by the Inquisition, others burned at the stake.

The Church as a whole has maintained its position. Some few advanced posts have been surrendered, but that is all. A Scandinavian writer, Dr. Sigurd Ibsen, has called attention to this powerlessness of science. He points out that several notable scientific truths are, even to this day, only accepted by ordinary people as "knowledge," without penetrating to their deeper consciousness.

"And this I venture to assert," (he writes) "applies to just those truths which are of the most far-reaching theoretical importance, the great discoveries associated with the names of Copernicus and Darwin. The earth flung out from its position as the centre of the universe, mankind deprived of its divine patent of nobility: no such dislocation of ideas has ever been seen before, for it touches the very foundations of our existence. Imagine a monarch, inspired with the highest ideas of his exalted birth and calling, faced with the discovery that he is but a changeling, the son of a common labourer: what a revolution must then take place in his mind! How then can it be that so enormous an alteration as that which science has brought about in our conception of the earth's place in the universe and the position of humanity itself in our planetary life, has not affected our whole fundamental attitude, and forced the race to reckon with an altogether new system of values? For none will venture to maintain that our view of life has been darkened, our self-esteem lowered, in comparison with those of generations that believed the earth to be the centre of the world, and man created in God's image. There can be but one explanation : we have accepted these results of scientific research in a purely intellectual fashion, as part of the sum of our knowledge, but they have not penetrated down to our feeling ; our motives, aims, our innermost ego, remain unchanged."

Science, despite all its victories, has not succeeded in shaking the position of religion. And why ?

The reason can only be, that science, in the field of religion and ethics, has been for the most part so busy with its destructive operations that it has not troubled to offer us any positive programme of life, such as our feelings demand, in place of the old. True, some few attempts in this direction have been made, as for instance by Goethe, Hegel, Schopenhauer, Nietzsche and Karl Marx. But Goethe's work was, after all, poetry, not a philosophy to live by; Hegel lost himself in dialectic vapourings; Schopenhauer clothed his teaching in a garb of pessimism that rendered it repulsive; while Nietzsche's system of separate moral codes for Master and Slave, with the glorification of the " Will to Power " as the supreme vital factor, was suited only to the few. The only one of these systems which has really proved of any great importance in actual life is Marxism ; and this, as a substitute for religion, is accepted only by the extreme communist section of the social-democratic party, that is to say, by a minority. Certainly it has not demonstrated its practical vitality as yet, and is hardly likely to do so, seeing that its origin is political rather than ethical.

The fact is, that the modern philosophers on their new natural science platform drawn up to oppose the Church, have not succeeded in giving humanity a theory of life with enough of the pure element in its composition to balance the appeal of revealed religion to our intellect and feeling. Consequently, the philosophers have not become what they should be in our enlightened age : the true spiritual leaders of the people. They have landed in a barren, renunciatory scepticism and almost fatalistic determinism ; they have collected a mass of psychological material, but have been unable to utilise it in practical ways except in the field of psycho technics ; and they are often apt to lose themselves in futile struggles with the theory of knowledge which ordinary people other than philosophers cannot and do not care to follow. And so we get the present remarkable state of things, in which the mechanists consider they have long since made an end of all religion, while the banner of the Church still waves aloft unscathed, never lowered, as it were nailed to the mast.

The question then naturally arises : how are we to get out of this deadlock ? Should it not be possible, on the basis of modern scientific results, to work out a theory of life combining the truths of natural science with that portion of religion and morality which is of positive value to life ? Why surrender the field to spiritists and theosophists, Christian Scientists and other obscurantists who find, in the present transitional stage between religion and science, an opportunity for themselves ?

One of the few who ever realised that science should put forward a programme of life in addition to its critical work, was the Danish writer Ludvig Feilberg. He pointed to the theory of *evolution*, and said : let us listen to the voice of Nature, and see if it be not possible to create, by proper interpretation, a theory of life to supersede these dogmas.—It was the conception of a genius. Feilberg was the first to realise that the theory of evolution is the neutral ground on which parties from the opposite camps can meet. If anything but religion can ever tell us what is the meaning of existence, what is the goal toward which life moves, and how we should proceed to bring ourselves into tune with Nature, it must be evolution.

The great philosophical authorities of the past, from Plato and Aristotle to Leibniz, Spinoza, Kant and Hegel, lived their lives in ignorance of this fundamental theory, which must revolutionise our views in all main points. The theory of evolution offers us an entirely new and invaluable means of building up a view of life, a theory of life not hovering in thin air or flimsily anchored upon myth and revelation, but firmly based upon the rock of Nature itself.

Philosophically speaking, we have still only taken the first

RELIGION, SCIENCE AND EVOLUTION

rough measures of the theory of evolution ; indeed, philosophers until Feilberg had mostly misinterpreted it themselves, by reading it, that is, from one particular point of view. That the theory of evolution has not become more widely known and of greater effect than is actually the case—it is over a hundred years old now—is doubtless due to the fact that it got itself mixed up with politics almost from the start. And especially since the Darwinists—or a certain class of Darwinists—were smart enough to grab the idea and transform it according to the needs of a mechanical view, the theory of evolution has been shut up in a prison where it is badly off for air. Darwinists like Huxley, Haeckel, Gunther and Nietzsche have, by their fanaticism, done more harm than good, and it is only of late years, since the Neo-vitalists began to criticise this one-sided view of evolution, that the theory itself has been able to lift its head and breathe again. Before, it was near being suffocated in the affectionate embraces of its " friends."

Ludvig Feilberg led the way in Denmark. He was one of the first to realise the full consequences of the theory of evolution by applying it to intellectual life. Feilberg sees man not as a casual whim of Nature, but as a calculated factor, purposely set in a definite place in the evolutionary process, with a task that must not be shirked at any price. Man is a spiritual transformer of energy. He receives from Nature a certain value in the form of food, light, heat and sense-impressions, and this he has to give out again, by means of work and effort, in a richer and refined, that is to say, in a spiritual, form. Evolution, through its various phases, teaches us a definite lesson, namely, that it is only when we serve higher powers than our little narrow selves ; only then are we worthy to live. Otherwise, we can only fumble blindly and miserably about in " spiritual meanness," and when we die, sink back into the earth again without having made any positive contribution to the economy of Nature. Evolution, again, teaches us further that life is ever fighting its way forward to higher and higher degrees of perfection ; and this should give us courage to make an effort ourselves. Feilberg was able to extract an essence from the teaching of Nature which he call *absolute value*, or *nature value*. Such values must be above all human criticism, simply because they are the dictates of Nature, and must be acknowledged and respected accordingly by all, by the scientists and the adherents of revealed religion alike. And in this manner he laid the foundations of an idealistic theory of evolution which we shall endeavour in the following pages to set forth and explain.

The starting-point of the philosopher, with no divine revelation to fall back upon, must necessarily be something purely and generally human. But while people generally think lengthwise, the philosopher has to think crosswise as well.

The purpose of this book is to interpret evolution, not from the specially scientific, but from the philosophical point of view. Great parts of the history of evolution still remain shrouded in mist and enveloped in semi-darkness; it must be left to the particular sciences to procure for us a thorough knowledge of the details; we have, indeed, our physicists, astronomers, geologists, biologists and sociologists for the purpose. And these are by no means agreed as to the progress of evolution up to now, and especially, as to its real cause; but all are fortunately of one mind in that an evolution has taken place. We can, for instance, by means of fossils, trace the different forms of existence from the highly complicated structures of the present day, back to primitive, ultramicroscopic parent forms, and farther back still to geological periods when life had hardly yet managed to assume organic form at all. The demonstration of this process of development must, we think, mark an era in the history of philosophy, as it has done in that of natural science. A new foundation is here created, a new light thrown on life itself.

True, not even evolution can afford any metaphysical explanation of why the world exists at all; or why there is such a thing as evolution. But in regard to other important problems, as the trend of this gradual ascent, and man's position in the same, man's future, and finally, how it is that our reason, comprehending a part of the world, yet understands it only incompletely, relatively, conditionally—in regard to all this, and a great deal more besides, evolution can tell us something, and it is therefore worth our while to consider it a little.

Our present programme, then, is as follows :

Having first laid down a rough outline of what science can tell us at present as to the progress of evolution, we will go through, and criticise briefly the various interpretations of evolution, laying particular stress on Feilberg's view, as that which, to our mind, points forward into the future.

On the basis thus given, we will endeavour further to formulate an idealistic theory of evolution. Here, perhaps, we may outstrip the conclusions of our master ; nevertheless, we believe that we shall not be going so far but that his *manes* would at least approve our endeavour.

Feilberg himself, it is true, does not directly mention *The Collective Spirit*. But when he says that conscience, for instance, is hardly a mere product of digestion, liver and lungs and education ; when he speaks of how we can take part in the great circulation of Nature by spiritual concentration, and how it is our duty to develop and pass on spiritual values, how we are taxpayers and purveyors to such a degree that hardly anything is left for ourselves ; when, again, he asserts that human beings at every moment of life are sending forth little ants'-eggs of thought out into the depths of the physical universe, whence perhaps in some mysterious way they will return if we but hold our " spiritual window " open—then, it seems to us, that he has also anticipated the idea of the Collective Spirit. And when he goes on to describe youth, looking out so hopefully upon existence that things themselves appear to shine in that projected light—then, we cannot but think that he has given us the key of that idealist philosophy which we now put before our readers. It is a difficult task, and one we should not have ventured to undertake had it not been for his friendly and fatherly guidance.

THE PROGRESS OF EVOLUTION

> The sequence of evolution of the earth, and that of its inhabitants, are closely related throughout.—*Lamarck*.

IN all branches of science it has at last, after much hesitation and opposition, been agreed that the planet on which we were born, with its mountains and plains, its gardens and ice-fields, its green fringe of vegetation and its multitude of animals and human races only gradually assumed the form in which it now appears. Something has taken place which we call *evolution*.

Science further teaches us that evolution is not an idea applicable only to this planet of ours. It applies to the entire solar system of which we form a part; and as this again is but a portion of the universe beyond, we may conclude that the farther fixed stars are also subject to evolution. We can, indeed, in our spectroscopes, follow the course of this evolution at different stages from new white stars of very high temperature to the older, yellow and red stars whose temperature is lower and more like that of our sun.

How matters may have progressed on other stars we cannot say, but as regards our own earth, we can follow the progress of evolution, roughly speaking, from the time when our planet was but a portion of a glowing nebula, until it attained independent existence like that of the other planets, cooled down, and formed a crust, in the fissures of which, in the sea and on the land, it gave birth to plants and animals of increasingly complex structure, until Man arrived on the scene, and crowned the whole work by taking a pen and setting out to describe what had taken place.

We say, roughly speaking. Unfortunately, it is but very roughly speaking that we can trace this process of evolution; for there are still so many gaps in our knowledge that the

THE PROGRESS OF EVOLUTION

theory must be said to be still but loosely put together. Steady work in the fields of physics, astronomy, geology and biology, however, is always filling up these gaps, and our knowledge to-day is greater, and rests on more solid foundations, than ever before.

Carved from the rock on which the Acropolis stands we may still see the ancient theatre where the poets of a past age gave utterance to the most beautiful sentiments, the keenest wit, the most penetrating psychological insight. The theatre was framed in an architecture and decorated with a sculpture never since surpassed. Centuries before the birth of Christ, mankind had attained so high a degree of culture that in certain respects it was, so to speak, nearing its culmination. At the same time, humanity was far behind in other respects, especially as regards natural science. Anaxagoras believed that the sun was not much bigger than the Peloponnese—and Aristotle died of vexation at finding himself unable to explain the phenomenon of the tides.

The ancient Greeks, cultured as they were in other matters, had a very primitive conception of the world. They placed the earth in the centre of the universe, surrounded by seven or eight " heavens," with a heaven of crystal outside, enclosing all the rest as in a cheese dish.

It was not until the Renaissance, with Copernicus, Galilei and Giordano Bruno leading up to Newton, that the conception of the world was formed which has prevailed until our own day; the world as an infinite universe filled with ice-cold ether, in which floated, miles apart, small pin-heads of glowing matter, suns, occasionally surrounded by dark satellites, held in their places by the law of attraction which regulates the celestial mechanism. True, certain changes do take place in this universe; a whirling nebula develops into a solar system, which, after the lapse of milliards of years, is again extinguished. But these are only superficial, not real changes. The sum of energy remains the same. Infinity extends on all sides; the universe has always existed and will never cease to exist; it is a piece of clockwork wound up once and for all; the world is endless and eternal.

This was the view that prevailed until recently. Now, however, we have entered on a new period in natural science, characterised by Einstein, Rutherford and Bohr. The view of the universe presented to us now is different from that of Newton's day, easier of comprehension in some respects, more difficult in others.

We have no difficulty in following Einstein and his disciples when they assert that the universe is finite. The finite is something we can understand at once, whereas infinity is foreign to all our natural habits of thought. According to the Einstein school, the universe is a field of force having a definite extent, containing between two and three milliards of stars and a great number of nebulæ at different stages of development. This universe is 100 million light-years in circumference, and it weighs ten septillions of pounds. The whole forms a planet-shaped sphere, and outside it is— nothing. Neither air, light, electricity, force of gravity nor sound. In this spherical universe there is no such thing as up or down, north or south. There is no common time valid for the whole, but only a system of various local times in the different regions, according as they are in motion or at rest relatively to one another.

That is the modern scientific view of the universe as a whole. But there is also a corresponding world in little, the world of electrons, as investigated by Sir Ernest Rutherford and several other English and American physicists, in Denmark by Niels Bohr. According to the modern atomists, each atom consists of a small positive electric nucleus and some still smaller particles, the so-called electrons, which are charged with negative electricity and race about the nucleus at an enormous rate of speed, like planets about the sun. In all substances we find these forces in motion; only when the temperature falls to 273 degrees below zero Centigrade does the movement cease, and the substance is then "dead." If some of the electrons be removed, this has the remarkable effect of changing the element itself into something else. Radium is an instance of an element in process of natural transformation; some of its elements are being continually thrown off, and in course of time the substance itself turns

THE PROGRESS OF EVOLUTION 13

into lead. Of the ninety odd elements known, all have the same atom nucleus, but the number of electrons surrounding it differs, and it is this which gives rise to the difference between one substance and another. On closer investigation, then, matter is found to be electric energy, and the atomic forces operating in different forms of matter seem to be closely related to natural forces such as magnetism, light, heat, attraction, etc.

In one respect, the modern atomic theory has already been of importance to the theory of evolution, in that it shows that matter is not as imperishable as was formerly supposed. Lavoisier's principle as to the constancy of matter is shaken. If elements can be altered by the removal of one or more electrons, it is reasonable to suppose that we could, by continuing to remove the electrons, get down to a substance which would not be matter at all in the accepted sense of the word, but a kind of preparatory stage towards matter; i.e. matter not yet charged with energy. It is possible that the mysterious light-ether, which is supposed to fill the space between the stars, may be some such raw material of matter, which only becomes true matter when the requisite energy is added, e.g. by an increase in temperature. It is not only possible, but seems likely, that in the gaseous nebulæ which we observe out in the universe, the initial stages in the formation of matter are taking place, the product being later, by the addition of new energy, formed into matter of increasingly complex character, with high atomic weight, that is to say, consisting of atoms whose positive nucleus is surrounded by a great number of electrons. It is important to note that radioactive substances—i.e. those which give off some of their electrons—are just the ones with the highest atomic weight, as for instance uranium and radium. These elements, however, are not represented in the gaseous nebulæ in which solar systems are being formed; here, on the other hand, we find substances with low atomic weight, such as hydrogen and helium. Plainly then, the forms of matter have gone through a process of evolution like everything else, until, at the upper end of the scale, we get elements with so high an atomic weight that they are literally overflowing.

It is of importance here to point out that all natural phenomena are manifestations of one and the same energy at different stages. The elements are the most stable form of the energy enclosed in atoms. Heat, light, electricity are less stable forms of the same energy, which is liberated when the internal atomic equilibrium is disturbed.

The spectroscope of the atomists then gives us, as it were, a glimpse of evolution at its very earliest stage; we can almost follow the process by which matter itself is formed.

It is interesting also to note that the formation of matter can, apparently, only be continued up to a certain point. As soon as the substance has attained a high atomic weight, the charge of energy goes no further, and if development is to proceed at all, it cannot do so by crowding more electrons round the nucleus, but has recourse to another method. Atoms of different weights unite, and form a new unit, the molecule. Molecules again unite in similar fashion, forming crystals and colloids, and it is by combination of these that we ultimately arrive at the products characteristic of the highest forms of life.

The atom, then, with its varying complement of electrons, from 1 to 92, is the first result of the physical process of creation. These atoms enter into combination with one another according to definite rules, and thus form the next stage of development, the molecule. The molecule consists of a certain number of atoms of different kinds—a molecule of water, for instance, consists of two atoms of hydrogen combined with one of oxygen. And since there are about a hundred different kinds of atoms, we can get a great number of different combinations. Some molecules show great mutual affinity, and unite in peculiar molecule families or groups, as in the crystals and colloids. The colloids become the seat of bio-chemical activity; it is in colloidal structures that life was first developed, and the colloids can therefore be regarded as a transition stage between the inorganic world and the organic. The marvellous processes which take place in cells are due to the interaction between crystals and colloids.

The Indian biologist, Bose of Calcutta, in particular has

shown that the transition from dead to living matter is less sharply defined than was formerly supposed. Bose has made a series of experiments with inorganic substances and shown that they often react in a manner similar to that of the organic forms. Metal, for instance, gets " tired " after use, just as living tissue does. Dead Nature reacts in response to stimuli to such a degree that one may at times feel tempted to credit it with feeling. We realise that there is really no unfathomable gulf between the dead and the living state, but that the transition may well have taken place. We find in the inorganic world processes very similar to some in the organic world, save that they take place at a lower stage of development.

There is no very cogent reason then, to believe, with Lord Kelvin and Helmholtz, that life must have come to this planet from other parts of the universe, enclosed in meteorites; or to resort to the even more fantastic theory of Svante Arrhenius, that life-spores are found in the cosmic dust of space and scattered about among the spheres by the pressure of rays. Such theories were also condemned by Prof. Schafer at the Annual Meeting of the British Association in 1912.

It seems more natural to suppose that there were forces at work in " dead " Nature itself, so that life came into existence on this planet by a natural process, forming first of all the inorganic colloids and then, with the aid of sunlight, organic colloids which are the raw material of life. Not until a far later period did the cells with protoplasm arise. These cells are the bricks of which organic structures are formed. Cell is added to cell—the human body alone contains more cells than there are human beings on the earth—and these cells are more closely united, and co-operate in finer harmony than the individuals in the best organised human society. If we regard only the final product, it seems a marvel, but on tracing the process step by step as far as we are able at present, we realise how it has grown by a succession of almost imperceptible additions. Even with the limited scientific material now at our disposal, we can dimly perceive the connection between the highest forms of life and the less complex forces operating at the time when life had not yet appeared.

How old our planet is we cannot say. Kelvin, in 1867, estimated the age of the earth at 25 million years; the discovery of uranium and radioactivity, however, has upset this calculation. The earth must have taken a much longer time to cool, and we now reckon generally with an age of 1000 million years.

Man has only lived on earth for a very small fraction of this time. If we put the age of the earth as equivalent to twenty-four hours, it would give us only a few seconds at the outside for the period of our sojourn up to now. We must, then, consider ourselves new-comers.

The succession of geological periods, both before and after the arrival of life on earth, would take too long to give in detail here. We know that the map of the world shows great differences at the different periods, with glacial and tropical phases alternating; Greenland, for instance, was once rich in tropical growths.

As regards the history of life itself on our planet, the relationship between the different species of animals and plants was observed even by Linnæus. It is only the theory of evolution, however, which has shown us that such relationship exists between all forms of life on earth, since all are derived from a common ancestral form.

In the two great groups, the animal and vegetable kingdom, if taken separately, we can point out transitions between most of the larger and smaller subdivisions; and at the lowest as well as at the highest stages, representatives of both kingdoms meet in common external and internal features respectively.

Sometimes, also, it might seem as if evolution had taken place from several different starting-points, inasmuch as we find parallel lines differing greatly one from another; some authorities nevertheless assume that there can only have been one original form to begin with, a creature of the simplest possible structure that serves as the mother organism for all living things.

In the vegetable kingdom it is believed that we can trace a natural development with fairly gradual stages from algæ and sponges via the mosses, ferns, horse-tails, club-mosses, to

THE PROGRESS OF EVOLUTION

the gymnosperms and flowering plants; and in the animal kingdom similarly from the protozoa via corals, echinoderms, worms, articulates and molluscs to the vertebrates. And within these larger groups again we can trace the process further, as for instance, among the vertebrates, from fishes to toads and reptiles, and thence in two lines of development, one leading to the birds, one to the mammals, with man as the latest sub-order among these last.

The course of evolution itself has been illustrated in an interesting manner by Bergson. He believes that the efforts of the animal kingdom were probably first directed towards the formation of very simple organisms, which were, however, capable of a certain degree of movement, and in particular, so indefinite as to shape that they could adapt themselves to all future needs. These organisms may have been rather like our worms, though the worms of the present day are exhausted and stiff degenerates from the infinitely plastic forms which had an unlimited future before them, and were the ancestors of echinoderms, molluscs, articulates and vertebrates.

They were exposed, however, to a danger that doubtless came near to exterminating animal life at the outset. When we glance at the fauna of geological antiquity, there is one peculiarity we cannot fail to remark. We notice that the animal was enclosed in a more or less hard envelope or shell, which could not but hinder, or often even paralyse, its movements. The early molluscs were, more generally than those of to-day, provided with a shell. The articulates were, like crustaceans in general, equipped with a carapace. The oldest forms of fishes had an extremely hard bony covering. The explanation of this generally prevalent phenomenon must be sought in a tendency on the part of the soft-bodied organism to defend itself against others by making itself as hard to swallow as it possibly could.

Some of the first organisms, then, had adapted themselves to animal life by relinquishing the vegetable method of producing organic matter from inorganic substances, and getting their organic food instead ready made from organisms already entered on the vegetable career. So, also, many forms of animal life adapted themselves to living on other animal forms—a labour-saving expedient. An animal—i.e. a mobile—form can, by virtue of its mobility, seek out the helpless animal forms and feed on them as well as it could on plants. Undoubtedly, therefore, the various species became more and more voracious and dangerous, as their mobility increased.

This must have occasioned an alteration of the whole development of the animal world in the direction of increased mobility. The hard, siliceous covering of the echinoderms, the shell of the molluscs, the carapace of the crustaceans and the bony plate-armour of the oldest fishes owe their origin to a common endeavour on the part of the species to protect themselves. But the protective armour hindered the animal in its movements, and often paralysed it completely. Just as the plant renounces consciousness by enveloping itself in a membrane of cellulose, so also the animal which encloses itself in a fort or armoured sheathing, is reduced to a semi-dormant state. Even to this day the echinoderms and molluscs live in that sort of trance. The articulates and vertebrates were probably also exposed to the same danger, but managed fortunately to escape it, and thus paved the way for the present development of the highest forms of life.

We can see how the progress of life towards mobility along two lines again takes the ascendant. The fishes relinquish their stiff bone armour in favour of the more plastic scale covering. And long before this, insects had arisen, and had similarly freed themselves from the armour which had protected their ancestors among the crustaceans. In both cases the inferior protective efficiency of the new covering is made up for by a mobility which enabled them to avoid their enemies, and even to take the offensive themselves, inasmuch as they were now able to choose the time and place of combat. Exactly the same thing may be seen in the military equipment of man; the knight in armour has had to yield to the foot-soldier who was able to move more freely about the ground.

The well-known American biologist, John M. Tyler, assumes, with Bergson, that the first form of life must have been represented by some ultramicroscopic bacteria which were able to maintain their existence by assimilating inorganic substances as food, just as do some bacteria of the present day.

From this mother organism, evolution has followed two distinct lines : the vegetative, which in the case of chlorophyllous plants followed the same principle as the earliest bacteria, viz. of procuring food from the matter afforded by lifeless nature ; and the animals, which chose organic substances for their food and were thus forced to live either upon plants or upon other animals.

The precise distribution of animals and plants in the different geological periods is still one of the most debatable questions of modern science as regards the details. Roughly, however, we have been able to work out lists of the flora and fauna of the different epochs, and it is believed that the pedigree of man can be traced back directly to the fishes.

During the Cambrian period, there were living in the sea worms, gasteropods, mussels and large crustaceans, living mainly upon marine algæ. In the Silurian period which followed, we encounter the first vertebrates, in the form of large armoured fishes, capable of swallowing their invertebrate competitors. Then come the amphibians, breathing both by gills and lungs, then reptiles breathing by lungs alone, turtles, serpents and crocodiles. In the Triassic, Jurassic and Cretaceous periods, many of the trees found in the earlier forests, such as equisetaceæ, sigillaria and others, have become extinct, and only those of the fern type remain. During the first part of the Cretaceous period, the flora takes a new line, with the foliferous trees ; now, also, we get the fantastic saurians : the ichthyosaurus, plesiosaurus and, finally, the giant dinosaur, whose fossil eggs were recently found in the interior of China. In the Jurassic and Cretaceous periods lived, *inter alia*, the herbivorous titanosaur, a creature forty metres long and weighing many tons but with a brain no larger than that of modern man.

During the later periods (Tertiary, Glacial) outstanding features are the birds and mammals, marsupials, mastodon, horse, dugong, lemurs, apes and, finally, the latest inhabitant and present ruler of the world—man.

It was Buffon, the French naturalist, who, as far back as the close of the eighteenth century, first put forward the idea of evolution in its modern form. It was received with enthusiasm in Germany by Goethe and in France by Geoffroy Saint-Hilaire.

The true father of the theory of evolution, however, is another Frenchman, Lamarck, whose epoch-making work on *Zoological Philosophy* was published in 1809. Like many other great men, Lamarck was not appreciated by his contemporaries. The idea of evolution was not yet understood; not until 1859, when Charles Darwin published his *Origin of Species* and Wallace stated that he himself, working independently, had arrived at similar results.

Since then, the theory of evolution, of a gradual process of development, has found confirmation in practically every field of science, especially in embryology, astronomy and geology.

There is complete agreement on this point. But when it comes to explaining how this evolution took place, what was the motive force behind it, then, we find, it is a very different matter. The adherents of evolution as a whole have split up into a number of different schools: Lamarckians and neo-Lamarckians; Darwinians and neo-Darwinians, mechanists, vitalists and psycho-vitalists; and wholesale confusion arose among them all when the Dutch botanist, Hugo de Vries, in 1900 published his great work on the Theory of Mutations. This seems, indeed, likely to be of as far-reaching consequence to the conception of evolution as the work of Lamarck and Darwin.

Both Lamarck and Darwin were of opinion that species merged one into another by variations which were hereditarily transmitted. De Vries, on the other hand, believed it possible to show that species were derived one from another by sudden "mutations." Every fresh unit added to the old forms a mutation, and separates the new form sharply and completely as an independent species from that in which it had its origin. The new species, then, appears all at once, without any transition forms between it and the earlier ones.

De Vries also bases his theory on the theory of evolution.

The principle of evolution itself has not been shaken during the century that has elapsed since it was first advanced. All the discussions as to its proper interpretation have only served to strengthen it. But the ancient saying *natura non facit saltum*, is now discredited; there is a decisive breach with the previous mechanistic period which denied all creation —and yet could not get away from it after all.

Now, the leaders of biological science all point to the conclusion that not one but many successive creations have gone to make up the world in which we live.

THE MECHANISTIC THEORY OF EVOLUTION (DARWINISM)

> My theory will lead to a whole Philosophy.
> *Darwin.*

IT is a prevalent error to suppose that Darwin was the father of the theory of evolution. We saw in the last chapter that he was not; he merely gave a particular interpretation of evolution, which is now known as the mechanistic theory of evolution. This interpretation is wrong, as even the most obstinate Darwinists are now forced to admit, and we should have no occasion to go into it further here were it not that it has played a great part in philosophy and thus hindered the progress of thought by leading it into a wrong channel.

The fundamental idea in Darwin's theory as to the origin of species is, of course, that all species of animals and plants have a tendency to vary, which becomes particularly marked when the animal or plant is moved from its natural environment into artificial conditions, as with domestic animals and cultivated plants.

Among these, races or varieties easily arise through man's purposely favouring the reproduction of those sorts which are most valuable for his own purposes, by choosing such specimens for seed or propagation. And similarly, Nature will favour the maintenance and further development of any little accidental change in shape, colour, structure, or instinct in so far as it renders the individual better able to grasp its prey, avoid or defeat its enemies, protect its offspring, propagate its species and so on.

The best-equipped varieties—the favoured races—will therefore have the advantage in the struggle for existence. That involuntary action on the part of Nature which picks

MECHANISTIC THEORY OF EVOLUTION

out races best suited to continue at the expense of the rest is called *natural selection*, as compared with the artificial selection which goes to produce new types in domestic animals and cultivated plants.

In Darwin's time, it was believed that peculiarities of structure, colour, etc., were easily transmissible to the offspring, especially when found in both parents. This hereditary quality should in course of time render the peculiarities permanent, and thus transform a fluctuating variation into an independent species.

Darwin, like Wallace, arrived at his conclusion partly through the study of Malthus, who—erroneously—maintained that individuals' power of propagation exceeds the power of their environment to supply them with adequate food. The weaker will then be at a disadvantage in the competition. Malthus puts it epigrammatically: if you come to Nature's table and find no place laid for you, you must leave the table. In the struggle for existence only the strong can survive; hence the phrase first formulated by Herbert Spencer and adopted by Darwin; the survival of the fittest.

According to Darwin, evolution is not, as Lamarck supposed, the result of a creative faculty inherent in the individual, but the effect of external natural causes. This gave a rational explanation of the mystery of evolution. Kant-Laplace had revealed the story of the creation of the solar system; Galilei and Newton had shown that even suns and planets were subject to iron laws; Darwin now applied these laws to life itself.

The new doctrine was received with enthusiasm, not only by the votaries of natural science but especially by the school of philosophers who, with Herbert Spencer at their head, held by the mechanistic conception of the universe, that is, sought to explain the universal processes as those of a physico-chemical system of machinery. Darwin's principle was pure mechanism; the function proceeds from the organ; we see because we have eyes (Lamarck maintained the reverse). Any question as to how such and such an individual had obtained such and such qualities was met by the answer: because, by developing this variation, it was enabled to survive in the struggle for existence. This mechanical element was largely responsible for the enthusiasm with which Darwinism was first received, and the rapidity with which it became a dogma.

The point in which we are interested here is not the theories of evolution themselves, or the discussions for and against them, but the philosophical consequences of those theories. In this respect the Darwinist hypothesis has been highly productive.

The first to base a philosophical system on this theory was Herbert Spencer, who obtained a large following in England. A considerable number of Darwinistic philosophies have been published, right up to the present day; one of the most recent and most talented is James Clark McKerrow's *The Appearance of Mind*, published in 1923, in which the theory of selection is very consistently carried to its conclusions as a philosophical interpretation of the universe. In this, as in so many other works of like character, it is maintained that man, like animals and plants, is merely an attribute of a chemico-physical activity and a bio-chemical process. Evolution proceeds, as Spencer himself believed, rhythmically; there is no definite goal, and all " progress " is merely accidental.

But it is more particularly the Germans, always noted for their powers of digestion, who have taken up the theory of natural selection; chief among them is Haeckel. His *Riddle of the Universe*, which has had a larger sale perhaps than any other philosophical work, puts forward a purely deterministic, monistic theory of evolution, with Darwin as a heavy gun to annihilate all teleological target shooting.

Höffding, in his book on Charles Darwin and Philosophy, writes that just as Greek philosophy developed particularly under the influence of logic and mathematics, so also modern philosophy has developed under the influence of natural science; and he placed Darwin's name beside those of Copernicus, Galilei, Newton and Robert Mayer. It is undoubtedly a fact that Darwin also did exert very considerable influence, especially in the field of ethics.

But what are the philosophical, and more particularly the ethical, consequences of a mechanical theory of evolution?

MECHANISTIC THEORY OF EVOLUTION

Professor Conrad Günther, of Freiburg, in his great work on Darwin and the Problems of Life, sets forth these consequences as plainly as could be wished:

In reality, the world has no place for duty from the scientific point of view. The cosmic process goes on inexorably. There are no ends towards which the eternal changes are working ; and there is no force that can arrest or control the rolling wheels.

The stars travel on in the infinite universe. They exist at one moment of the world's history, and are gone the next. On a small body in a corner of the universe certain beings were produced in one of these moments, to perish for ever with their planet in the next. Such is the story of mankind.

How ridiculous and aimless it must be, in view of this conception of things, to direct a man how he shall act. As if he could make the slightest change in the inexorable march of cause and effect ! How is it possible to set before a man aims that he shall strive to realise, when there is no " teleological " occurrence in the world, when even human actions are determined by causes that lie behind, not before them ? (There can, of course, be no question of free will to the scientifically minded man.)

The utmost that science can say is that an ethic, a setting up of ends to be attained, has no meaning. It can only direct a man to let himself be borne in peace on the stream of cause and effect, without doing anything, because his action could have no aim and no result. The only possible scientific ethic is resignation. . . .

The principle of selection is not a principle of progress. It does not lead up inevitably to the " highest being," to man ; he is the accidental outcome of one branch of the organic system. Even in the evolutionary series, of which man is the terminus, we cannot speak of progress ; it would not be scientific, but anthropomorphic. In the eye of science, man is not " higher " than the other animals. It is precisely one of the elements of the success of the scientific view that it brings man into line with the other living things. It is illogical suddenly to raise him again to the position of the " highest being."

Further, it is entirely wrong to say that selection gives increasing value to the frames of animals, because it makes them increasingly fit to maintain their existence. Maintenance of existence has nothing to do with maintenance of value. Science has only attained its great results by studying the world independently of all considerations of value. It sees nothing but changes. . . .

The scientist has only to determine that there are human beings and animals, and that some survive and others perish on account of their bodily characteristics. He cannot wish that certain animals, or even man, should maintain their existence as long as possible. . . .

The whole cosmic process is aimless. There is no such thing as a sense of life.

It is only fair to Darwin, however, to remember that he himself was considerably less materialistic in his philosophy. He maintained, for instance, that the theory of selection also contained ethical values, as the sense of duty can also arise as a product of evolution. He considered that the ethical " should "—answering to Kant's categorical imperative—originates in the social, maternal and paternal instincts which, like others—the instinct of self-preservation, for instance—are more deeply rooted than the feelings of pleasure or pain, and to some extent independent of them. Among many species, not least among human beings, these instincts are aided by natural selection, and when the power of recollection and comparison is developed, so that individual actions can be judged by the standards of profound social instinct, the consciousness of duty and remorse will then be possible.

The question now is, whether Darwin or his disciples are the more logical as Darwinists. It cannot be denied that the disciples have shown a more and more materialistic tendency, and that even the mechanistic theory of evolution seems inspired with a highly materialistic spirit !

A very sound application of the mechanistic theory of evolution is given by Nietzsche in that section of his philosophy which deals with the Eternal Repetition. He argues roughly as follows :

The sum total of the forces of which the universe consists appears to be constant and definite. We cannot really imagine that it should decrease, for if it did, then it must long

MECHANISTIC THEORY OF EVOLUTION

since have been exhausted, seeing what an infinity of time lies behind us.

Nor can we imagine that the total should be capable of infinitely increasing, of growing, for instance, like an organism. For in such case it would require nourishment, and where is the nourishment to come from? To believe in a constant increase of the force existing in the universe would be the same as believing in a miracle constantly repeated. There remains, then, only the hypothesis of a constant total of definite forces—and consequently it must be finite.

Let us imagine that these forces reacted accidentally against one another; what would then take place in the eternity of ages? First of all we must admit that these forces have never reached a point where they balance and settle down at rest, and that they will never reach such a point. If such a point of quiescence were within the bounds of possibility, it would have been reached long before this—and the universe would have come to a standstill, unable to resume its motion.

We find ourselves, then, face to face with the fact that there must be a ceaseless interplay of forces going on within the universe, and that this interplay must sooner or later repeat itself, as all possible combinations must ultimately become exhausted and a new series of the same kind will have to begin.

And this will go on to all eternity. Each individual life is but a fragment of the great cycle. Consequently, each individual has lived its life an endless number of times before and will continue to do so throughout all eternity. This world of ours has already reached every possible stage, not once but an endless number of times.

The whole life of man is as the sand in an hour-glass, turned and turned again and again to repeat its course.

This doctrine of eternal repetition is, of course, the reverse of encouraging, for it is based on the supposition that evolution is only an illusion, its innermost being is but moving in a circle. Altogether, there is little encouragement to be got from further acquaintance with the conclusions of the Darwinist philosophers. Haeckel regards man as nothing more than a "social vertebrate"; Ostwald regards culture as merely the expenditure of the least possible amount of energy; Mach sees in the human will only a pressure differing little from that of a stone on the ground where it rests; Avenarius considers the physical and the psychical of equal value; Petzold sees all values as relative; Taine looks upon virtue and vice as mere products, like sugar and vitriol, and McKerrow finds consciousness nothing but an illusion (perception an hallucination, knowledge a delusion).

Darwin rightly perceived that his theory would lead to a whole system of philosophy, but he was not able to foresee the materialistic consequences necessarily involved by a doctrine which made the struggle for existence the sole motive force of life.

Nietzsche, though he differs from Darwin on some points, evidently worked out his philosophy and ethics under pressure of the mechanistic theory of evolution and the positivism which followed in its wake. Nietzsche draws the logical conclusion which Darwin himself was loath to draw; he demands that all values shall be re-stated according to the new doctrine. Since Nature teaches us that only the strongest can succeed, then this must also apply to human life; for man is only a product of adaptation, a product as accidental as all other beings. And if existence is merely a struggle for life, why trouble to choose the good in preference to the evil? Why truth rather than falsehood? The only thing that counts in a struggle of any sort is to win. Nietzsche is certainly the most typical of the Darwinian philosophers. His philosophy stands or falls by the mechanical theory of evolution—and *vice versa*.

It will readily be understood that stubborn Darwinists are not to be ousted by ethical-philosophical arguments. Any such would be regarded as mere anthropomorphic nonsense. If a strictly biological attitude be adopted, the only convincing argument will be biological facts.

One is tempted, then, to quote the main points in the mass of material which biologists of the vitalistic school in particular have in course of time collected as an armoury against Darwinism; or refer to Kropotkin's criticism in *Mutual Aid*. All this, however, is superfluous. The researches of recent times have given us something more, namely, the results of modern experiments in genetics. *These overthrow completely the principal stronghold of the mechanical theory of evolution; the doctrine as to hereditary transmission of acquired characters, and consequent formation of species by variation.*

A new era in the study of heredity was introduced already by Hugo de Vries' Mutation Theory, mentioned in the last chapter. In that work, De Vries brought forward some researches previously overlooked, namely, those of the monk Gregor Mendel. These have since become one of the principal foundations in the study of genetics, and proved of importance *inter alia*, to the eminent Danish scientist Professor W. Johannsen, to whose pioneer work on the question of genetics the reader is here referred.

Professor Oluf Thomsen, in a recent work (*Religiös og Biologisk Opfattelse*, Copenhagen), sums up the results of research in this field, pointing out that it has been scientifically demonstrated that " acquired characters " are not capable of affecting the offspring; they apply only to the individual and die out with it. All that we have painfully acquired in course of time is lost again, and the new generation has to start afresh like the one before it. A selection due to the struggle for existence should then only be capable of producing a more and more complete pure culture of the fittest, but nothing more. Selection can only affect what is already given; it cannot itself produce anything new.

Similarly, Professor Weis writes:

Theories that were considered as facts in Darwin's time—hereditary transmission of acquired characters, hereditary succession of the innumerable variations produced by as adaptations to environment—have given way before the results of modern genetic research. But it was just this—false—faith that made the theory of evolution so easy to believe in. We now know that these variations are individual, affecting only the ontogenetic character of the organism, and having nothing to do with its phylogenetic character; these individual variations then, provide no basis whatever for the theory of evolution to work on.

Another question is: does the science of genetics now offer no point of vantage from which a theory of evolution can be built?

Here, first and foremost, we have to note the question of mutations. The difference between a mutation and a fluctuation (individual variation) is not by any means a matter of extent (a mutation may and often will be a matter of very slight divergence only) ; the difference lies in the fact that a mutation is an incident in phylogenetic history, whereas a fluctuation is an incident in ontogenetic history.

The difficulty of basing any theory of evolution on mutations instead of fluctuations as Darwin did—he regarded them as hereditary—lies partly in the fact that mutations are of comparatively rare occurrence. A further difficulty lies in the fact that mutations, whether occurring " spontaneously " or produced by external conditions, do not appear to be in the least degree affected by or suited to the environment in which the organism has to live, whereas this is the case to a very high degree with the individual variations. If, however, we are unwilling to relinquish the theory of evolution—as most biologists are nowadays—there is, as far as we can see, nothing but the mutations and new combinations produced by crossing to reckon with.

From this, then, it will be seen that the mechanistic interpretation of evolution rests on a very slight support.

But can we not then explain evolution by the natural selection of mutation forms specially fitted, and new mutations in course of time—in a word, by a succession of mutations in a particular direction together with constant selection ? Professor Thomsen leaves this point untouched. He writes :

Some think this can be done, others are inclined to regard most mutations as involving a degeneration which can hardly be taken as the basis for progressive evolution. The question cannot be decided at present, and to sum up, we can only say that we know nothing for certain as to whether evolution has taken place, and nothing at all as to how it has taken place, if so. But that there has, in some way or other, been a process of evolution from lower to higher forms is a view which few biologists would contest. It is supported, moreover, by the finds of fossil remains of animals and the first traces of man at a very late period.

In other words, Darwinism has been ousted, not by " dreary philosophers," but by biologists, by scientists using purely empirical scientific methods, and not concerned with speculations. As regards evolution, we have nothing to go upon whatever. No wonder, then, that the Darwinists are at a loss. They have made a brave show with their mechanistic interpretation of the universe for the past generation, and confidently pooh-poohed all doubt and criticism as mere superstition. They have built up a mechanistic philosophy, the consequences of which we have seen, for instance, in Professor Gunther's work above quoted, and this they held out as the last new truth of science, not only with regard to evolution, but with regard to existence itself.

Nietzsche has been quoted as a particularly virulent example of the Darwinian philosophers. But are the others any better? The best of them have little left now beyond the assertion that a species becomes extinct when the struggle for life proves too hard for its powers, when it cannot adapt itself to the allotted conditions of existence. And this no one is likely to deny. Undoubtedly, the struggle for life has played a part in the process of evolution, as it does in all forms of life. But there is a difference between admitting the importance of environment as a factor to be reckoned with, and making it out to be the cause responsible for the direction of evolution. It is this last idea which was erroneously maintained by Darwin and the philosophically inclined among his disciples.

It is now evident that the mechanistic theory of evolution has gained the victory by what lawyers would call a miscarriage of justice. Its rapid success was due to the fact that it offered an explanation which seemed obvious and easy to understand. The struggle for life, natural selection, inheritance of acquired characters, the survival of the fittest—these are things any child can understand. And the doctrine was supported by analogies from practical life until it seemed incontrovertible. It appeals to our sense of reality, and our logical sense. It does not need to have recourse to unscientific fantasies about a vital force invisible and beyond measure ; and it disposes once and for all of religious ideas as to the existence of some mysterious divinity and creator beyond.

The great thing about it is that it " explains " things ; and we poor human beings are so hungry for an explanation that we would rather have a bad one or half a one than none at all.

And that is how the delusion arose, how it was spread and how it managed to take possession of philosophy. Led by Herbert Spencer and by Germans like Haeckel, whose speciality is trying to improve on other people's work, the philosophers grabbed at the Darwinian theory without first troubling to find out whether it fitted in with all the facts. And we have seen the result !

Unfortunately, the mechanistic philosophers of the Darwinian school have shaken the faith of many in evolution itself. It will, however, be strong enough in itself to withstand the shock. Professor William Bateson, addressing a meeting of scientists at Toronto, gave a resumé of the progress of modern genetic research, noting the facts which had led people to doubt what had actually been the course and progress of evolution. Such confessions of uncertainty were, he pointed out, an excellent opportunity for the enemies of science. When it appears that we are unable to explain the origin of species at once, they immediately put forward interpretations satisfying only to obscurantism. His own faith in evolution, Bateson declared, was unshaken ; all the facts are on our side, and the obscurantists have nothing to offer at all worthy of our attention.

It is on such considerations as these that the future work of the evolutionists must be based. The mechanistic interpretation of evolution is dead beyond recall, and with it disappears a great deal of philosophy which has been accepted as sound for the past generation.

But is there no other to be found ?

We shall in the next chapter see what the vitalists have to say on the subject, and consider whether their interpretation is better qualified than Darwin's to solve the riddle of evolution.

THE VITALISTIC THEORY OF EVOLUTION

> Life does not consist of physico-chemical elements any more than a curve of straight lines.—*Bergson*.

IN contrast to the mechanistic interpretation of evolution we have the vitalistic.

Neo-vitalism distinguishes between a negative and a positive side. The former, starting from a biological point of view, seeks to demonstrate the inadequacy of the mechanistic theory; the latter embraces the theories advanced by neo-vitalism itself.

It is this latter, the positive side, we shall consider. We encounter at once two names standing out among a host of others: those of the French philosopher, Henri Bergson, and the German biologist, Hans Driesch.

The following pages give a very brief and therefore incomplete summary of the theory of evolution put forward by Bergson in his great work, *L'Evolution créatrice*, which has already achieved world-wide renown.

Bergson views the whole known universe—matter and life, the earth, the planets, solar systems, milky ways and nebulæ—as derived, metaphorically speaking, from a huge reservoir somewhere inconceivably far off.

Let us imagine, he says, a steam boiler at high pressure, with here and there a leak through which the vapour escapes up into space. Nearly all the steam thus escaping condenses and falls down in the form of small drops. The fall is the expression of a loss of something, an interruption, a deficit. A small proportion of the escaped steam remains for a few moments in an uncondensed state. This portion seeks to lift the falling drops up again, but cannot at the outside do more than delay their fall.

In the same way, let us imagine a continual rise of vapour from an immense reservoir of life and matter, each portion falling down and forming a world (e.g. a milky way). The development of living species within this world is what remains of the original upward trend of the vapour, and a progressive tendency in the direction of matter.

The reservoir, then, from which the worlds are derived, is filled with a " vapour " consisting of two component parts : life and matter. Life, which is a kind of explosive, is ever moving upwards, but matter, which is thick and heavy, tends ever to fall, and in falling drags life down with it.

Here on our earth—a single drop among the millions flung out from the immense column of vapour—life has assumed the form of plants and animals, and in this form, under the particular conditions prevailing on our planet, it has taken up the struggle against matter. On other planets, life and matter are also to be found, acting against each other like two opposing currents, but the struggle there may be of a different character. It is not necessary to suppose that life elsewhere, as on earth, is concentrated into absolute organisms of definite contour, into finite bodies leading the current of energy into certain marked channels, elastic though these may be. We can imagine—though we cannot, it is true, form any clear image of the condition—that energy could be gathered up and released by passing through matter which had not yet assumed any definite form itself. Between this vague, indefinite vital force and the clearly defined vitality we know there would be little more difference than exists between dreams and waking consciousness in our psychological life. Such conditions of life may have prevailed in our nebula before the condensation of matter was completed. On other planets, life will certainly have assumed other external forms than here. Given other physical conditions, the life impulse would perhaps have remained the same, but it would have split up differently and altogether have taken another course, possibly shorter, possibly longer.

The struggle between life and matter on other planets is a question which we are for very good reasons prevented from discussing. Biological development on our own earth, how-

VITALISTIC THEORY OF EVOLUTION 35

ever, has been subjected to scientific study, and we can, in the rough, trace the progress of this development.

Going back as far as ever we can, we find certain very low initial forms, as to which we cannot even determine whether they are merely of chemical and physical nature, or to be regarded as vital; we do not know whether we are dealing with life or matter as yet. From this we may conclude that life conquered the opposition of inorganic matter by making itself extremely pliable, slipping in adroitly among the physical and chemical forces. Life had to adopt the habits of inorganic matter in order to magnetise it gradually and draw it over into another course. The earliest forms were simple. They consisted doubtless of small slimy masses, externally resembling the amoebæ of to-day, but possessing, in contrast to these, a mighty inner force of potential progress which was destined to raise them up to the highest forms of life.

At an early stage life split up into two distinct lines of development, those of plant and animal; the immobile and the mobile, the unconscious and the conscious form. As we know, plants derive their nourishment directly from the air, water and earth, which provide them with the materials requisite for their maintenance, especially carbon and nitrogen. Plants are thus equipped for life in a manner which renders it unnecessary for them to move or feel. Animals, on the other hand, which have to go about in search of food, have developed in the direction of mobile activity, and thus also of increasing and extended consciousness. There is no need to postulate the influence of any mysterious power in order to explain this divergence, for living beings incline naturally to the side most convenient in every case, and plants and animals have chosen each their own way out of the two convenient methods of procuring the necessary carbon and nitrogen, In other words, plants and animals represent the expression of two different views of work, or one might say, of comfort and economy. The same advance which in the animal forms led to the formation of nerves and nerve centres, produced the chlorophyll and its action in the plants. The plant chose to develop in the direction of accumulating energy on the spot, whereas the animal acquired the power of giving off energy from time to time with intervals of freedom between its "explosive" acts. At first, the explosion takes place haphazard, with no particular choice of direction; the amoeba thrusts out its processes to all sides at once. But as we rise higher in the animal scale, we find certain definite lines of direction indicated in the very shape of the organism, nerve chains which the current of energy follows.

After life had split up into plant and animal, a further important subdivision took place in the latter, giving articulate and vertebrate forms. Along the two lines followed by vertebrates and articulates respectively, evolution has consisted mainly in an improvement of the nervous system. The aim was to attain mobility, agility and—not without much hesitation and bungling and an attempt at exaggerated hyper-development of bulk and brute force—a greater complexity of movement. To attain these qualities, however, different methods were tried. This can be seen by considering the nerve system of articulates and vertebrates. In the former, the body consists of a series of laterally connected rings of more or less extent; the freedom of movement, then, is distributed throughout a varying, often considerable number of parts, each having its own special function. In the latter, on the other hand, movement is concentrated in two pairs of limbs, and these organs then perform functions far less dependent upon their form. Perfect independence is seen in the human hand, which is capable of executing any kind of work.

So much can be seen by actual observation. But behind what we observe lies something more which can only be dimly discerned: two inherent forces in life, fused into one at first, but gradually differentiating out in process of growth.

One of these forces is reason, which reaches its culmination in man, the Lord of the Earth; the other is instinct, seen at its highest development in the ant, which is lord under the earth.

In vegetative lethargy, instinct and reason, we have the elements which coincided in the vital impulse common to plant and animal alike; elements which, in the course of an

VITALISTIC THEORY OF EVOLUTION

evolution assuming the most unforeseen forms, separated off one from another by their mere growth. The fundamental error which has been handed down from the days of Aristotle, and has rendered most philosophical interpretations of Nature erroneous, lies in regarding the vegetative, instinctive and rational forms of life as three successive stages of one and the same progressive tendency; whereas in reality, they are three distinct directions of an activity which has split up in course of its growth. The difference between them is not a matter of different intensity; it is a difference not of degree but of essentials.

Just as the fungus is an unsuccessful attempt at a plant and the plant an unsuccessful attempt at animal form, so also the animals are unsuccessful attempts at human form. Evolution on our planet has tried many ways; only one, however, namely, that which runs *via* the vertebrates to man, was broad enough to give space for the strong breath of life unhindered along its course. Admirable discipline and unity prevail among the bees and ants; but the communities of the insects have come to a standstill, whereas that of man lies open to progress. *Homo sapiens* is not merely a being capable of releasing its energy in an endless number of " explosive " acts; it has the possibility of advancing beyond itself.

True, man does this only to a lesser degree than man could wish; less indeed than man imagines. The purely formal character of reason deprives it of the ballast needful to give complete understanding. The requisite real nature, on the other hand, has instinct, but cannot seek its object far enough away; it lacks the speculative faculty. The cleavage in evolution which took place when the articulates separated off from the vertebrates is evident from the fact that there are things which reason alone can seek (though it can never find them unaided), whereas instinct could find these things but will never seek them.

What has happened, then, in the evolution of our planet, is that matter became magnetised by a broad stream of consciousness, charged with an immense multiplicity of possibilities, interpenetrating one another. Consciousness has effected the organisation of matter, but its own movement has been infinitely retarded and subdivided. Consciousness has either had to sink into a torpid state, like that of the chrysalis, or its manifold tendencies have been distributed among divergent series of organisms, transforming those tendencies externally into motion instead of inwardly into ideas. In the course of evolution, some sank deeper and deeper into their trance, while others awoke.

Life is one long movement in opposition to the downward trend of matter. Life is an ascent, from generation to generation, binding individuals as well as species together. Life makes the whole series of living things one immense wave rolling forward over matter.

And just as the minutest speck of dust is one with the rest of our entire solar system, so all organic beings are related, from the lowest to the highest, from the earliest origins of life to the time in which we live.

Everywhere, in all ages, we find but a single impulse, opposed to the trend of matter, and indivisible in itself. All living beings are united in mutual support, and are carried onward by the same mighty force. The animal is supported by the plant, man by the animals, and the whole of humanity, both in time and space, is one mighty army racing forward at a gallop.

Thus Bergson concludes his exposition; but on the question as to whither the galloping race of life so pictorially described is to lead, and what purpose it really serves, he tells us unfortunately very little. We cannot, he says, ascribe to life an aim or goal in the human sense of the word. To speak of any such is to imagine a pre-existent example. But life is progressive and enduring. Human thought can say nothing as to the road which had first to be traversed, since the road itself was gradually formed by the act of traversing, and was no more than the direction of that act.

And here we come to the weak point of Bergson as an evolutionary philosopher. In setting forth his view of evolution he is not so much concerned to interpret it as to provide a background for his theory of knowledge; which is, that reason is inadequate as an instrument of knowledge, and that we cannot, by reason alone, penetrate into the innermost

VITALISTIC THEORY OF EVOLUTION 39

depths of life and its manifestations. He too, then, like the mechanists, albeit on altogether different grounds, is unable to perceive the object of existence.

The mechanists regard evolution as a fan, unfolded only to close again. Everything is given, everything can be calculated beforehand, for it exists already. The future lies like a roll of film on its spool; if we have but the key to the chamber where it is kept, we can look into it; and it is a matter only of individual skill whether we can foresee it. Bergson argues that this is not the case. Evolution is a creation constantly renewed; producing gradually not only the forms of life, but also the ideas which enable reason to comprehend them. Its future extends beyond its present; it is not merely reflected in an idea within it. Within the evolution of life, the doors of the future stand wide open. It is a creation continued to infinity, by virtue of a movement imparted from the beginning. This movement forms the unity of the organic world, a fertile and infinitely rich unity, rich beyond the dreams of reason, seeing that reason itself is but one side, or one product, of this movement.

Bergson defines life as a struggle against matter, a struggle which, in so far as it succeeds, leads upward step by step towards the world of the spirit. In the course of this struggle life represents the principle of liberty; and the aim is to introduce as much liberty as possible into the automatically downward-tending world of matter. Matter is ruled by the Carnot principle of a constant tendency toward distribution of energy and thus to equilibrium. According to the law of entropy, mechanical energy is gradually transformed into heat. The opposite process cannot be imagined as taking place, as it would require mechanical energy to effect it, and this again would occasion a loss. The processes of Nature are, as Dr. Richard Eriksen points out, determined by a difference of intensity between the different quantities of energy. Experiment has shown that the difference of intensity on the whole decreases, and that the course of Nature tends towards equilibrium. This is chiefly apparent in what Max Planck calls the preference of Nature for heat as a form of energy. From the stock of energy existing in Nature, more and more is ever being transformed into thermal energy, which is dispersed as the differences of temperature in relation to environment are balanced. This thermal energy once dispersed cannot again be transformed into other forms of energy. Ultimately, then, all energy will be transmuted into heat, which will exhibit no difference of intensity, as the intensity of heat—the temperature—will be evenly distributed throughout. This is, in brief, the explanation of the principle of entropy, on the basis of which it has been prophesied that the whole of nature will ultimately perish by fire. According to Bergson, life combats this tendency, binds it and checks it for a time. Life and spirit oppose the trend of matter towards a state of equilibrium.

From an idealistic point of view we should not suppose that spirit and the highest forms of spiritual life would provide Bergson with an object for evolution; for, according to his own theory, the fruit of victory in the struggle between life and matter is spirit, liberty of spirit.

But here we encounter the difficulty mentioned above, to wit, that Bergson, in his theory of knowledge, had already in his youth discarded reason as an instrument of knowledge and set up intuition in its stead as a kind of super-knowledge. Reason, he says, is only a narrow enclave within a more comprehensive whole. Life extends beyond the scope of reason. Reason, by its practical point of view, has cut itself off from the great unity of life. Reason is, in its essentials, only a power of producing implements. If we would understand the activity of life and comprehend growth and creation, it is no use viewing them through the spectacles of reason alone; we must use intuition, which is defined as the vital instinct itself, but disinterested, conscious of itself and capable of reflecting upon its aim and extending it to infinity. Life has, in course of evolution, split up into instinct and reason. But it is possible to grasp the synthesis of which blind instinct and analytical reason are only parts. When we relinquish the practical motives which have guided evolution, and cultivate the disinterested sense of the rich reality of life, intuition becomes possible; and intuition is the highest form of soul life.

We need not here enter into a critical examination of Bergson's theory of intuition. We mention it merely to show that Bergson's inconsistency in rejecting the spirit acting through reason and yet declaring it the culmination of development, is due to his enthusiasm for intuition. This, the discovery of his youth, has led him so far astray that he is unable to draw the right conclusion from his own theory of evolution. His imaginary hatred of the intellectualists—to whom, after all, he belongs by virtue of his type of mind, whether he will or no—has forced him to stop at a purely vitalistic interpretation of evolution.

Bergson stops at the door which leads to the idealistic theory of evolution. We realise this when he tells us that the ideas of growth and creation are one, and that we know these activities from our own soul life; when he adds that the aim of his own principal work is to show that the cosmos is of the same nature as the ego, and understandable by completer study of the self; and, finally, when he concludes that life itself aims at bringing the greatest possible sum of indetermination into matter. It is here that he introduces the magnificent term: "*évolution créatrice*," creative evolution, which is a plank of salvation for all those who do not believe in a gloomy determinism or an equally gloomy finalism. He has fumbled at the keyhole of the idealistic shrine, but turned away at the critical moment without opening the door, simply because he feared to find within an altar to the spirit as the goal of evolution, and its noblest product; that spirit to which, from his theory of knowledge, he could not bow the knee.

This, to our mind, is the tragic point in Bergson's philosophy. He was unwilling to take the step from a vitalistic philosophy to a philosophy of value and spirit. Consequently, like the old vitalists themselves, though far superior to them in insight, knowledge and brilliant intellect, he sees in evolution nothing beyond a continual vital ascent, an ever stronger and ever more intense manifestation of life, but without aim, without even any definite tendency at all. He thus debars himself from offering any plausible explanation of the highest phenomena of life, such as art and ethics. We can no more found a system of ethics on vitalism than we could on

Newton's law of gravity, which some rationalists are said to have attempted.

By a curious freak of fate, this brilliant thinker not only reached no farther than vitalism, but even became a vitalist in the narrower sense of the word ; his bridge of intuition does not lead us up into higher and clearer worlds of spirit, but over into mysticism.

Bergson is like Moses looking out over the promised land with all its wealth and beauty ; it was not vouchsafed him to enter in.

The German vitalist, Professor Hans Driesch of Cologne, has, like Bergson, rendered great service in the collection of material to oppose the Darwinian theory of natural selection. In contrast to Bergson, who loves to speak in poetic imagery, he appears as the sober biologist, pursuing his work in a strictly scientific method of research.

Quite empirically, he has demonstrated the inadequacy of Darwinism. He shows that the Darwinian theory of selection and adaptation affords no explanation of the origin of species, it does not explain mutual adaptation, such as that which exists between plants and insects ; it does not explain the organisation of physical parts composed of different materials, such as the eye ; and it certainly does not explain how an eye should have arisen in such widely different evolutionary lines as those of mollusc and mammal, by entirely different evolutionary roads ; and finally, it offers no explanation of the remarkable and important biological fact that we can, by cutting up certain primitive marine organisms, produce from a single specimen as many as eight new individuals capable of sustained existence and even of reproduction.

Driesch agrees with Bergson that there can be no question of understanding evolution unless by premising an organising force flowing from within. Lamarck, the father of evolution, also reckoned with this. According to his view, the different species were capable of adaptation in different directions according to wish or need. Lamarck's psychological vitalism then, is, although Driesch on other grounds rejects it, nevertheless a more valuable theory than that of the mechanists, who only acknowledge influence from without, and therefore

VITALISTIC THEORY OF EVOLUTION

interpret evolution negatively, leaving no room for any positive factor. The Darwinists' answer to the riddle of evolution is rather like answering the question: "Why is that tree covered with leaves?" by saying "Because the gardener has not cut them off." The positive element is disregarded; and it is this which Driesch introduces in his theory of entelechy.

Entelechy is an expression used already by Aristotle to denote the living actual functional power inherent in the individual. Driesch defines entelechy as "a spaceless, material, individual, energy-suspending, regulating and organising vital principle." Entelechy is not physico-chemical in its nature, it is not a cause in space, though it acts upon that which is in space.

Positive proofs of entelechy are to be found, according to Driesch, especially in embryology and in instinct. The organic forms, in their character as wholes, cannot be regarded as a mere interplay of inorganic elements. Driesch points out that in the earliest embryonic stages, the relative arrangement of the cells can be altered by mechanical interference, and the embryo nevertheless develops normally. So also, a developing sea-urchin can be cut up into several parts, and an individual will grow out of each, proving that the "plan" of the organism is contained in all parts of the body. And as in physical formation, so also in instinctive acts, the organism behaves as a whole, guiding and determining the direction and relation of processes, now by inhibiting one, now by changing direction, or again by altering the relation between one process and another.

Wherever there is life, we find this determining purposive factor, which is superior to the law of energy. Entelechy acts on matter, but is itself immaterial. All other forces of nature can be measured and compared, they have a certain quantity and can be defined in calories, kilo rammes, etc. Entelechy, however, has no quantity. Entelechy cannot produce any movement which does not exist beforehand, it cannot make substances enter into combinations which they would not do by purely chemical means. What entelechy can do is to suspend a process for a period of greater or less duration. Entelechy can neither annihilate nor create energy, it cannot increase intensities, but only suspend and again release the same amounts of energy. The process of assimilation in particular is, according to Driesch, supra-chemical in its character, and can only be explained by entelechy.

When we consider the vital processes, we very soon perceive a factor of totality acting purposively, and this cannot be of physico-chemical nature. It is seen not only in the fact that new combinations of parts give rise to altogether new qualities, as for instance with the molecule in relation to its atoms, but also in the fact that it first creates the parts of which it consists.

In the organism, this factor of totality is apparent. We are forced to reckon with something which cannot be expressed in the language of physics and chemistry. Life is never a part in the sense of a link or section; it is the comprehensive process which produces the living structure itself and regulates its function. No biological phenomenon is explained until we have found out what purpose it serves. In every organism there is a directing factor which does not increase or reduce the velocity of molecular movement, but furthers or checks activity in certain directions. Anything useful to an organism seems for this reason better able to assert itself, whereas anything likely to prove harmful is met by preventive and precautionary measures.

This purposive activity does not radiate from anything outside the organism, as the latter would, if so, come under the heading of an artificial product. The organism is precisely a natural product. Nature cannot then, as the mechanists assume, be a merely physico-chemical process. The determination of direction can be studied in the growth of the organism and its pre-determined development from the egg to the finished state. It is apparent everywhere in the simple growth of propagation, and in assimilation, which is the basis of all life, a maintaining and renewing of the individual.

The difference between Bergson's vital force, " *élan vital,*" and Driesch's entelechy is, that *élan vital* is a directly creative force but acting blindly, whereas entelechy is only directive and regulatory, but with a definite purpose.

VITALISTIC THEORY OF EVOLUTION 45

Bergson says that life is a creative evolution, whose purpose is merely to create. Driesch says that life is an ordering and determining principle, but reveals its aims to us only in minor units, namely, organisms. That some greater purpose may lie behind is possible, but we can say nothing for certain as to this.

Driesch does not offer us any positive theory of evolution. He rejects both Darwinism and Lamarckism as inadequate, without formulating any better theory himself. He follows entelechy as far as the individual, but no farther. He recognises that this is insufficient; but he is a biologist.

Nevertheless, both have undoubtedly rendered great service in the effort towards an interpretation, not only by demonstrating, each in his own way, the inadequacy of Darwinism, but more particularly by indicating roads which may lead to a deeper understanding of the problem.

We shall see in the next chapter how Bergson's creative élan and Driesch's entelechy meet and can be comprised in a higher unity of nature which we have called the creative power, a power not only regulative but directly creative, grasping a material and fashioning, not blindly, but with definite purpose, a new and nobler form of the material in which it works. It is this power which forms the link between matter, life and spirit.

The vitalists can give us only a limited interpretation of evolution, because they stop quite arbitrarily at life and its manifestation as the culmination. To them, the bacillus that destroys man is of equal value with man that exterminates the bacillus—it is life itself that is the highest standard.

It is owing to this point of view that the vitalists have not, philosophically speaking, advanced much beyond the mechanists, and it is this which has called forth the protest of the philosophers.

Professor H. Rickert, for instance, points out that the vitalists are wrong in thinking that to live, to vegetate, should be reckoned among the greatest of good things. Life as life cannot of itself be reckoned as a good thing. That I am alive is nothing, he insists. The value of my life depends solely on the manner of my life, or the peculiar experiences of which it is composed.

The vitalistic theory of evolution, then, is no more suited than the mechanistic to the construction of a philosophical view of life. Philosophically speaking, it cannot get beyond a purely external pragmatism; everything will then depend on utility, conservation of energy, mass-production of offspring, exercise of force, strength and the power of longevity. The world of ideas counts for very little here; morality and art, ideals and hope are empty names.

Several of the vitalist philosophers have realised that this is a serious drawback. Some have sought refuge in Eimer's theory of orthogenesis, which demonstrates a craving and tendency in evolution to development in a given direction. Erich Becher's psycho-vitalism is related to this.

That vitalism should become psycho-vitalism, that is, be twisted in an idealistic direction, is most significant. It shows that vitalism in the long run does not satisfy its own supporters, at any rate not when they step out from the biological laboratory into the turret chamber of philosophy.

THE IDEALISTIC THEORY OF EVOLUTION

> One can feel so thoroughly down-hearted at times. One feels that Nature is saying something, but one can see nothing, understand nothing of it all. And yet we would so gladly understand what our own Mother is trying to tell us. And then again at other times, one feels that one really understands it all well enough.
>
> *Ludvig Feilberg.*

WE have in the foregoing chapter briefly summed up two theories of evolution, and arrived at the conclusion that neither of them gives an adequate explanation.

The fundamental error in the theory of the mechanists and vitalists is, in our opinion, that both seek to explain Nature from below upwards, and do not, as did the natural philosophers of the previous century, attempt to interpret it from above down at the same time. Neither mechanists nor vitalists pay sufficient attention to evolution in its finest and noblest form, as the evolution of culture and mind.

The purpose of this book, then, is to formulate and, as far as we are able, to give grounds for a new interpretation, a new view of evolution, which we will call the idealistic theory of evolution.

There is an essential difference between this theory of evolution and the two others, in that it is concerned not only with the evolution we see taking place in Nature, but is first and foremost interested in the evolution that takes place in human life, endeavouring to ascertain if analogies cannot be found between this and evolution at more primitive stages. That is to say, it takes Man as its starting-point—the only natural thing for Man to do—and reasons thence backward to organic and physical activity, assuming that the forces prevailing on the higher plane must have manifested themselves in some way or another before.

It is evident that the mechanistic theory of evolution, if of any importance at all, is restricted to a low material plane. The vitalistic theory gives a certain relief to its picture of evolution, but does not rise beyond the biological: like the mechanistic view, it comes to a standstill because it fails to reckon with mind as the noblest and most important factor in evolution. It is only when we take the phenomena of mind into consideration that we can hope to give the theory of evolution its proper depth; only then does it comprise all phenomena.

The chief objection, then, from a philosophical point of view, to the mechanist and vitalist schools is that they do not pay sufficient attention to what we regard as of decisive importance in the everyday life of communities. To find all higher forms of life, the things we honour and respect, such as art, genius, invention, fine feelings and lofty ideals, unselfishness to the point of self-sacrifice—to find all this disregarded as inessential and accidental, is revolting alike to our feeling and our intelligence. The vitalists often do not distinguish between primitive and more developed forms of life; they do not give mind the highest place, but lose themselves in admiration of a mystic *élan vital*, a force creating blindly and aiming evidently at nothing at all beyond its own continuation. And this we feel, is not sufficient.

It is but natural that a reaction should arise against so shallow an interpretation of evolution. In summing up the course of evolution so as to draw conclusions, if possible, as to its aims, it is only reasonable to dwell on the results generally acknowledged as of principal rank. By their fruits ye shall know them, say the pragmatists; and it is no use commencing our studies by hermetically closing our eyes to the finest and most precious fruits of the tree.

It is not strange that we should feel sceptical towards a philosophy which adopts an attitude either of indifference or of actual opposition to the hard-won foundation of values in our whole civilisation, the result of thousands of years of struggle. We cannot really respect the philosopher who asserts that the phenomena of mind are not of greater natural value than physical phenomena ; that a fly is really as valuable as a human being ; that the *Divina Commedia* or Beethoven's Sonatas are a mere by-product in the struggle for life, a variation of no real use whatever ; and that law and conscience, ethics and the sense of art are merely accidents, which might have turned out quite differently, might have been opposite to what they are, if evolution had chanced to take a slightly different course.

The mechanists' assertion that evolution has no aim and the world no meaning cannot but seem to us as astonishing as it is discouraging. If we consider ourselves and our own life, we find that we, practically speaking, never do anything else but set up aims for ourselves, and strive with more or less success to attain them. That the universe—of which we ourselves after all are a part—should in this essential respect be altogether differently constituted from ourselves seems suspicious at once. In a novel, a play, a limited company, or a community, we find a course of development, subject, it is true, to many accidental influences, but nevertheless aiming at a definite object just as a steamer steers a definite course, and does not allow its route to be determined by accidental gales. When an organism, a plant, or a child grows up, we see, as Driesch has shown from a purely biological point of view, a purposive development ; the process moves towards an end. Wherever we can discern a course of development in the individual, we find an aim. But the development which has taken place in Nature, evolution as a whole ; this, according to so-called science, is to be understood as having no aim ! We find it hard to believe.

Why should Nature take all this trouble to no purpose ? Why stage the great struggle for life when nothing is to be won ? It seems to us that the very term evolution in itself contains the promise of a goal, and this is confirmed when we see that evolution does not oscillate and vacillate at hazard, but can be followed evenly and harmoniously from one degree of condensation to the next above.

Undoubtedly, Charles Darwin is one of the great men of science. Moreover, he was always straightforward and strictly honourable in argument and his polemics. But it cannot be denied that his contemporaries, and still more his later disciples, set him upon a pedestal where he should not stand.

Darwin the evolutionist has been confused with Darwin the selectionist. His work, *The Origin of Species*, appeared at a time when the world was at last ripe for the understanding of the idea of evolution. It was successful accordingly, and readers swallowed the theory of natural selection into the bargain, more especially since it could be used as a weapon against the Church, which had been a persecutor of science from time immemorial.

This view, however, needs to be revised. We must give Darwin the credit he deserves, as an evolutionist, but none the less we must reject his theory of natural selection; not only on scientific grounds, as the vitalists and the students of genetics have done, but also on philosophic grounds. The struggle for life is an important factor in evolution; but it has not been, as the mechanists suppose, a struggle merely for possession of the best feeding-grounds. Looking impartially at the evolution of the human mind, we find quite other motives; ethical principles, faith, hope and charity, ideals and idealistic effort; these are the elements which in spite of all take the decisive place; and they cannot be merely in the air.

If the evolution of humanity can teach us anything, it must be this: that man, despite all difficulties and reverses, is ever setting his ideals higher and higher. And these ideals are not only of individual scope, but reach beyond the individual aim.

Fortunately, the mechanists have never succeeded in effectively implanting in humanity the belief that every one of us, even the best, is but a little insignificant wheel in a clockwork system insignificant in itself. The common sense of the ordinary man rises in revolt against a supposition which stamps the whole of evolution as an illusion, a harlequinade.

It is remarkable, indeed, that such views should ever have come into existence. One would surely think that the discovery of evolution, of the fact that we are in process of evolution from a lower to a higher state, would be grasped at by mankind as the most welcome of gospels. There is in every human breast a longing for a better world. And when science comes and tells us that this longing is not unwarranted, but is shared by all Nature, that the whole development of the world shows a trend upward and forward from lower to higher forms—then, we should think that science was offering us support and encouragement such as we had never before known in all our wanderings. But instead of holding up the evolution of Nature as a great example for our guidance and aid, the mechanists have used evolution to damp our courage and have tried to persuade us that this evolution was itself blind, accidental, without aim or end. All that martyrs, poets, great artists, idealists, have sacrificed of their heart's blood, all this is of no avail. All that millions of human beings through hundreds of generations have been able to foster and exert in the way of enthusiasm for noble causes is of no use. It is all an illusion; whether we live or die is immaterial; the highest type of humanity is, properly speaking, of no more value than the meanest worm.

We have seen with shame how the ideas of great martyrs have been exploited in the service of some selfish purpose; as for instance the teaching of Christ by the papacy and priesthood. A man of genius comes forward with a new message to the world, but the message is misunderstood, perverted, trampled in the dust and exploited to the personal advantage of lesser men. The idea of evolution has fared but little better. Since it was first advanced, it has been monopolised by a narrow-minded clique for party purposes.

How can it be that no prophet has arisen to protest against this? To tell us, in simple words, that the theory of evolution is the most beautiful gospel ever uttered, since it brings with it a confirmation of our hopes, and a vindication of optimism, such as no religion, no philosophy has ever been able to offer? Why have we not been told that we have here, for the first time, the word of Nature itself to assure us that we have not lived in vain as long as we, each in our own sphere, strive to better ourselves and the world we live in? Why have we been denied the encouragement of knowing that we are acting in accordance with Nature's plan when we place spiritual interests above material ones, when, by effort and sacrifice, we press forward earnestly towards scientific, ethical or artistic aims ? Why has the word evolution been misinterpreted and perverted until it ceases to mean evolution at all ?

It is perhaps hardly too much to say that the idea of evolution has from the first fallen among thieves ; and that it is high time the philosophers stepped in and reinstated it ; that is, built for it the great all-embracing temple where the whole of humanity can gather and draw strength for the daily task from the sight of its purity and greatness. If there be an evolution taking place on this earth, then no one of us has the right to hold aloof ; that is the practical teaching of evolution. To pervert and misinterpret it is to murder the best that is in us, for it thrusts us out, makes us passive observers only, and lets evolution pass us by.

This, of course, will not be the case. The influence of the mechanistic theory is over, though it certainly has been disastrously prevalent in its day, at universities and in literature.

In the great speculative philosophers of the previous century, Schelling, Fichte and Hegel, we find the first vague attempts at an idealistic theory of evolution. Schelling in particular divined what was to come.

Unfortunately, these philosophers gave themselves up too much to speculation. Schelling, indeed, went so far as to reject the ordinary methods of physics, and proposed to replace them by "speculative physics."

It must be borne in mind, however, that the science of that day was far behind that of our own times. The material of natural science at the disposal of philosophers was inadequate and often incoherent, and the theory of evolution itself was unknown. Consequently, these philosophers had recourse to thought-structures of so fantastic a character that "philosophy of nature" has been in bad odour ever since, and scientific investigators have shunned it like the plague.

Schelling in particular has been condemned as a fantastic ; and it must be admitted that he often went to a depth of speculation and mysticism where few would care to follow.

Nevertheless, he was something of a philosopher in the true sense of the word; he possessed a quality which our own short-sighted age appears to have lost: the power of comprehensive vision, of regarding phenomena as a whole. He realised that if a system of natural philosophy were to be formed, mind must have a decisive place in it, and if he had lived at the present day he would have been better qualified than any other to give us an idealistic and spiritual interpretation of the theory of evolution.

In his principal work, the *System des transcendentalen Idealismus* (written in 1800, or nine years before the epoch-making work of Lamarck appeared), Schelling speaks of the world-soul that has developed along two lines, of Nature and mind. Nature is a living whole, and natural development is the gradual awakening of the spirit to consciousness of itself. The thing that moves in Nature as its blind force is spirit, which is still in an unconscious, dormant state, and only attains to complete understanding of itself and its content in the human consciousness.

" Dead and unconscious natural products," writes Schelling in his *Philosophy of Identity*, " are only unsuccessful attempts on Nature's part to reflect itself, and our so-called dead Nature in nothing but an immature intelligence; wherefore the intelligent character already shows through in its phenomena, albeit as yet unconscious."

Schelling was already aware that there is an ascending principle in Nature, a tendency to ever higher forms of life. The organic world has developed out of one and the same organisation. The individual is only the means, the end in view is the propagation of the race. The world is a giant spirit, partially petrified but struggling towards consciousness. In living man, the universal soul becomes aware of itself, and discovers that it is the force which moves in everything. This soul has developed along two lines—mind and Nature. Mind and Nature are therefore identical.

Schelling touches one of the leading problems in philosophy when he asks how the human faculty of sense has arisen in Nature, how Nature with its causes and effects comes to exist for us. He explains this in another way than Kant. Kant held that beyond Nature there exists *das Ding an sich*—the thing in itself, which we cannot grasp and never shall be able to grasp by reason of the limitation of our understanding. When he discovered purposiveness in Nature, he believed that it was there because man had put it there; it was ideal, not real. To Fichte and Schelling, on the other hand, it is real, for, they argue, if mind can rediscover itself in Nature, this is not due to the fact that it " creates " Nature, but because it discovers its own principle there. Nature must therefore be a sort of mind, albeit a dormant mind. All matter is in reality living and has a soul; and that is why the spiritual life is so intensely connected with that of Nature.

Schelling regarded the relation between Nature and mind as similar to that between two brothers, one of whom, Nature, was poorly developed, almost torpid, while the other, mind, was powerfully alive, constantly developing and flourishing in art. If he had been acquainted with the modern theory of evolution, he would perhaps rather have viewed the relationship as that between father and son, Nature being the father, old and blind, acting now but automatically, and the begetter of mind, the young, alert and active son with the quick eye and idealistic endeavour towards ever greater liberty and ever higher ideals. Schelling did not get beyond the formulation of a certain systematic relationship between natural forms; he divined the connection, but was not able to interpret Nature and mind as created by a progressive development, the process which we call evolution. He did not realise that one stage arose out of the other; that mind was a later product of Nature itself.

But Schelling was one of the first to characterise the fundamental principle of Nature as a will to mind, and for this alone he deserves immortality.

The German Romantic philosophers came into the world too soon. They did not get as much out of their philosophy of Nature as they would have done had they been born half a century later. The theory of evolution appeared in the meantime.

We have seen how it was misinterpreted from the first. But the road lay open for a deeper and more comprehensive inter-

IDEALISTIC THEORY OF EVOLUTION 55

pretation of Nature, and that road has already been followed by the Danish physicist and philosopher Ludvig Feilberg (1849-1912). Feilberg pursues the theory of evolution to its full consequences by applying it to the highest forms of life we know, namely, those of the mind. Similar ideas are also discernible here and there in the works of German vitalists and English writers of the neo-Hegelian school, but nowhere so clearly formulated as in Feilberg's works. He sets down his thoughts on this subject clearly and distinctly, uninfluenced by any other writers; he is himself the first to deal with it.

Evolution, says Feilberg, teaches us that the daily alteration which takes place in Nature is not accidental, tending this way to-day and another way to-morrow; there is a definite direction in its movement. There is a meaning in it all.

It is further evident from this phenomenon of natural development that Nature is not perfect or complete, but is ever working its way forward from a lower to a more perfect state, slowly overcoming a certain opposition (natural antagonism).

When we see a sheet of asphalt bulging up before the pressure of a toadstool, which, after all, cannot force its way through; or a man's life-work spent apparently in vain, with no visible gain; these are instances of Nature's battle against powerful resistance which it is unable to overcome. And it may often be difficult then to discern a meaning through the failures in the foreground. But taken on the whole, viewed from one geological period to another, the evolutionary progress of Nature appears as an unmistakable fact.

The study of evolution leads Feilberg to the conclusion that the world consists not of many kinds of Nature but of one only, that which surrounds us all. And evolution has a certain definite direction; it proceeds undeviatingly "from a thinner to a more condensed state."

If we ask on what he bases this theory of "condensation" Feilberg answers:

On the phenomenon of *effort*. That there exists a psychic phenomenon of effort and that it invariably occasions a momentous change in the psychic content wherever it occurs, is a matter of incontestable experience, a fact as certain as any practical observation can offer.

This condensation is discernible not only in the life of the soul; we find it at all stages of natural development. Fine linen, for instance, represents a higher degree of condensation than coarse. Coal, the product of many centuries, has a higher condensation of potential energy than peat. Fruits are more highly condensed than leaves. The brain of a scientist will contain a greater number of work-units than that of a peasant. Self-sacrifice, then, we may conclude, will demand a greater condensation of natural energy than mere unruly enthusiasm. Effort must always be a sure sign of condensation.

The different degrees of energy contained in different natural products will as a rule be apparent in a difference of the power of work contained. Some are stronger than others, able to conquer, check, expel or oppose the action of others; they have a greater vital force. Coal has more vital force than peat. Man is able to master animals far superior in bulk and physical strength—it is the condensed form of natural energy present in psychic activity which conquers the more primitive brute; primitive in the sense of being at a lower stage of condensation. A small nation may conquer a greater one at a lower stage of progress.

Observation clearly shows us that something is taking place in Nature; that the part we call " living " Nature is at open feud with another, which we call inertia, or dead Nature; and that the struggle results in a slow movement which we call natural development. We can, moreover, no longer doubt that we ourselves are partakers in the strife, since we know we originated in living nature as a part of it and a stage in its development.

But, it may be objected, Nature does not distinguish between good and evil. You and I and all things are equally products of Nature; even the meanest represents a stage in evolution. All is naturally justified and therefore good. There cannot possibly be anything naturally evil.

Feilberg answers:

" It is true that everything produced by Nature does to a

certain extent help forward natural development, and is thus good ; otherwise it would not have existed at all. But there are very different degrees of goodness. Just as cold is a very poor degree of heat, and darkness a very poor degree of light, so also in Nature, despite the fact that everything is naturally good, we nevertheless find things which must relatively be called naturally evil, namely, those which represent the very lowest degrees of goodness. Nature creates many things that are very poor in goodness ; it is inherent in the principle of evolution to begin with the poorest. And where there is evolution we cannot have everything equally good.

Any impartial observer of natural development will perceive that the work of Nature tends in a direction from less to more complex (condensed) forms. The earth was a glowing mass before trees grew on it ; the crustaceans came into existence before the mammals. A glance at Nature shows us all degrees of condensation. Some products are found in enormous quantities, evidently produced at no great cost, while others of rare occurrence are plainly the result of long toil and sacrifice and effort. We can actually measure the high cost of one as against that of the other.

Feilberg regards man and the mind of man as the costliest product of Nature. But man is not the end, only the means ; he has a task assigned to him in the process of evolution. What is this task ?

Man can improve the sum of Nature's energy by transforming it from a poorer quality to one more condensed, a richer form. We find this actually done again and again, willingly or—more often—unwillingly. The business of all creation is really to improve and intensify creation ; to act as Nature's transformers of energy.

It is this transformation of energy which takes place when a wheat straw produces its concentrated grains of wheat. And the same process is seen wherever man, by the exertion of effort, intensifies his spiritual force;

If human beings were not capable of thus transforming energy by condensation, we should be unable to make any real contribution to the work of Nature. If we could do no more than give back the talent we have received, nothing would be gained on either side.

Valuable as are Feilberg's ideas on the subject of evolution, we have not space here for a further exposition. What has been said already will suffice to show the great difference between his conception and those of the mechanists and the vitalists.

He interprets evolution by applying a measure of value. He distinguishes between natural products as more or less "naturally good," and therefore, not only more or less endowed with vitality but also of greater of less value. He is not content with the assumption that the whole evolution of Nature is based on mechanical accident, or that its sole aim is life and the maintenance of life. He finds an inner leading principle in evolution from less to more condensed forms, he follows this principle through many stages, and sees it blossom out at last in human life, where it assumes various forms such as self-control, mental effort and sacrifice. He gives us a more profound interpretation of evolution as a whole than we find elsewhere. His most important contribution, however, is undoubtedly his placing of man himself as an important factor in the evolutionary process, by virtue of this transformation of energy, whereby man, receiving a certain value from Nature, retains it in a richer form.

Ludvig Feilberg is thus the founder of the idealistic theory of evolution, and gives us a basis upon which we can build further.

Our hypothesis is in the main as follows :

The great process of evolution, or condensation, observed by Feilberg has up to the present had a certain aim, to wit, that of producing transformers of energy capable of producing mind.

Man is one of the results—a successful result—of this process.

Animals and plants are other products of the same process, but unsuccessful results. That there must be something wrong with them is evident from the fact that so many have perished in the course of evolution, never to arise again ; also from the fact that the development of the others is evidently now at an

IDEALISTIC THEORY OF EVOLUTION

end. There is no further progress to be looked for in the animal or vegetable world; we find only a retrogression.

The form best suited to fulfil the purpose of Nature is evidently that particular type of transformer we call man. It is this form that has passed, and passed with honours, in the great competition of evolution.

Man stands now as the ruler of the earth. Since first man entered on the scene, the human race has been in constant progress. Racial types have arisen and disappeared again, but the race as a whole has only been strengthened by this alternation. At no stage in the history of our planet has man been so powerful and so widely distributed as now. It is a steady advance throughout. All other species have declined in comparison. If we retain the term transformer of energy as indicating an organism, it must be admitted that man is the type of transformer which Nature has preferred and specially endowed.

This result has been attained by evolution. Immense forces must have contributed to the work, for the condensation could not have taken place of itself; it needs a force behind to effect it.

Of what sort is this force? We do not know. All that we can say for certain will be mostly negative. We can, for instance, definitely assert that it is not mechanical, for in such case it would not have been capable of transforming matter into life, which evolution shows us has been done. Nor can it have been a merely vital force, for in such case it could not have effected the transition from primitive to spiritual life. Again, it can hardly be a merely spiritual force, such as mind, in the human sense, for mind is a comparatively recent product of evolution, and is itself a product of the unknown force in question; the two cannot therefore be identical.

The one thing we can say positively is, that the force has been busily at work, and has manifested itself in sudden changes from time to time—as in De Vries' Mutations. It worked in matter to begin with, later, in the vegetable and animal forms, and finally in humanity. It is a creative force producing ever new forms. The idealistic theory of evolution calls this force *the creative power*.

Whether this power at the beginning found matter ready to its hand, or itself created matter, we do not know. But we must assume that it gradually built up the elements from which is has created life, and thus laid the foundations for spiritual life.

The creative power, unlike other forces of Nature, cannot be seen or measured or weighed. But we need not therefore regard it as a fiction of the imagination. A thought cannot be seen or measured or weighed, yet it is none the less a reality. Unless we postulate a creative power, x, it is impossible to explain evolution. Without it we can find no relation between the phenomena of evolution.

Following the creative power on its course through evolution, we find that it has been constantly aiming at a certain end, namely, that of producing spiritual transformers. If then it be not itself mind, then it must at least comprise a will to mind, analogous to Schopenhauer's will to life.

Its *modus operandi* at all stages of development has been identical. It took a material, dissected it, let the individual parts meet in combat, and the strongest, most concentrated, emerge hardened from the fight to encounter new opponents of like calibre on a higher plane. The progress of evolution from atom to molecule, from molecule to amoeba, from amoeba to man, has been effected by Nature through a system of heats just as one would select the best team for a game from among a whole population.

Man, then, was Nature's goal; but is the ultimate goal attained with man? The idealistic theory of evolution holds that this is not the case. Man is only a temporary goal. Nature has, by a long and painful process of struggle and creation, produced a great number of transformers, to wit, the human race, capable of in turn producing mind. Mind, spirit is the ultimate goal.

This interpretation may perhaps at a first glance appear surprising. Similar ideas have, however, been put forward earlier, as, for instance, in a paper by Professor Armand Sabatier delivered at the Institut Général Psychologique in Paris in 1904.

Professor Sabatier regards the human brain as an apparatus

IDEALISTIC THEORY OF EVOLUTION

where the lower cosmic forces are accumulated and transformed into mind; he likens the function of the brain to that of an accumulator. The brain effects a transformation of energy, and stores and directs the higher energy thus formed. The soul is defined as a bundle of energies, built up by ourselves, with our brain acting as accumulator and transformer.

The French scientist has here, with a striking similarity to Feilberg, indicated the place and task of man in Nature by the same terms, accumulator and transformer. The whole process of evolution has been directed towards the production of these transformers.

But what happens to the spiritual force, thus refined, by the action of innumerable individual transformers working together?

It is here that the idealistic theory of evolution comes forward with its hypothesis. It says: a great portion of the force is lost at once (which by the way proves that it is not " force " in the ordinary sense of the word); but part of it is preserved in the form of what we might call the common spiritual property; the common stock of spiritual force. When someone thinks a new thought, he does not keep it to himself, but communicates it to others. If his fellows consider the thought of value, they keep it, and it lives on thenceforward not only in the brain of its originator, but in many other brains. Thus, in course of time, we get the common store of mind, the group mind.

It is this product of man in the aggregate that the idealistic theory of evolution regards as the aim of evolution, the aim which Nature has had in view. Our doctrine seeks as far as possible to show that a perishable physical world is gradually creating, by a process of refinement, a spiritual—i.e. non-material—replica of itself.

In order to attain this result, the physical world has by gradual evolution created a series of apparatus (brains and nerve systems) capable of transmuting physical into spiritual values. The process of evolution is now at the present stage where the transformers are made and beginning to work. The spiritual world which is to take the place of the physical world is thus now in its first stage of formation. The solidarity of culture, the spiritual life of humanity, has its first foundations laid.

This new spiritual world is at present centred in the accumulator section of the human transformer system (memory) and thus is still associated with the bio-physical world. But there is much to suggest that this is only a temporary arrangement. In time to come, the spiritual world will break away from the bio-physical world and enter on an independent existence as spirit alone. The Collective Spirit will be the quintessence of all that is greatest and best in the mind of man.

There is nothing in this assumption which need affright or even discourage us as human beings. There by the roadway stands an electric transformer, apparently no more than a tower of steel. But within that insignificant-looking shell immense, invisible forces are at work, transforming energy from lower to higher forms. Innumerable wheels are driven, machines and factories are kept going, whole cities lighted and heated by the work that goes on in that dark, chilly tower. Similarly, man has been entrusted by Nature with a task of the greatest importance and responsibility, as the producer of spirit, of the Collective Spirit. Generations are born and die, whole races arise and live their span and perish, but all these human units are working toward one and the same ultimate end; all are engaged in the production of spiritual force, and each individual thus contributes his share to the refining process of Nature.

It may be objected that this common spiritual property in process of formation is only to serve as a means of ethical development, one generation aiding its successors by means of the accumulated store of spiritual force. But this assumption will hardly be correct; for the work of individuals, indeed, of whole generations, becomes insignificant in comparison with the overwhelming sum of the whole. As the leaves of a tree continue to change, though the tree is all the time growing greater and stronger by their aid, so also human beings have their task in the service of the Collective Spirit; they are a means, not an end. But as the tree could not lift its mighty branches to the light and grow in strength and beauty unless aided by its faithful servants, the leaves, so also the Collective

Spirit cannot grow save by the earnest effort and self-sacrifice of mankind.

Work for a great cause ennobles all who serve it. The thing that gives to man his touch of divinity, and in the great moments of life as it were a halo of light, is his effort in the service of the Collective Spirit.

We feel within us forces urging us forward toward the Collective Spirit. Religion and ethics have given these feelings their first fine expression, naive as it may be. Now, science points to the theory of evolution and says: study the course of Nature, range facts in their order and relation, consider evolution from the lowest to the highest! And lo, in the manifold picture-book of Nature we find all needful confirmation of the vague feelings within us. Everywhere about us we find a process of development, we ourselves are partakers in the same, and the more we aid and support the process, the nearer we get to the purpose of Nature.

In regarding the Collective Spirit as the end, not as a means of evolution, we base our view upon the following considerations:

1. We cannot otherwise explain the presence in man of strongly developed artistic and scientific instincts which often rather hamper than advance the individual in the struggle for existence. These instincts are plainly designed to serve, not the individual alone, nor even the race; they have a still higher purpose: that of the whole. They may at times be so strong as to drive the individual, or a whole generation, a whole nation of individuals to self-sacrifice. Social feeling, science and art have their martyrs as well as religion. Men sacrifice themselves in the cause of the Collective Spirit.

2. The law of entropy teaches us that the whole universe will perish by dissipation of energy. All material and biological development will thus be brought to a standstill sooner or later. All the work effected will be in vain. That is, unless the costly fruits of evolution can be preserved in some imperishable—that is, immaterial form. Such a form is provided by the Collective Spirit.

If it be asked, whether the Collective Spirit is a reality at our present stage, the answer must be : it is a reality in the making.

To take a simple illustration, we may say that the Collective Spirit is a house in process of erection. Millions of human beings have carried stones to the site, but only a few of the best and finest stones have been selected, the rest are thrown aside. The house has not yet reached its first floor, and fresh material is constantly being brought in; but we can already discern the greatness and beauty of the edifice to come. The house of the Collective Spirit is already far enough advanced to act as a mighty inspiration upon those who gather about it.

That such a spiritual edifice is under construction, and has been so as far back as the history of culture extends, will hardly be denied. The only possible question will be as to the purpose for which it is intended.

We believe that the house is the aim of all creative development here on earth, now and in the future. The position of individual workers in relation to the edifice as a whole is like that of the ancient Egyptians towards the great pyramid. Individual workers are dead and gone, but they have left behind them a monument through which they live, and will live, as long as the world exists. All men will die, but the Collective Spirit will remain.

If we attempt to find an explanation of ourselves and the phenomena about us, it is useless to look at facts in their externals only, as science does; we must look within, to reasons deeper down. Various instincts are at work within us —psychologically as well as physiologically we are built up on instincts. Some of these we find again in the animals, as for instance the instincts of self-preservation and of propagation. Others, however, such as the ethical and artistic instincts, are only developed to any extent in man. If we would know what is our task in the world, we must first of all ask our instincts. Their direction and aim must tell us what it is that Nature asks of us—if indeed there is any meaning in life at all.

On consideration, it soon becomes evident that just these higher instincts in man would be sadly out of place if they were only grafted on the individual to serve individual aims.

Man could get along very well in the world without art or science or ethics; that is, from a purely material point of view, like that of the beasts. If, nevertheless, we find ourselves equipped with these instincts it seems evident that Nature has some end in view for the individual which lies beyond the individual himself. When Nature gives a bird the nesting instinct, it is not out of regard to the bird itself, but for the sake of the brood to come, that is, for the race. Similarly, we may say that when Nature has given us artistic and scientific and ethical instincts, it is not out of regard for the individual or the human race alone, but with a view to the higher world that shall some day take the place of this, the world of the Collective Spirit.

The presence of higher instincts in the human breast explains the curious fact that humanity, despite all rationalism and practical sense, has adopted the mystic religions of the Asiatics, which are in several respects at variance with our ordinary views of life, but nevertheless form the spiritual food of many to this day. Man has discovered a craving within him, and certain myths have adapted and accommodated themselves to that craving. The so-called religious feeling, which the Church exploits to the uttermost in the service of its own, often far from worthy aims, is nothing but the feeling of our own instinctive tendency towards the Collective Spirit.

It is altogether erroneous to suppose that we think with our brains alone. We think, as a matter of fact, much more with the heart. " The heart " is our halting, clumsy term for the sum of feelings, our love and need of ennobling ourselves in a multitude of ways, a thing we cannot explain by any logic. If we seek to convince anyone of anything, it is not enough to proceed by reason alone, we must speak to the heart, for the heart is in reality the master, and reason the servant; the heart is the current of steam, the reason only the valve that regulates it.

The enormous power of religion over man is due to the fact that it goes, unlike dry science, directly to the heart. It has ennobled the world in agreement with our feelings, and has always been capable of spreading light, even during its darkest age.

It is not religion, still less the religious feeling, we are here seeking to oppose, but the teaching of the Church, the hard, inhuman shell in which religion has been enclosed.

In place of a Church, man will in time build a temple to the Collective Spirit. For the thought of the Collective Spirit will be capable of giving man far more than the Church. By means of the idealistic theory of evolution we shall attain to a deeper understanding of our existence, we shall view things as a whole, realise what is our own task, and learn to take the right place among our fellow-humans. We shall realise that it is to our advantage to do our duty to the utmost; we shall feel ourselves as citizens of the earth, and understand that *this* life—this life that has been so misnamed and so misused—is our grand opportunity.

The idealistic theory of evolution is no dry science. It seeks by the aid of reason to comprehend the great material of science, but at the same time urges its adherents to think with their hearts as well. It is more idealistic perhaps than any doctrine, for it says: do your duty without reserve, without self-righteousness and without thought of any reward in another life. It gives us a religion of this world, yet without denying that another world will arise out of this in time to come.

The ancient faith held that God created Nature and man. The idealistic theory of evolution teaches us that the reverse is the case; it is Nature that creates God, using man as an instrument for the purpose of that creation.

THE CREATIVE POWER

> Neither God nor Man has created this world.
> *Heraclitus.*

IF you, Reader, will consider what you consist of, you will find that three different principles are united in your being. These three principles, each of which constitutes a world in itself, we term the material, the biological and the spiritual.

1. The Material Principle. Your body is built up of a series of organic substances, which are compounds of inorganic elements such as those we find in " dead " Nature.

2. The Biological Principle. There is something in you which is called life. You have a *living* body, which was born, grew up and in course of time will die. There is in you a vital principle which finds its physical expression in instincts, growth and propagation. You are a living individual, constituting a biological unity answering to those you see in other human beings and in different forms of animals and plants. Biologically speaking, you recognise the factor of totality which was the object of Driesch's investigations.

3. The Spiritual Principle. You possess something which we call a soul-life or spiritual life. You have the power of thinking and exchanging thoughts with other human beings. Something similar is found among certain higher forms of animals, but only rudimentary, without the wealth, extent and possibilities of development which characterise the spiritual life of man.

The doctrine of evolution, especially through geology and embryology, teaches us that the highest and most complex human types were not created all at once. During the different phases in the history of our planet, we see life at various stages of development, and if we go back far enough, we come to a point where there was no life at all, but only matter in a fluid state, at a very high temperature.

Life has evolved gradually, commencing with the material principle, after which the biological principle (life) entered on the scene, and last of all the spiritual principle in its present form.

These facts are incontrovertible.

The question now is: what has been the motive power in this process of evolution—from matter to mind?

The mechanists evade the question and regard evolution as an outward appearance only, the mere expansion of something already given which will again contract and expand again, in rhythmic repetition (Herbert Spencer, Nietzsche). Darwin's spiritual relative, Huxley, has formulated the idea very clearly. If the fundamental principle of evolution be correct, namely, that the whole of the living and lifeless world is the result of a reciprocal opposition of the molecular forces which constituted the original nebula of the universe, acting by definite laws, then it is also certain that the present world was potentially present in the cosmic vapours, and that a sufficiently mighty intelligence with a knowledge of the qualities of the nebular molecules might have predicted, for instance, the state of the fauna of Great Gritain in 1868 as confidently as one can say what will happen to the vapour of the breath on a cold winter's day.

If we cannot accept this theory, and assume that evolution is not a mere mechanical expression, but a creative process, there will then be two possible explanations:

1. We may assume that there is, behind the process of evolution, a creator and architect, a maker of the world, who has set the whole in motion and still guides the process in order to serve his own higher ends, which are incomprehensible to us. This theory is supported by most of the so-called revealed religions and acknowledged by most civilised states, where it is given the official stamp of an authorised interpretation of evolution.

Or,

2. We may assume that evolution is the work of some force or power manifesting itself thereby.

It is this latter theory which the idealistic doctrine of evolution adopts, since it seems to us, all things considered, the most reasonable.

But we may at once admit that we cannot offer definite proof that the theory is correct ; we can only show that it is most likely to be so. If it be asserted that all evolution is an illusion, and that all that takes place is but the expansion of something previously existing ; or if it be maintained that there exists a God guiding and directing all things in the universe, then we cannot, at the present stage of scientific knowledge, produce any incontrovertible proof of the contrary. It must therefore be left to the individual judgment to decide which theory is the more likely ; a judgment which, when all is said and done, will depend on the individual acumen and mental capacity.

It will be asked : can we consider it at all an acceptable explanation, to say that the world has created itself ? Is not that at variance with the whole of our experience, based on the iron laws of cause and effect and conservation of energy, declaring that nothing ever perishes, while on the other hand, nothing new is ever formed ? Must not a world created by itself be, as Nietzsche puts it, a miracle eternally repeated ? We cannot find any instance anywhere of something being created out of nothing. On the other hand, we do see that energy and matter continue to exist, changing their form, but adding nothing to their sum. We cannot imagine how the sum total of the universe should ever increase.

Such an argument is false. To say there is nothing new under the sun is the greatest fallacy that ever was uttered. Look about you in the spiritual world. Every time a new thought is conceived, or a new work of art created, a permanent increment is added to the economy of Nature, far exceeding the subjective minus of the energy expended. And this is continually happening. In the spiritual world, creation is a phenomenon so general that we never notice it as anything unusual. But creation it is none the less. (Where were the tragedies of Shakespeare before he created them ?) How can we deny creation when we see that the whole of our civilisation is itself a continual spiritual process of creation ? How can the man who conceives a new idea deny that it was created in his mind?

The mechanists, however, disregard all this. They assert that nothing is ever created; everything was there beforehand (Shakespeare's works, for instance, the products of mind, were present in embryo in certain physical atoms!)

Why should the mechanists cherish this hatred of the idea of creation? We can only explain it as a reaction against the uncritical acceptance, in a previous period, of the existence of a creator somewhere beyond, the author and cause of the whole. Maturer views reject the assumption of such a creator, but here we have the not uncommon error of throwing away the good with the bad. Not content with deposing the Creator, the mechanists assert that all creation, as a process, is an impossibility.

It must here be pointed out that though creation itself is a wonder, and hard to understand, yet it is surely no more wonderful or harder to understand than the very fact that there is a world at all; that it should be there, instead of nothingness. That the world is real will hardly be doubted; but is the fact that it is, any less strange than the idea that it should gradually have created itself? The mechanists' theory of expansion and contraction does not by any means do away with the mystery of creation; it only makes the whole thing more mysterious by pushing the act of creation still farther back in point of time. If the world we know was already potentially present in the cosmic vapour, there must still have been a creative principle to form and arrange the infinitely complex distribution of atoms in that vapour in order to render its subsequent development possible at all. The idealistic doctrine of evolution assumes that creation has been a successive process, a gradual development, one stage providing the foundation for the next; The mechanists, on the other hand, assert that everything was created all at once, and gradually unfolded as a bud from its sheath. But in either case a miracle is required to explain creation at all. And it seems to us that the miracle involved in the idealistic doctrine of evolution is less miraculous than that which the mechanists assume.

THE CREATIVE POWER

Recent philosophers, also, are not afraid to admit, as do the Buddhists, the reality of a creative power working by gradual stages. It is to Bergson that we owe the term: *évolution créatrice*, and we cannot be sufficiently grateful to the French philosopher for this idea. Whether the creative process has followed the course he assumes, and is due to the causes he suggests, is another matter. We shall have occasion to consider that later on. For the moment, it will suffice to note that we agree with Bergson in regarding evolution and creative evolution as synonymous terms. If we deny the attribute creative, then the word evolution has no meaning at all.

But it is not only Bergson who appreciated the reality of evolution. One of the most prominent German scientists and thinkers, Wilh. Wundt, whose work includes important researches in the field of psycho-physics, puts forward the principle of creative resultants, a principle which fully recognises creative power in spiritual life. According to this, psychic combinations and products are always rather more than the sum of the elements of which they are built. Wundt writes: "The product, in comparison with the elements which go to its production, is something *new*. Its essential qualities cannot be identified with the factors which went to its formation." In this way, we get a spiritual creative process, inasmuch as the co-operation of the spiritual factors is always capable of bringing into the world something new, and that, moreover, of a higher order.

We may also quote, among many others, the American writer, E. W. Lyman, who entirely supports the hypothesis of creation. Lyman considers not only that the world is the product of a creative evolution, or of a series of creative syntheses; he goes even further, and suggests that the world "is creating creators." This, according to our theory, is entirely correct; the creative power lends its forces to man, especially to great artists and scientists.

These three names alone: Bergson, Wundt and Lyman, show that the theory of creation is by no means lacking in supporters and advocates among the best philosophers, besides the ever-increasing number of biologists of the neo-vitalist and neo-Lamarckian schools, who likewise adopt it.

The idealistic doctrine of evolution builds on the following assumption:

As entelechy is the ultimate cause of the growth of the individual organism in the form it attains, so also there must necessarily exist a " force " which is the ultimate cause of the occurrence of all vital phenomena ; of the whole mighty system of evolution leading up from dead matter to the supreme product of life, namely, man.

This force we call the creative power.

The term creative power is far more comprehensive than Driesch's entelechy ; it is not only regulating, liberating, purposive, limiting and organising, but also, as the term itself indicates, directly creative. On the basis of the material world it has created life, and from this again, at a later stage, mind. Without a creative process in the most positive sense, evolution could never have got to the point where matter began to feel, and feeling in turn became transmuted into thought.

The creative power of the theory of evolution is again not identical with Bergson's *élan vital*. According to Bergson, the creative power is an attribute of life—of all life. Life and creative force are identical. As soon as life gets hold of matter, creation begins, and this creative process goes on until life has conquered matter, has exhausted it. Bergson has not realised that there is a great deal of life in which creative power is no longer positively manifested. It is true that all life—and, we may add, all matter—is due to a creative evolution, but the creative power need not therefore be still *actively* present in all the phenomena we see around us.

But so it is. The creative power must originally—in some manner which physical science cannot yet explain, though we can dimly discern it—have built up the elements then left them to automatism, which preserves, conserves and as far as possible protects all that the creative power has produced. The automatic side of the creative power is apparent in Nature in the form of inertia, the conservation of energy. Then, having carried the elements to the point of perfection, the creative power set about a new task, the creation of life. Here, however, the same thing occurred ; after having clothed the vital principle in a series of forms, plants, animals and human beings, it concentrated its efforts on another task, the creation of a world of mind.

All that we see on earth, then, is the product of creative power; but this power is no more actively present in the products of its work than the power of the artist in the works he has produced. Creative power is, at the present stage of evolution, only active in the mind of man; all else that it has created has long since been handed over to automatism and follows its laws.

Driesch calls the creative power a purposive and liberating force. Bergson considers it identical with life, and, like life, creating blindly. We on the other hand say: that creative power is higher than matter, life and mind, since it is the creator of these; it is the positively new-creating principle of existence, and this principle has, as the course of evolution plainly shows, worked not on one plane throughout, but by rising from one to another.

In order not to make this new point of view too complicated for the reader, we will for the moment disregard automatism and consider only the creative power itself, following, as nearly as we can, its process through the different stages.

First Stage. Creative power in the material world.

With the material accumulated by physical science up to date, it is impossible to say anything as to the work of the creative power at the earliest stage of evolution. Several theories may here be advanced. Did it create the atoms, ether, magnetism, electricity, the force of gravity, etc? Or did it find these forces in the form of dormant energy, which it released and set in motion, allowing them to act upon one another in new states of equilibrium? We cannot say.

One night, when Herschel the astronomer was watching the Milky Way through a telescope, he suddenly discovered a dark, starless patch. There must be a hole in the sky! It was subsequently found that the patch was not a hole, but a dark mass of enormous extent, obscuring the stars behind. It is now called Barnard's black nebula in Orion, and is still one of the greatest riddles of astronomy. There are, then, in the universe, not only milliards of suns connected one with another through the radiation of light across the ether, but also non-luminous continents, colossal areas fixed in the ether as apparently dead masses. Here perhaps we have a key to the creation of the universe, the first chord in the mighty concert of the world. It is not impossible that the universe may originally have consisted of some such mass, subjected to the action of the creative power, and providing the basis of the gradual evolutionary process, which has led, *via* nebula suns and solar systems, planets and life on earth, to the spirit of man as the finest evolutionary product we know. The latest researches of Professor Niels Bohr seem to suggest that energy is actually *created* in nebulæ at high temperatures. That is to say, that the law as to conservation of energy is valid here on earth, but not out in space, where new worlds are being formed. By the aid of our spectroscopes and telescopes we are able to observe actual processes of creation in the material world. These new researches are annihilating to old-fashioned ideas of physics. Up to now, we have never been able to see the creative power at work in its earliest stages, but only the results.

These results we found, in physical Nature, as a state of equilibrium between the series of " wills to power " which we call natural forces and elements. Schopenhauer has given us a magnificent description of how these natural forces are constantly meeting in conflict and co-operation, ever seeking new states of equilibrium. Magnetism, electricity, gravity, chemical qualities and the like struggle one against the other, fighting to gain a place for itself against the rest. The world of Nature is dominated throughout by the will to power.

How matter was formed we do not know. But the atomic theory offers a certain support for the assumption that substances were formed at a comparatively late stage as the result of a creative natural process, gradually assembling several electrons about a common atomic nucleus. This produced elements of different atomic weight. The creative power then proceeded to unite several atoms into molecules, which, again, formed larger units, and thus paved the way for the colloids, the raw material of life.

One might almost say that the creative power had realised

that pure mechanism would not have sufficient stability ; if left to itself it would, as we know from the law of entropy, lose its potency and gradually sink to a state of equilibrium at a low level, when all energy would be dissipated and depreciated to heat energy.

In order to avoid, or at any rate to postpone, this termination, the creative power then aimed at the formation of a new principle, that of life, which, supporting itself on matter, but refining it, would be able to oppose the entropic process under more favourable conditions. Thus life was formed.

Second Stage. The creative power in the biological world.

As long as the creative power was content to operate in the material sphere, it might be defined as a purely physical power, stronger, it is true, than the other forces of Nature, since it was able to control them, but still of a purely physical character. But the course of evolution has shown us that the creative power was not content with manifesting itself in a physical form ; it had a higher aim in view. And accordingly, it achieved the masterpiece of passing from stage one to stage two, and creating life. A marvellous development took place. When the physical forces had been brought to a certain degree of evolutionary maturity, the creative power concentrated on a fresh task, that of bringing into the world a hitherto unknown phenomenon, life ! It was a miracle, the miracle that strikes the mechanists dumb.

In this new world thus formed, the world of life, the foundation is still that of the elements, material energy, consisting of atoms and molecules ; these elements, however, now appear in far more complex combinations than hitherto ; they are transformed from inorganic to organic matter.

It is not this, however, which gives the world of life its peculiar character ; not even, perhaps, the fact that this world has the faculty of propagation. The decisive difference lies in another sphere. In the world of life we find something hitherto unknown, feeling and sensation, an inner life.

If we strike an object in the material world, it is affected in some way or other, but only in a purely external, mechanical way. If we strike a living organism, exactly the same thing takes place in a material sense, but also something more. The material effect is accompanied by a phenomenon hitherto unknown, an alteration of feeling takes place within the organism. As long as dead matter was all that existed, only external effects were known; here, however, we suddenly come upon an inner life. The material changes occasioned by a blow could be directly measured, but how can we measure the sum and intensity of feelings? We find ourselves now in a sphere where material measurements can no longer be applied. The miracle that took place when the creative power moved from stage one to stage two can be summed up in this: a quantitative world gives rise to a qualitative one.

As soon as life is present, we have to reckon with a duality in place of unity. And this applies to flora and fauna alike. Trees have no inner consciousness in the higher, human sense, but they are sentient to a far higher degree than " dead " Nature. They stretch their branches up towards the light, and send their roots down to the water-bearing strata, struggle with their surroundings and strengthen themselves for the task by healing their wounds as best they can; in manifold ways they reveal an inner life which inorganic phenomena cannot show. And the higher we move among animal forms, the stronger is this sentient life.

All the same, life has not cut itself aloof from matter. It was engrafted on matter, and uses matter as its support; and, most interesting of all, it betrays its material origin to such a degree that we are tempted to define it as being merely matter in a new form. On closer consideration, we find that matter itself reappears, only in a refined, non-material form.

But even though life, on analysis, proves to be matter idealised and refined, it cannot be denied that there is a very essential difference between the two, the same that we find between life and death.

But what is the difference between life and death? What is the difference between a turtle lying dormant, motionless, and a turtle lying dead? What is it the latter has lost? Here is the entire organism; yet there is something lacking, a vital principle with the power of growth and organisation, a responsiveness to sense-impressions and instincts, a supra-material, purposive factor of totality that was the master of the organism as a whole. It is this vital factor that has been formed as a world in itself, above matter, subject to laws different from those of matter alone.

Life is a supra-material something, though we can never see it at work save in physical form, as plant, animal or human being.

We have no real knowledge as to how and under what conditions the various species have arisen. Fossil remains show us only a certain succession, proving that the creative power has moved tentatively along innumerable roads, most ending in some blind alley, where the species became extinct.

It is none the less evident that the creative power at the biological stage was never at rest. It was continually experimenting and working by what De Vries has called mutations. These mutations take place comparatively rapidly, and the biological creative period on our earth need not have taken such an enormous period as the mechanists assume. It was a period of growth in hothouse atmosphere, when the species propagated, met in conflict, leaving the strongest and fittest masters of the field. During this period of mutations, the creative power made numerous mistakes, furnishing individuals with qualities which proved only of temporary value and later, under altered conditions of life, detrimental; to such a degree, indeed, as often to involve the extinction of the species. Life in the great biological mutation period developed much as the automobile industry in our own day. It began with a few tentative and clumsy types, experimenting in all directions. Some forms were tried, lasted a while and were then dropped as unable to compete. The final result was a limited number of the best and most suitable types; these were turned out by mass production, and all others became extinct. The term " survival of the fittest " is of great importance in helping us to understand the biological mutation period, but we must remember that the creative power cannot be eliminated itself; it played the same part in regard to the species as did the manufacturers with the automobiles. The numerous extinct species answer then to the obsolete types of car.

And now, what was gained when the creative power

managed to step up from stage one to stage two, the world of life ? Bergson has pointed out that the principal advantage was that the entropy threatening matter could at least be put off for a time. Force was accumulated and concentrated in the individual organisms, and by propagation it was possible not only to preserve the centres of force, but also to increase their number, with a prospect of thus postponing their extinction.

But the biological world has also a kind of entropy hanging over it—a nemesis of matter ! For life, in seeking its own further development, has not been able to escape the principle of conflict, the will to power, which, in the material plane brings forces into opposition until they ultimately reach a state of death-like equilibrium. The will to power has, it is true, at stage two assumed the form of will to life, but this again was at first only a higher form of the will to power, and thus arose the Darwinian struggle for existence. Life inherited from the lower plane the element of conflict, and it was found that this also was needed in the higher plane. Hence the apparent contradiction that life set itself to combat and exterminate life. Previously, only natural forces had been in opposition one to another ; in the biological world, it was now the different species which fought and swallowed up their fellows, each species thinking only of its own maintenance and paying no regard to the interests of the rest.

It is this battle of life against life which forms the great mystery of evolution, and has been a source of so much speculation to the natural philosophers, leading some of them indeed to pessimistic conclusions. Why should Nature create life, and arm it, only to destroy innumerable lives thereby ?

The idealistic doctrine of evolution offers an explanation. True, the creative power is a magician, but its magic power is subject to certain limitations. It cannot work wonders after the manner of the Slave of the Lamp, turning out a finished and furnished palace to order in a moment. This sort of thing is never found in Nature. The creative power works in a different fashion. It takes a material, works on it and shapes it and takes impressions of it in another kind of matter— much as a sculptor fashions a statue first in clay, then moulds it in plaster, then casts it in bronze, until finally it appears in marble. Plainly, the sculptor in his work is only free within certain limits; he is tied down by considerations of subject and materials, and, inevitably, some of the faults which occur in the earliest stages will be found again in the later forms. In the material stage of evolution, there was a constant struggle between natural forces and the elements. And when the creative power proceeded to form the world of life as a finer and nobler copy of the material form, the principle of conflict had to be introduced here as well, since it was an important, not to say vital, factor on the lower plane.

Yet it is by no means certain that the creative power regarded the struggle of life against life as a contradiction. Rather the reverse indeed. For what Nature was aiming at was not life in its primary form, but life in what Feilberg calls " condensed form," and to attain this result there could hardly be any better way than the introduction of conflict and competition, as a stage in the condensation process. We find exactly the same thing in schools and universities, among students at examinations. At all stages of evolution, including the stage of mind, we find the creative power continually making use of conflict and competition in order to further its ends. Properly speaking, then, there is nothing inconsistent in the fact that the will to life, in course of development, often involves the extinction of lives.

It is evident, however, that this struggle of life against life can only have been of service in a qualitative, not in a quantitative respect. And if the merciless conflict goes on, we can easily foresee that the great majority of species will become extinct, leaving only some few of the strongest and fittest, just as in the automobile industry. These forms will continue to exist until the day comes when they too must succumb, owing to the cooling of the planet to a point at which no life can exist. But this means that the law of entropy will have conquered after all; firstly, because the struggle for existence, quantitatively speaking, reduced the number of power-accumulating centres, and finally, because life cannot endure the terrible cold that will crush earth in its mighty fingers when the sun is gradually extinguished.

Bergson's *élan vital* does not reckon with this gloomy end.

It is only calculated to postpone the action of entropy, not to defeat it. Fortunately, however, the creative power has had more foresight. It realised, we might say, that if entropy were to be conquered definitely, this could not be achieved either on the material or on the biological plane; evolution must first be lifted up to a still higher stage, the spiritual plane; then and then only would there be any prospect of salvation from the threatened annihilation of the natural process.

Very early in the second stage of evolution the creative power began taking measures to this end, dividing its work into two fields.

It concentrated on the purely physical side, constructing and plastically forming the many different species in the animal and vegetable kingdoms, and often attaining physical perfection, i.e. a stage where any further alteration would only be detrimental to the individual and the species. Here the creative power presumably started with the sexual cells, transforming and improving them so as to give a series of mutations.

But it was not only the sexual cells which were the object of its attention and interest. It was also occupied with the development of the nervous system and the brain, not only to provide the individual with a serviceable instrument in the struggle for existence, but also to afford a material and biological basis for spiritual development, the construction of a spiritual world as a further stage in the evolutionary process.

The sexual cells were formed to serve the individual vital principle; brain cells, on the other hand, to further supra-individual aims, and in this world of the spirit, or of mind, the creative power soon found so wide a scope for its activity that it left the biological field altogether and concentrated exclusively on the spiritual. This brings us to the stage of evolution at which the creative power is working now.

Third stage. The creative power in the world of mind.

The transition from material to biological was doubtless more or less gradual, possibly indeed almost imperceptible from without, as is mostly the case with the work of the creative power. The biological principle was grafted on the material ; and in the same way, we find the spiritual principle grafted on the biological element. Mental or spiritual powers were at first only designed to serve the same purpose as instinct, as an aid to the organism in the struggle for life. But with the creation of the biological form to which we belong, the human type, spiritual life gradually changed its character, acting now not only in the interest of the individual, but also furthering that of the family, tribe or nation, nay, the whole of humanity. Mind ceased to be purely egoistic, and assumed a more altruistic form ; a common stock of mind or spirit was created, giving a peculiar world in itself, distinct from the plane of matter and life, an entirely new phenomenon.

And thus we enter on a new phase. The first stage might be characterised as the will to power, the second as the will to life, but with the third a new type of will appears : the will to mind.

From the moment when the creative power had produced the world of mind, it seems to have concluded its work on the biological plane, just as its work on the material plane came to an end with the commencement of the biological mutations. Races of plants and animals propagated from henceforth automatically, or disappeared, the entire biological machinery went on its round, but the creative power was now occupied with its new purpose, working with the mind of man, steadily striving to link all individuals closer together, uniting them in work for a common end.

The world of life and matter is more or less clearly defined in our consciousness ; in the world of mind, however, all seems vague. There are two reasons for this. First and foremost it is, from an evolutionary point of view, only quite recently that the creative power reached this stage. It is still at work there, and this gives rise to alterations and uncertainty. We have not here, as in the earlier stages, reached the phase of automatism. And, further, the world of mind as we know it is evidently only a transition stage. The human transformers of energy produce innumerable thoughts ; but Nature's aim is evidently something more than mass production pure and simple ; it aims at the formation of a spiritual whole on a still higher plane again. This spiritual whole is the Collective

Spirit, the world of pure mind, a form of being above and immune from entropy and all other laws of things that perish.

We know that matter will some day come to an end in death-like equilibrium; we know that the alternating forms of life will become extinct. But the spirit is imperishable, it has no limitations, it follows other laws than those which apply to matter, plants, animals and man. Therefore mind is the ultimate aim of the creative power. But it is mind of a certain type. Just as life is a finer form of the natural forces on the lower plane, so also the Collective Spirit will be a finer, idealised reproduction of life—its quintessence.

The existence we know, the world in which we live must at its present stage be regarded as a nursery in which a new and better, superhuman and extra-human form of being, the Collective Spirit, is being developed.

Even to this day we still have with us the ceaseless conflict from the material and biological planes. But the difference is that it is often fought out between thoughts and ideas. And every time a higher view gains the victory, it means a fresh stone laid in the construction of the Collective Spirit.

We ourselves are in the midst of the conflict We have brought with us from the biological plane our body, in which instinctive passions still prevail; but our shaping thought, ever stimulated and fertilised by the common stock of spiritual life, brings us into contact with the form of being that is to be the next stage of evolution, the Collective Spirit.

Man has, therefore, a double battle to wage; downward against the animal instincts, the whole armour and armoury of the biological world; and upwards, in a spiritual struggle with his equals for a share in the formation of the Collective Spirit.

When we contemplate this remarkable world in which we have been assigned a place for a brief span of time, it is hopeless to think of understanding its many apparent contradictions unless we realise that it is the birth of the Collective Spirit that is taking place, that it is the birth-pangs of this new being that fill us alternately with wonder, sorrow and joy, fascination and hope.

And now the critical reader may ask: how are we to know

THE CREATIVE POWER

that it is the creative power, this mysterious, anonymous, undemonstrable force, which is at the root of evolution as a whole? How dare we postulate that it has been here and there and done so and so? Are we not drawing very bold conclusions?

To this we reply, that the creative power certainly is, at present, no more than a postulate, an unknown quantity, x. But *if we are to find any meaning in evolution at all, we cannot do without this unknown quantity.*

How else could we find any cohesion in the chaos which surrounds us? No acceptable theory has ever yet been offered. True, the mechanists have endeavoured to arrive at a certain unity by reducing all processes to motives of a physico-chemical nature, but this hypothesis has been shown to be entirely inadequate.

We have only to look out of the window, and we see how difficult it is to find any unity in the general view of the world. From our little narrow outlook we mark the blue sky with a slender pale new moon, the trees in the plantation, a road with stones and gravel, a chauffeur cleaning his car and whistling at his work, and a dog. The whole complicated process of evolution that has led up to all this has to be brought in under a definite category which also has to include ourself and our desire of finding unity in it all. Is it strange, then, that in formulating the equation we must have an unknown quantity?

This unknown quantity we call the creative power. It must be either *in* matter or else it must have come *from without*—we can turn and turn about between these two possibilities; the main point is simply, that not even the most radically mechanistic interpretation can get away from the *fact* of evolution, the fact that matter has, under the influence of some unknown quantity, *advanced to higher forms*. Every attempt to derive life or spirit from mechanical matter has always proved a failure. It is only successful when life or mind has somehow been smuggled into matter beforehand.

The evolution which has taken place must therefore be designated as a continual process of creation; it cannot be explained otherwise. But if some delicate souls with a lurking inclination towards mechanistic views object to the term creation, we can substitute for the present a more physical term, which will also serve to illustrate what has taken place. We can call it a distillation process. From the world of matter an essence is distilled which we call life ; and out of this life again emerges a finer and more volatile ingredient which we call mind. That is what has taken place ; and no one can study the course of evolution without perceiving that these stages were a part of it, and in the order named.

That there are these three planes, each with its laws and systems of causality, was recognised already by Schopenhauer, though he did not, in his philosophy, draw the conclusions that follow from this division.

In his *Fourfold Root of the Principle of Sufficient Reason*, Schopenhauer points out that there are three forms of causality, viz. : (1) causes of a material nature, (2) irritations (*Reiz*) and (3) motives—answering to each of our three planes : matter, life and spirit.

When two spheres collide, the cause and effect are a matter of externals only. If the sphere collide with a living being, the cause gives rise not only to a material effect, but produces an irritation which again gives rise to feeling. And if the living being thus affected be of a higher, spiritual type, then there will be the further effect of setting thought in motion ; the collision produces, not only a material effect and an effect of feeling, but also a thought-effect (a higher form of feeling). It has passed through all three planes, and its effect is different in each.

It is most significant that Schopenhauer should note these three types of cause and effect, for it shows, as clearly as could be wished, that he realised the triple nature of things. And this further shows, we think, how impossible it is to find unity in the conception of the universe without due regard to all three stages, each, as evolution plainly shows, gradually developed from the one before.

Taking the historical aspect of evolution, then, we find ourselves compelled to divide the process into three great epochs : a material, in which the physical world assumed its form; a biological mutation period, apparently just concluded; and a spiritual phase which has just begun.

It is in these three forms that the universe presents itself to our mind. And we find all three forms represented also in ourselves. It is but reasonable, then, to divide things first and foremost along these historical lines.

But there is another division to be made before we can attain to any deeper understanding. We must divide the world into that part in which the creative power is actively at work, and the portion dominated by its natural counterpart, the automatic power, a preserving, persisting, conservative, conserving, repetitive power.

The relation between the two powers is as follows: The creative power takes up a substance, whether of material, biological or spiritual nature, gives it a form and composition previously unknown, and that is all. We can see this for ourselves in our minds; a thought occurs to us; the process takes but a moment, and it is over. But the thing thus created does not disappear again at once. And this we can only explain by assuming that a new power immediately enters on the scene and takes charge of the new creation, seeking to preserve it in the form in which it is received. This power we call automatism. The creative power is the maker, automatism is the keeper, endeavouring by every possible means to preserve the product, help it to maintain and reproduce itself, to continue its existence in despite of any unfavourable influence from without. Evidently the creative power would be of no importance whatever if it were not for this auxiliary, the automatic power of preservation; save for this, all creation would be lost as soon as created.

All that we see about us in Nature is a result of the work of the creative power at different stages; the power itself, however, is no longer actively operating in these phenomena; it has long since handed over to automatism as far as these are concerned. Consequently, Nature appears to us to be automatic throughout.

At our present stage, the creative power is only active in the sphere of mind, and here again only where new spiritual creations are in progress.

We can trace the alternating action of the two powers very distinctly in our own mental and spiritual structure. When we think a new thought, we are creating something; but as soon as the thought is there, it ceases to belong to the creative department; it is handed over to the charge of " memory "—a name we use to designate what is really the automatic department. Every time the thought crops up again, it is automatic, and does not now require the mental effort that went to its creation. The pattern once made, further copies are cheaper to produce.

Our assimilation of the thoughts of others also calls for a certain amount of creative power on our part, though not in the same degree. The process here is a receptive one, but costs us, nevertheless, a certain mental effort; less than the effort of first creation, but still an effort. As soon as we understand the new idea, this, too, is handed over to the automatic section, and no longer calls for any creative effort.

Obviously, any active operation of the creative power must be a phenomenon of comparatively rare occurrence in proportion to the immense number of phenomena controlled by the automatic power. It is therefore easy to understand, if not to justify, the mechanists when they go so far as to assert that none but automatic processes exist.

But the mechanists must understand that the only explanation of the heterogeneity of automatic processes and their different stages of development is that the creative power at some time brought them to the stage where they now are. We can, by digging a canal, create a waterfall which will go on acting automatically as a waterfall for centuries. But the waterfall would never have existed had it not been for the canal which created it. Everywhere in Nature we find continuous processes in operation; but this does not mean that they have always been going on automatically. In order to be there at all, they must at some time or other have been *set* going by some power distinct from the power which *keeps* them going; they owe their origin to a power which, having brought them into being, has long since transferred its activity to other spheres of work.

If the mechanists deny the existence of the creative power,

it is because they lose sight of it in the overwhelming mass of phenomena that do come under the charge of automatism. Compared to the wealth of automatic forces which we find in matter, life and mind, the creative power is a small thing, quantitatively speaking, like the eye of a whale. Even our own thoughts are mostly automatic. It is difficult to realise that anything ever is created, and easy to imagine that everything goes on automatically in a circle, for the simple reason that we ourselves consist, materially and biologically speaking, exclusively of automatism, while our mental and spiritual life is at least 99 per cent automatic. This leaves but a very small share for the creative faculty. And the result is, as far as the mechanist is concerned, that his fundamental view disregards this small percentage and reckons only with the remainder, though in reality this quantitatively insignificant element is the essential ingredient, without which all the rest could never have existed.

According to our theory, the whole of Nature works automatically, and the animals, as well as the plants, are automata; even the human body is an automaton, and most of our feelings and thoughts are likewise automatic; all is but a repetition of earlier processes, only in different combinations. When we eat and digest our dinner, it is a purely automatic process which takes place, just as it is when we delve into our memory and draw forth old recollections for our after-dinner stories.

When a dog lies down to sleep in its basket, it rolls round once or twice before settling down, a habit which owes its origin to the conditions which prevailed when its ancestors lived in the open and had no other couch than they could make for themselves in the grass. A cat covers up its excrement by scraping up the earth; and will try to do so even where a floor or carpet takes the place of earth, when the movement is of no use. In both cases, automatism is evidently at work, since the action is obsolete and purposeless.

" Routine " is a word particularly used in cases where automatism has superseded the creative power. There is a touch of contempt about it, suggesting something distinct from, and inferior to, creative work. But the existence of routine in any sphere of work involves the previous action, at some period or other, of creative power.

Routine and habit play an enormous part in the world. We are constantly falling back upon habit; it is our natural state of rest, our "stand at ease," which does not call for the same condensation as creative power. We should soon collapse from overwork if the creative power were constantly operating in us. There is little danger of this, however. We should rather be on our guard against relapsing too completely into automatism, habit and routine, stock phrases and repetition, the hackneyed in life as well as in art. Being bored simply means wandering round in the circle of automatism. And, therefore, let us have anything rather than boredom, which is spiritual death. Voltaire was right in saying that any form is preferable to that which bores us.

If the creative power were suddenly to cease operations, the world would be able to continue for quite a long time without any very perceptible difference. Everything would go on in the same old way, to the delight of conservative souls. But it would be a world at a standstill, or rather, on the decline. When nothing new was created, evolution would imperceptibly tend in the opposite direction; thoughts, life and matter would in time be worn out, and entropy would mercilessly make an end of all creation.

That automatism prevails in Nature is easy to see, for the natural processes themselves form an ever-repeated cycle. But animals and trees are also automata, although of more complex form and higher degree of development than the forces of Nature. Typical examples of automatism in the animal world are the bees and the ants, creatures which practically work in their sleep all the time. Only where spiritual life is apparent do we find anything better, but even this is constantly sinking down into automatism again. In many people, the creative power is so faintly developed as to make them conspicuous. It was these phenomena of "circulation" which Feilberg studied so keenly—and so mercilessly exposed. "A strange ghost-walking of dead things!" he exclaims. "It is rare to find anything coming up with life in the soul, any fresh shoot of something new. Always the ghosts of the old.

Thousands and thousands of us go about as miserable, suffering creatures, themselves the cause of all their woes. Their misery is simply the result of a simple sum which anyone could have worked out for them with ease. It could not possibly be otherwise. But they no not care; for they are dead."

But the creative power is always present in human beings, even though they may seem " dead " for a time. We feel the power every time we make a mental effort, whether working on a new idea, considering a decision, assimilating some new and difficult piece of knowledge, or resisting the temptation to act on the automatic impulse of the moment, and acting ethically instead, following the inner voice of duty.

The creative power soon tires, for it has to work against a mighty resistance, the whole weight of automatism in full. It is not easy to bring anything new into the world ; we sometimes feel, like Hjalmar Ekdal in Ibsen's play, that all possible inventions have been invented already. The creative thought glides imperceptibly from one thing to another. Otherwise, perhaps, it could hardly create. It has always to avoid all previous creations and seek new fields of work.

And that is why there is so much unrest in mental work, and in human communities; the creative power here works by leaps and bounds, so that the human world looks rather like a caravan of emigrants, ever on the move. Among the old, worn-out nations of southern Europe there is more rest, for automatism prevails; in America, on the other hand, the newest country in the world, there is a constant flux of creative processes, and endless unrest and spiritual mutation, rather like what must have taken place during the biological mutation period, when the animal species were being created and formed, and animals had not yet become determinists.

The creative power acts rather after the fashion of the nervously energetic American business man, keen and enthusiastic, working with intense concentration on some new understanding, only to leave it as soon as it becomes a going concern, and devote his energies to something else. Such businesses have sufficient vitality to keep them going for a time ; but the freshness of their initial period wears off and is supplanted by automatism, and sooner or later they decline.

It is just these phenomena of determinism, things once created, then left to themselves, which we see around us everywhere. The only thing in the world that is really free is the creative power, and even that is only free at its extreme point of contact—like the diamond point of an electric drill.

Modern genetic research has given us the best possible confirmation of the importance of automatism among animal species, by showing how firmly the type is implanted in the race. Environment may differ, and may occasionally give rise to certain alterations, but these are only superficial; the genotype remains constant. Since the various species were created in the great biological mutation period, no new ones have arisen, and it is impossible to create new species, because the creative power has long since deserted the biological field, handing it over to automatism, and transferring its own energies to the spiritual field. And there is consequently something predetermined about all animal life, an inexpressible melancholy of habit and routine, with no hope of anything beyond. The animals are Nature's throw-outs, with no future before them; that is why they easily become extinct. Numerous species have already done so, and all will do so in time. The creative power has long since left their sinking ship and hoisted its pennant in the world of mind.

Civilisations, too, die out in time; whole peoples die; but, in this case, we find new ones growing up to take their place. In the animal world, however, this is not the case. No renewal has taken place here since the glacial period; and Chinese girls are still born with normal, finely shaped feet, though the feet of girl children in China have for thousands of years been subjected to artificial deformity from birth.

Evolution, in the positive sense, is found only in the sphere of mind; all else is now automatism. If Darwin's theory were correct, it should be possible, by pure cultures, to produce pumpkins and strawberries of ever-increasing size, and stallions of ever-increasing strength. But this can only be done within very narrow limits. The process suddenly comes to a stop. Nature will go no further. And then it declines. It is much the same with highly gifted families and those of noble descent; they attain a certain culmination and then decline. The race cannot advance beyond the limits of its genotype (automatism). But there seems no limit to the progress of mind; that is, to the common spiritual attainment of the human race as a whole. Here, since the glacial period, we find astonishing progress, more especially when viewed against the background of the rest of the world in its decline.

Creation is going on in every sphere of spiritual life; in our childhood and youth particularly we can discern the creative element. When we look back upon that time, it has a strange glamour, something almost magical; "the glory and the freshness of a dream." This is due to the fact that we were then " discovering " the world; facts poured in upon us in all their freshness and abundance, unsmirched by the wearisome repetition of automatism. It was a first intoxication, though it was only the receptive aspect of the creative power working within us. And youth is the great spiritual mutation period. Original thoughts and ideas come easily to youth. Ideas rush in upon us, and are often carried out but imperfectly, without order. But there is power in them. The *Sturm und Drang*, the storm and stress of youth will always have an attraction and a beauty of its own unparalleled in any other period of life. Men may achieve great work in their maturity, but it is mostly on the basis of thoughts and ideas born in them long before.

The creative power manifests itself in all spiritual fields, great and small. The cobbler who improves upon the last his father left him, the business man who puts a new article on the market or starts a new concern, the actor who gives life to a character on the stage, the teacher who explains a difficult subject to his pupils, the man who resists a temptation, the inventor who gives us new implements and apparatus —all these are working creatively. In art, science, philosophy and ethics there is constant creation; but there is creation also in our every-day life, as soon as we use our mental equipment in a manner beyond the merely automatic. It is these creative processes which render man a free agent in contrast to all the other products of Nature.

But, the determinist objects, can we really speak of freedom here? Is it not rather that the so-called " free " creators are urged onward by two forces, one external—the total sum of automatism, and one internal, which is also automatic in a way, since it is inherited, and the individual is not himself responsible for possessing it. When we create, we are in reality acting of necessity after all, and have no right to call ourselves free agents.

If we consider the single individual, we cannot deny that he is, as such, not free, but crushed in between the sum of automatism from without and his own inherited material, biological and spiritual constitution, within. Man is thus himself an implement. But within this implement is a force, itself free and capable of raising the implement to an ever-increasing freedom. This force is the creative power, and through it we are given a share of freedom; thanks to it, we are able to stem the current of automatism itself.

Again, the determinist objects that the creative power is itself inborn in us, a part of our individual nature. When we create, it is not a miracle, but merely the manifestation of our nature.

This, however, is a one-sided argument. To take an illustration: A man inherits ten thousand pounds, invests his capital in some productive undertaking and in a few years possesses a million. He is now a different man, a millionaire. We may say it is the ten thousand pounds that made him a millionaire; for without them he would not have become so. But the man may very justifiably argue that he himself has contributed to the process. In the same way, we are all born with a certain capital in the shape of a creative faculty, but we make our capital productive, and turn it into more than we originally received. This is evident when we make ourselves better human beings on the whole, greater and finer than we were. The artist who creates a number of spiritual works grows in the process. So we have a miracle after all, since the creative power, in the course of its operations, raises our whole ego to a higher plane. The automatic portion of our being and the creative power together form a partnership, to the enrichment of both. The partnership cannot be dissolved. The creative faculty with which we are born is itself free and untrammelled, but it cannot act without its partner. The other partner in turn is magnetised by it, becomes a part of it and may fairly claim a share of the freedom attained.

Man is thus free inasmuch as he possesses creative power, and the more this operates through us, the freer we are. To say that the individual is not free because it is only the inherited creative faculty within him that is free, is equivalent to saying that a negro is not black; it is only his skin that is black.

The only way the determinists could make out a case for themselves would be by proving that the creative power itself was not free, but a product of determinism. This, however, they cannot do, for the peculiarity of the creative power is precisely that it does create something always distinct from the sum of the previously created; it defies automatism, and in working through us, gives our ego as a whole a status of freedom in Nature, distinct from all the rest.

All of us possess creative power to some extent, but it is most pronounced in men of genius. If we wish to study the faculty at close quarters, and find out how it can best operate, we must turn to the great creative artists. Every time an artist creates a work of art, we have a miracle of mutation in all its glory; the same thing that, from a lower stage, built up the whole of dead and living Nature.

That the world should have been created in the complex form in which we know it is no more wonderful than that a poet can go into his study and come out half an hour afterwards with a poem which may be immortal. The power that produced the poem is the same which produced the poet—and the whole of the world besides.

When a great animal painter paints a lion, we have a mutation on the third, or spiritual plane, answering to the mutation which took place at the second, or biological stage of evolution, when the lion as a species was first created. And if anyone says it was God who created the lion, we simply answer that it was God who painted the picture as well.

The great artists themselves give us, unfortunately, but fragmentary information as to how the creative power works in them. A writer, a painter or any other artist can tell a great deal about the preliminary studies for his work, external influences and other factors, " atmosphere " and the like, but the main thing, the process itself, he cannot explain, still less teach.

There are one or two exceptions. Alfred de Vigny, for instance, in the preface to *Chatterton* tells us how the creative power acts upon a poet :

Within his burning brain something forms and grows, something resembling a volcano. The fire glows faintly, imperceptibly in this crater. He does not know when the outbreak will take place ; one might almost say that he is a stranger looking on at what takes place within him, so unforseen, so divine, is its coming.

Nietzsche gives us a somewhat clearer view of the inspiration under which he worked when writing *Zarathustra*. The creative power acts on him like

an ecstasy, the enormous tension of which finds vent at times in a flood of tears . . . a sense of being utterly beyond oneself, with the distinct consciousness of innumerable tremors and shivers down to the tips of the toes, a depth of happiness where the darkest and most painful things do not appear as an opposite, but as a necessary colour in a sea of light, an instinct of rhythmic proportion embracing a widespread realm of forms. *All this is involuntary to the highest degree, taking place as in a storm of freedom, of unrestriction, of power, of divinity.*

It will be seen that the poets themselves regard the creative state as involuntary, a state in which something like a higher principle grips them and acts through them. They cannot explain how the mutation takes place ; but it is none the less a reality.

Ludvig Feilberg, in his first book, *On the Utilisation of Soul-Power*, refers to certain changes of mood, glimpses of feeling, which he calls potential values, or " direct current," but which can perhaps be characterised as manifestations of the creative power. This direct current is seen " as often as we open ourselves to anything beyond our own finite state."

Whether this is sufficient to describe adequately the creative power we will not venture to say. Nietzsche has defined life as "that which ever seeks beyond itself," and this is perhaps a better characterisation of the creative power. It is a power that never repeats itself, and is therefore allied to the nature of the gods, who never repeat themselves—as Æolus pointed out to Odysseus when he begged a second time for a favourable wind.

Everyone knows that a poet cannot write until the spirit moves him. And this particular spirit will not come at his call, as with the rest of our spiritual stock-in-trade, which is automatic and stored ready to hand in the memory. Even under the most favourable circumstances, inspiration may often be lacking; while at other times, when circumstances are anything but favourable, it will appear, operating irresistibly in spite of all.

More haste less speed does not apply to the artist working under the influence of inspiration. Dostoyevsky, Balzac and many other writers turned out their best work, so to speak, in one breath; Rossini composed "The Barber of Seville" in a week. The inspired artist must strike while the iron is hot; he knows to his cost that if he wait till the morrow the chance may be lost. And so he writes at such a pace that the words tumble over one another; the pen is too slow for the flight of thoughts; ideas come crowding in upon the mind, clamouring for shape and form, for existence in reality.

Assuming the creative power which produces a work of art to be the same power which has built the structures of life in all their various forms, we must conclude that this creative power works in a similar manner in matters other than those of mind and spirit. Life remains long at a standstill, marking time in automatic repetition, altering only from the point of view of externals, when subjected to some mechanical influence; then suddenly it gathers itself for an effort in the creation of something new, something hitherto unknown, and we get the "mutations" known to biologists.

The geological strata show us, not only transition forms, or varieties, but also examples of the innumerable attempts at new types, which, however, soon proved failures and perished accordingly. A typical instance is that of the archæopteryx, which, the Darwinists maintain, represents a transition form between reptile and bird form. This is hardly correct. The archæopteryx is rather a form distinct, a mixture of bird and reptile, produced as an experiment by the creative power, but proving a failure after all, owing to its bastard character; it could not hold its own either against reptiles or against birds proper. The bird, then, is not a descendant of the archæopteryx, any more than man is directly descended from the monkeys. The archæopteryx is an unsuccessful attempt at a bird, just as the monkeys are unsuccessful attempts at man. And similarly, we find innumerable unsuccessful mutations in the products of the mind. Every bad book written, every bad picture painted, is an archæopteryx!

But when the creative power does turn out bad work, this is not the fault of the power itself; it is due to the fact that the instrument it had to work with was unsuited to the purpose. The creative power is one, as the waters of the Nile are one. But just as the Nile flows more or less strongly, according to the channels through which it has to pass, so also the creative power manifests itself more or less richly in proportion to the limitations of the medium it works in.

The organisms best equipped by Nature's hand for the furtherance of creative aims are men of genius. In these the creative powers flows freely and strongly (Feilberg's "direct current"). In others, it circulates, stagnates, meanders away into unproductive marsh. And we can see from the outward appearance of a man something of his equipment in this respect; the physical structure shows in some degree how far the organism offers adequate channels for the creative power.

The individual may indeed be regarded as itself a channel for the creative current. This channel is the product of automatic forces acting together, and its adequacy depends on how it is built. But we cannot conclude from this that its character is already determined from birth. Just as the water of the Nile can improve its own channel, cutting a broader or deeper bed of its own force, so also the creative power, acting through an individual, can render it more suited to the purpose in view; the individual itself is gradually improved. A man's creative potential may thus increase as he himself becomes ennobled by his work for the creative power he serves. Were this not so, it would be idle to talk of artistic development or moral improvement. Given specially favourable conditions, human character can be changed for the better—just as it may degenerate in others.

But how can it be that we find such difficulty in describing a creative act, when creative work is constantly going on within us ? There are several reasons, one being that creation is not a separate process that we can isolate and consider as such, but is interwoven with the automatic thought processes. And again, we ourselves are not mere spectators of what takes place, but participate in the process ; we are cast hither and thither like the golden apple in a fountain, till we are blind and dizzy—or at any rate, too greatly moved for cool, objective observation.

There is, however, a state in which we can observe the creative power directly at its work, albeit through a veil, namely, in dreams. In our dreams, the power seems to operate unaffected by the logical rules of automatism ; it is freed from the trammels of its armour. Here, one situation arises directly out of another without reference to cause and effect. This shows us the mutative possibilities of the creative power. There is always a certain coherence in dreams, one vision being linked to another, though it may be but the slightest thread that holds them together. But the new vision arises as a thing complete in itself, with astonishing suddenness, yet with a fascinating delicacy and wealth of detail. Our dreams show us new things, improvements on what we know ; often cities and landscapes of a character transcending all reality. We can all be Shakespeares in our dreams. But why not when we awake ? Because reality now resumes its sway ; the steam-roller of automatism brings us back to earth. Only at night does it rest, and we can raise our heads . . . no great harm can come to us in the world of our imagination !

This shows that the essence of our mentality is something other than what we might call the mentality of action. The latter is the product of creative power in conflict with automatism in broad daylight. But the true essence of creative power is imagination ; and this imagination, which in day light is hampered by the reality of automatism, is, in our dreams at night, given free play in all directions.

Hence the importance always attached to dreams, which the modern school of psycho-analysis has tried to provide with a scientific foundation. The things we dream are often incomprehensible nonsense to all seeming, yet we cannot but feel ourselves brought into contact with subconscious forces in ourselves, an idealising power that the daylight scares away.

The fact that people can become the slaves of stimulants which intensify, though but temporarily, their sense of creative activity, is really due to the peculiar satisfaction we experience in feeling the creative power at work within us. And if we cannot get it to work in any other way, we have recourse to alcohol, opium or hashish. The opium-smoker says good-bye to the world of automatism and goes off on a grand tour through the golden realms of fantasy, the wonderland of the creative power.

The word intoxication is used with reference to drugs, such as opium or morphia; but it applies also to the ecstasy of artistic creation. And it is worth noting that the term is used both for a state so passive as a form of sleep and for the most intensely active state we know, as when a man is engaged upon a work of art. But the common term is right enough, for in both cases we have a manifestation of a higher force, the creative power. The opium smoker's trance and the ecstasy of the artist at his work are but a sleeping and a waking form of the same thing. In sleep the result will be visions, phantoms, fantasy; waking, it gives us art, invention, new ideas, a moral exaltation. It is the man whose temper is mainly of the automatic type, the creatively impotent, who gives himself up to artificial intoxication; great men have no need of this. And when they do resort to it, they are not merely pitiable, like the poorer sort, but contemptible as well.

We noted some time back that the creative power had ended its work on the biological plane; and we characterised it then as a power of mutation. But how can this be made to agree with the fact that De Vries in Holland, Tower and Morgan in America, W. Johannsen in Denmark, and others, have produced artificial mutations in the biological world?

We must here emphasise the word *artificial*. For the mutations produced are in reality of such a character that they cannot be said to give us more than a pale reflection of the biological mutations which must have taken place in earlier times in a degree of wealth and abundance hard to imagine nowadays. Nearly all the mutations experimentally produced are of a negative character, their dominant feature being the *loss* of some quality found in the parent individuals; the addition of fresh qualities has been known to occur, but very rarely. These occasional positive mutations should also, perhaps, be regarded as a form of atavism.

In any case, biological mutations are of very infrequent occurrence, and no longer any part in Nature itself. They seem to be but the last dying flicker of a natural process which has ceased to be of any practical use. Faint traces of it are also found in the so-called hybrids, in which we observe the division and redistribution of hereditary tendencies.

The biological mutations produced by experiment thus only show that mutation is possible in the biological world under certain natural conditions, doubtless widely different from those now prevailing. They are of the greatest importance historically, since we cannot explain evolution without them; but that is all.

In the world of mind, on the other hand, mutations are not accidental, negative or atavistic, but entirely positive and constantly occurring. Here we find new creations ever going on; showing, we think, as clearly as could be wished, that mutation has now been transferred from the biological to the spiritual plane, just as in earlier times it was transferred from the material to the biological.

But here it may be objected that even granting the occurrence of mutations both in the biological and in the spiritual worlds, this does not necessarily mean that the processes originate in one and the same power.

We have only to compare the two planes, however, and we find that the mutations in both have so many points of similarity that we need have no hesitation in giving them a common origin.

Considering the mutations in the biological world, we find that they take place not so much by breaking up earlier forms as by the constant addition to, and improvement of, existing forms. We find, for instance, in the human body, a number of rudimentary organs, not only the vermiform appendix, the coccyx and other superfluities, but a skeletal structure and a system of blood circulation seemingly more suited to the needs of a fish than those of a human being; the human body may be said to be merely a transformation and improvement of the body of a fish. This is particularly apparent when we compare the early embryonic stages of the two forms, which are astonishingly alike. Similarly, the mind of man has developed by constant additions to existing material, with no mutations or abrupt transitions, but always carrying over a series of rudiments from the animal period, besides a quantity of dead weight in the form of superstition, and childish, religious and artistic ideas dating from a period when man was, spiritually speaking, a far more primitive being than at present.

The course of evolution is marked by two features: improvement of existing forms or total extermination of existing forms. So it has been in the biological world, and so it is also in the spiritual.

The forces at work in our mind must originate from the same mother source as those which were present in life ere the lamp of the spirit was first lit, though they are of a nobler type, and different in appearance from these. Every spiritual phenomenon has its biological or material counterpart; our mind is not a world in itself, independent of life and matter; it is merely an improved edition of these lower values, and the force to which it is due must be the same at all stages.

It is important to note in this connection that this improvement, this steadily continued refining, tends to exhaust the material with which it works. This is seen, for instance, in the fact that individuals tend to become less fertile the more they are possessed by spiritual forces. When we find, for instance, that the birth-rate of a nation decreases as its culture increases, this can only be due to the fact that the vital forces at its disposal are now devoted to ends superior to the biological plane. A mosquito can produce a trillion of its kind in the course of a single summer; a cod lays millions of eggs; a Russian peasant has a big family of children; whereas educated people as a rule have few. The fact that highly cultured nations tend to die out should not therefore, be reckoned to their discredit; it simply means that they have sacrificed their biological existence in favour of their mental development.

The creative power is, as we have already noted, still scientifically anonymous. In the course of evolution it has appeared under so many disguises that its identity, its very existence, has been doubted. But the time has come when we can no longer deny it; for unless we recognise it as the innermost reality of life, we cannot find and hold the clue that runs through all evolution.

The creative power has suffered the remarkable fate of being denied the credit which is its sole due, because it has from its nature always handed over the results of its work to automatism, and these have in course of time accumulated to such a degree as to hide it from view. Much as in the case of the Egyptian king who built the great pyramid; his mummy has never been found, and the credit of the work is given to others.

Automatism is itself a mighty pyramid, which all can see and feel and handle and photograph and measure and weigh. But we should not allow ourselves to be so overwhelmed by the work as to deny the existence of its architect!

NATURE'S AIM

*The evolution of the world is identical with
the judgment of the world.—Schiller.*

The aim of Nature is a spiritual aim.
Rasmus Nielsen.

HAS Nature any aim, and, if so, can we discern it?
The mechanistic view of life answers the first of
these two questions negatively, and the second thus
ceases to exist. The teleological view answers both in the
affirmative.

Kant, in his *Critique of Judgment*, observes that only two
interpretations of the universe are possible; the mechanistic
and the teleological. Bergson follows Kant in saying that
once we discard the purely mechanistic view, we thereby
adopt the teleological, in some form or other.

Teleology is a doctrine which has been stubbornly opposed
by the philosophers, from Lucretius to Bacon, Spinoza and
the Darwinian determinists. It has been said that it is
ridiculous to suppose the grass exists for the cow, the lamb
for the wolf and the whole of Nature for man. Man is a
product of Nature like everything else, an accidental product;
and when we look at Nature itself, we cannot find anything
suggestive of a definite aim. If we do think we can discern
something of the sort, in the fact that one stage succeeds
another in evolution, this is due to the fact that we attribute to
Nature's progress, guided as it is by the law of cause and
effect, a meaning which is not there. In the opinion of the
mechanists, teleology is merely the law of causality read
backwards.

The mechanists forget that there are two sides of evolution,
a positive and a negative. The positive side is that which has

gone on up to this day (and it is this which the mechanists gaze and gaze at, interpreting it as causality reversed); but there is a negative side, which must also be considered when we seek to interpret evolution as a whole, namely, all that part of evolution which at any time came to a standstill, which has fallen out. It is no longer of any practical importance, but it is of great importance theoretically for an interpretation of evolution. For we must not only find out what succeeded, but also what perished in the process; otherwise our picture lacks all shadows.

Unfortunately, we know very little about the failures of evolution as compared with its positive successes; geological research does, however, provide us with a certain amount of material in this respect. Since the Glacial period, a great number of animal and human races have perished, evidently without any tendency on the part of Nature to worry about them or regard their disappearance as a loss.

The idealistic doctrine of evolution holds that Nature's purpose with our planet as a whole must be characterised as a wish to produce spiritual force in the richest, most varied, and at the same time most condensed form possible. This view is based not only on the fact that the mind of man, as shown in the field of science, art and ethics, is the finest product of evolution up to the present; the costly drop of essence, the attar of roses distilled from innumerable individual blooms; but also on the fact that all that has not aided in this process, in this distillation of the spiritual power that forms the soul of the world, has perished or is perishing.

Schopenhauer was right in discerning behind all phenomena a Will; but it was not merely the Will to Life; in the course of evolution it condensed and became the Will to Mind.

Nature's economy is lavish of life. Life is born and perishes, there is a superfluity of life, and a single life counts for nothing. Mind, on the other hand, is of value, its products are guarded and preserved, and the individual organism becomes itself of value in proportion as it contributes to the common store of mind, the spiritual property of the universe. Every organism which does not directly or indirectly help to increase our wealth in this respect is harmful, and to be exterminated without mercy. Plants and animals are suffered to exist only as far as they serve the needs of beings which themselves produce spiritual force. What has taken place here on earth since the birth of the spiritual element is, that the creatures of the spirit exterminate all those organisms which are not of use to them in some way or another.

During the biological phase, animal life had its flourishing period. Now, owing to the activity of man armed with explosive weapons, it is rapidly declining. Species that may have taken millions of years to produce become extinct in the course of a few centuries, and Nature does not lift a finger in their defence. Kropotkin relates that when the Europeans first came to America, they found the country so overrun by buffalo that the earliest settlers were sometimes obliged to halt for days owing to the hordes of buffalo crossing their line of march. And when the Russians took possession of Siberia, that region was so densely populated with deer, antelope and squirrels that the conquest of Siberia was really a hunting expedition which lasted a couple of centuries.

And it certainly will not be many centuries now before the flora and fauna of our planet are reduced to those forms of plant and animal which are of use to man. All others will then be relegated to the zoological and botanical gardens and museums. The process of extermination is already far advanced, and science is now arming for a magnificent campaign against the harmful microbes. Many species have already been conquered, and we can hardly doubt that the science of medicine will in course of time master them all. Nothing is so insignificant to man as creatures unproductive of mind. We have no respect for life as such—the mere existence of a human being involves the destruction of millions of animal and plant forms. Life is only suffered to exist as far as it can serve the cause of spiritual progress.

Animal species one after another are degenerating or dying out, and no new forms are created by Nature to take their place. The only spiritual form now extant on earth is man; and man has attained, or is attaining, complete mastery of all the rest, which live now, practically speaking, on sufferance. Millions of species of animals and plants have already relinquished the unequal struggle, have laid down their arms and received the *coup de grâce;* others again exist with an appearance of life, in that they still propagate unceasingly, but with no hope of any progress for the species; they are like a man adrift with a life-belt in the midst of the wide ocean, still struggling to keep afloat but knowing all the time that the struggle is hopeless and must sooner or later come to an end. These races of plants and animals are the shadows in the picture, and we cannot disregard them if we wish to realise what is Nature's aim. Their hopeless struggle tells us that Nature has no use for them in the long run; they are flawed creations, the waste products of evolution.

Even these waste products, however, have been of use in their day. Bergson realises this when he writes:

" Evolution as a whole proceeds as if some indefinite and changeable being, man or superman, were endeavouring to realise itself, and could only do so by leaving part of itself behind on the way. These relics appear in the rest of the animal world, and even in the vegetable kingdom. . . .

" From this point of view, the discords of Nature are softened to a great extent. The whole organic world appears as the soil from which either man, or a being spiritually resembling man, must spring forth. Distant as the beasts may be from our own species, and hostile as they may be to us, they have yet been useful travelling companions, upon which consciousness has thrust the superfluous burdens it had to bear, enabling man himself to attain to heights from which again he sees an unlimited horizon opening out before him."

Bergson is right in regarding the beasts as our allies inasmuch as we have grown great on their disaster. We have both used them as a support and fought with them, and thus hardened and ennobled ourselves.

The well-known fact of human life, that the wise consciously use the less wise to their advantage, is a thing we find, in an unconscious form, at very early stages of evolution in Nature, and it is carried on throughout the whole process. The plants, for instance, have been able to make use of microbes binding atmospheric nitrogen and those which alternately transform ammonia compounds to nitric forms and these again to nitrates. With the aid of these microbes, the plants have advanced. Vegetation again has been exploited by the animals, which draw their nourishment from the solar energy accumulated by the plants through the action of chlorophyll.

Again, some races of animals hit upon the method of devouring others; and as the highest product of evolution, we have man, consciously and deliberately utilising animal energy for his own needs by breeding domestic animals and cultivating plants. Finally, in the world of man we see how the mentally superior classes have managed to exploit the labour of these at a lower stage of mental development, and to utilise the surplus thus obtained for spiritual ends. Evidently, Nature has throughout encouraged the types which were capable of utilising others to their own development, and it is hardly too much to conclude that Nature here, in this system of prizes for any advance throughout all stages, reveals to us its true purpose.

Even the struggle for existence itself, however, has been of service to the cause of mind, in that one race has served as the enemy on which another whetted its blade and sharpened its wits. None can deny that man's final triumph in this struggle has been due to mind and not to physical force. But mind was not merely an instrument; it was the very object of the struggle itself, as is shown by the fact that man has not been content to rest on his laurels after having overcome the animal world, but devotes the force thus liberated to spiritual ends.

Physically speaking, man is weak, but this weakness has been a source of strength in the struggle for existence, for it is an outcome of the dominant position occupied in the organism by the sensori-motor system; the nerves and muscles, in the human frame; an upper-class position, Bergson calls it. All the rest of the organism is plainly in the service of this system, designed to support and nourish it, provide it with potential energy and bring forward supplies at the precise moment, and in the precise quantity needed. It is also this part of the organism which is protected to the utmost. It has been found, for instance, in animals dying of starvation, that the brain is almost unimpaired, whereas the rest of the organs have suffered considerably. The sensori-motor system is the master, commanding the service of the organs of digestion, respiration, circulation and secretion. The reverse is never found. To deny that Nature here distinctly reveals its purpose with the higher organisms is equivalent to denying that the printed sheet delivered by a rotary press is the purpose of the machine. And it is not only in the highest organism that we find this preference of Nature for the nervous system. From the lowest protozoa to the best equipped insect forms and the most intelligent vertebrates, the progress achieved has been essentially an improvement of the nervous system.

A study of the struggle for life in Nature shows that Nature has by no means sought to protect the largest and strongest types, but rather the wisest. The largest animal forms which have existed on earth were the giant saurians; but Nature was evidently aiming at mental capacity rather than mountains of flesh, and as these huge creatures were relatively deficient in mental capacity, they soon became extinct, despite their mighty bulk and strength.

At a very early stage of biological development we find the creative power endeavouring to provide its creations with some mental capacity. Even very primitive animal forms were furnished with eyes, providing an invaluable outlook on the world about them, through which they could receive impressions and thus advance their consciousness.

According to the Darwinian theory, it is impossible to explain why the evolution of many species should have been carried forward to a certain culmination, only to come to a standstill there, with no further alteration since. Many of the animals now living had at comparatively early geological periods the same form as now. The explanation, in our opinion, can only be that the creative power, in its innermost essence aiming at spiritual development, gradually wearied on finding that the road it had chosen here did not lead to the desired result. It was like a ship which finds itself beset by drift-ice, and therefore draws its fires, as there would be no use in keeping up steam any longer.

The evolution of the higher animals also tells us something of Nature's aim. We find here a specially developed form of instinct, that of the herd. This gives not only a will to mutual protection, but also a desire for mutual encouragement, as may be observed very plainly among the cranes, beavers, parrots, penguins and apes. The higher an animal form, the more developed its mental power, and the forms with highest mental capacity will certainly also be the last to succumb in the struggle against man, save, of course, those which man protects from egoistic motives.

If there existed on earth other races, lacking mental capacity, but in possession of other faculties which counterbalanced this deficit, and placed them on an equality with man, then we could rightly query the Will-to-Mind theory; this, however, is far from being the case. There are no races whose power of achievement is even approximately comparable with that of man, and, therefore, the dominion of the earth is rightly man's. Mention might perhaps be made of the ants in Brazil, which are said to have exploited the country there to a higher degree than man. But how long will this state of things last? Hardly longer than man is content to suffer it. And if the ants have assumed such a dominant position it is due to a power which can perhaps hardly be called mental in the human sense, namely, instinct, which may be defined as a kind of biological forerunner of mind. Instinct is a peculiar form of mind, an unadaptable form, useful, it is true, to the possessor and to the community to which it belongs, but also liable to involve the individual in great difficulties without the power of its younger, but more clear-sighted and intelligent successor to adapt itself and learn from experience. Instinct is a biological precursor of reason, capable of leading the species to a certain stage of evolution, but inevitably subordinate in the long run.

We disagree entirely with Bergson when he says that to speak of an aim necessarily implies thinking of a pre-existing model or example. True, we human beings often work from a model when aiming at a certain end, but we do not always, and it is highly unlikely that the creative power would do so.

A Danish writer, Dr. Severin Christensen, in his work *Looking Inward*, writes:

" Purpose in Nature ? Certainly, both evident and still more potential. A plan thought out in detail to be realised is not the highest. In human life our aims are formed by unconscious growth, and often alter during the process of realisation. Think of a creative artist at his work ! We should, therefore, always distinguish between productive will, the unconscious tendency which creates the purpose, and the realising will which achieves it.

" Can we will without willing anything particular ? Can we, in other words, imagine the productive tendency without ideas ? Must we not imagine the position as being that ideal conceptions are the product of the creative total will, raised to clear consciousness, becoming a distinctly contemplated purpose for the conscious will and making the means easier for the same ? "

This is well observed. We cannot simply declare that the creative power has no purpose before it because its purpose does not appear as clearly as a railway station does to us when we are hurrying to catch a train.

If we go to the source, to the creative faculty in ourselves, and ask whether it sees its purpose clearly, we find that this is just what it does not. When Victor Hugo sat down at his writing-table and commenced his novel of *Notre Dame*, he had nothing to go upon but the white paper before him and a vague idea that the book was to be something about the mystic atmosphere of the church of Notre Dame. How the purpose was to be achieved he could not say until he had achieved it. And it is generally so in great art. The creative power is not a mathematical formula, but rather a tendency. But the very term tendency involves the idea of something teleological and purposive.

The mechanists are scornful of the teleological point of view, which attributes a purpose to Nature ; they say, it is easy enough to be wise after the event and point out the course of evolution when we see the road it has run. But the mechanists are here taking the word purpose in a different sense. The word is, indeed, ambiguous, inasmuch as it denotes both a definite objective decided on beforehand, and also a mere line of direction, a seeking forward along a given line without knowing what milestones the road will pass. Instinct gives us the best example of something so incomprehensible to the mechanistic view as an unconscious idea of purpose. Among the animals—and also in plants—we perceive a constant working towards certain ends. A bird one year old has no idea of the eggs for which it so busily fashions its nest. Young spiders spin their webs without any idea of the flies they are to catch. The ant-eater can have no idea of ants when it first constructs its trench. The larva of a stag-beetle, if a male, makes the hole in the bark where it awaits its metamorphosis twice as large as that made by the female, to leave room for its horns—of which it can have no conception in its larval state. Such actions show us as distinctly as could be wished that Nature works towards certain ends even where no *conscious* motive is present.

Similarly, life, without being conscious of it in the human sense, has aimed at producing spiritual life of rich and highly varied composition. In order to attain this end, innumerable methods have been tried, but only one, that leading by way of the mammals to man, has proved suited to the purpose.

And so we find that life on all other roads has come to a standstill; it has stuck fast. True, the struggle for existence still goes on, but all these animals which live their lives in strain and conflict, the great majority perishing at a terribly early stage, all must be regarded as the mere relics of evolution, doomed to extermination. The tragical and ridiculous struggle of the animal world resembles the panic at a railway station on a holiday, when the gates are suddenly shut in the faces of struggling excursionists because the train is full. People keep on elbowing their way in chaotic confusion, all to no purpose, for the train has already gone.

When we look at the many helpless, futile and hopeless organisms still fighting their miserable battle throughout the world of Nature, we should be thankful indeed, as human beings, that our lot is happier than theirs ; that we are on the main road, wherein evolution, overwhelming and triumphant, strides forward to its goal. When we compare our fate with theirs, we should, indeed, be ashamed to let any temporary difficulty or distress lead us to pessimism, which may be justifiable among the others, but never in ourselves. The human pessimist is a traitor to the cause of life ; Nature has no use for him, he deserves to be left behind in the ditch. A pessimist is a theoretical suicide.

With all due respect to the many scientists who still hold by a pessimistic, mechanistic view of life, we must protest against their trying to persuade us that our earth is a kind of madhouse on a larger scale. But this really is what it amounts to when they tell us that ethics and spiritual life, morality and art, are but blind accidental growths in a senseless struggle for existence. Why strive for higher ends when there is no higher end ? Why all this trouble and effort when all is meaningless, and there is no future to encourage our endeavours ? If it be only a question of securing existence to the highest possible degree, then a great percentage of human effort, and that the part generally adjudged the noblest of all, will be useless, and those engaged in it fools for their pains.

Pessimistic mechanistic views are plainly useless as a theory to live by—and there is no optimistic mechanist view. Nor is it, indeed, accepted in practice by any save the suicides—the practical, not the theoretical suicides ! We feel, every one of us, in more or less degree, a call to something beyond the mechanistic range ; and it is this call which we call the Will to Mind.

Schopenhauer himself, pessimist as he is, is forced to admit that both science and art have taken root and flourished among mankind. The race has carefully preserved the works of Homer, Plato and Horace for thousands of years, copied them, guarded them and ensured them against oblivion, no matter what disasters and atrocities have harried the world. The race has here shown its appreciation of mind.

It must be something more than accidental that while all material things are constantly being reformed, melted down again and again, the products of the mind remain imperishable.

THE COLLECTIVE SPIRIT

All that remains of ancient Greece, materially speaking, is a certain quantity of ruins and fragments of stone; and yet, Attic civilisation is radiant still, it lives on in unimpaired brilliancy; each one of us has something of its making within us. Great thinkers have been burned at the stake or poisoned, but their thoughts could not be suppressed.

The only permanent Great Power on earth is the power of mind, and no one can seriously believe that the lamp of the spirit should have been first lit by accident only. All human beings, and even the animals, have something of the Will to Mind. And it has again and again led them to individual disaster. The history of mind shows us in every sphere a roll of martyrs who sacrificed life and health for ethical, scientific or artistic ideals. Sir Thomas More, imprisoned by Henry VIII for refusing to take oath against his conscience, was reproached by his wife for his obstinacy. Why should he choose to lie in a dungeon, with the prospect of the scaffold, when all the good things of life lay open to him if he would but do as the bishops, and the best and most learned men in the kingdom were content to do? Why, indeed?

More chose the scaffold. And a like choice has been made by many of the greatest benefactors of mankind. Why? Can the mechanistic or the vitalistic point of view explain it?

Evolution moved gradually forward until mind awoke in man. And then it suddenly took a mighty leap and, in the course of an astonishingly short time, altered the whole conditions of life on our planet. Even the most obstinate mechanist must admit that if mind be a product of accident, then it is an accident that looks very much as if done on purpose. Accident or not, the result has been an overwhelming success. The only outward means we have of deciding whether anything is of value or not is by asking quite pragmatically: Is it a success, a lasting success? Does the thing persist, does it grow, does it increase, does it show any development? We know nothing that shows such continued and flourishing development as the human mind. All else has had to give way to it.

Mind is a late-born child of the body, a very wise child eager

NATURE'S AIM

for knowledge, growing at an astonishing rate. But while the body is long since come to its full growth, mind is still at the awkward age. And so it is that mind often abuses itself and its father the body, it is capricious, unstable, prone to over-confidence and discouragement alike; if suffers from growing pains and is apt to behave at times as an *enfant terrible*.

The creative power has not yet advanced to the stage where it can gauge and survey its own creation. First create, then understand—this is the curious sequence of evolution. Life is not yet fully explained; there are many unsolved riddles in our bodies alone.

We say that mind is a creation of yesterday, a thing hardly begun. In the organic development which took place at the earlier biological stage we have a standard by which to estimate something of the great spiritual development to come.

The fact that evolution has accelerated from the time when mind began to assert itself as an independent factor proves that evolution was aiming at mind. One might, indeed, be tempted to say that it was not until the appearance of mind that evolution really got properly to work; for from this time forward it concentrates instead of scattering as before. It is as if Nature at last found its feet; things went on at a very different pace; now at last Nature found room to work as it would, and a fever of activity resulted.

The creative power had now no longer to fear the loss of its results, for all results were gathered up in the common stock of mind, on which not one, but all succeeding generations could draw at will. On the spiritual plane, evolution took on a new, more practical and therefore rapidly growing form. Consequently, mind has in many respects forged ahead of biological development—in technical things, for instance—though mind is but a few generations old compared with the age of the body. The common stock of mind saved the creative power a series of mutations; single individuals could attain development without the need of individual mutations.

Evolution on the biological plane was subject to the curse of its transient nature: all that a single generation gained in the way of experience perished with it when it died. The common stock of mind does away with this. Mind is the savings bank of all humanity; individuals deposit their surplus, and the sum bears interest, increasing endlessly to the advantage of the species. Mind, then, must be regarded as a new institution in evolution of immense importance to its progress; from the evolutionary point of view, it is the greatest advance ever made.

This new institution is of so recent date that it has hardly yet adapted itself to the world. We find the curious phenomenon of an old body, sternly trained in the biological struggle for existence, a strong and durable piece of mechanism, ingeniously equipped through a series of purposive mutations in the war of each against all, appearing as the bearer of a wild young devil-may-care mind, in certain respects far superior to the body itself, and yet so inexperienced that it has but an imperfect knowledge of the functions of this body. Mind is like a wealthy parvenu coming into possession of a fine old estate—the body—and mismanaging it. It is this which gives rise to so many astonishing situations and developments in life; the things that provide matter for the humorist and room for mirth.

Mirth is unknown to the animals; for they act in animal fashion, regarding themselves with a natural seriousness. We, on the other hand, are for ever laughing at ourselves, as one laughs at a parvenu; we are constantly reminded of our frailty, we have a sort of feeling that we have too much money in our pocket all at once. Evolution, in the breathless acceleration of its course, has furnished us with Thought, which can put a girdle round the universe quicker than the bolts of Jove; and who are we, thus marvellously equipped? Gods maybe? Alas, we know but too well that we have physically speaking barely cast the pelt of the beast.

No wonder, then, that we are still, spiritually speaking, in a state of chaos, where all manner of views and theories collide and wrangle. We are like the first gold-diggers of the Klondyke, all bewildered by the sudden find, and still shouting in confusion.

But over this camp, the new, raw settlement of mind, a

vapour is condensing imperceptibly; the dust remains below and the confusion still goes on automatically, but a golden cloud is formed in the sky.

This golden cloud, that holds the best of the past and the present, with rich and splendid promise for the future, is the Collective Spirit.

THE COLLECTIVE SPIRIT

> Man hungers after knowledge as a lion after food.—*Nietzsche.*
>
> A planet is really not ripe for progress until all its inhabited parts have attained the intimate association which makes of them one living organism.—*Renan.*

HITHERTO we have been taught to regard ourselves as the centre of the universe, and our spiritual and physical constitution as predominant in the economy of Nature; we imagine that our little soul—even our body—is to live on as an eternally independent unit after death. It is hard for us now to realise that this is not so; that we are not the ultimate aim of Nature, but merely one of the channels through which the stream of evolution flows.

But this is what the idealistic doctrine of evolution tries to make plain.

We have in the foregoing chapters sufficiently shown that we have little sympathy with the determinists and their view of life. But here for once is a ground on which we can meet, namely, in demonstrating the utter fallacy of considering ourselves at all important as independent souls.

It is true enough that man, as an organism, is both spiritually and physically a complex, advanced, interesting and, in many respects, admirable product; he is so, however, not on his own account, but by procuration, so to speak, as the agent of the creative power. It is this power, and the results of its work, we must admire in man; it is its soul, not the soul of man, that deserves the credit. Nay, more, we must accustom ourselves to the thought that the individual has not a soul at all, metaphysically speaking, whether it be a cat or a human being we are considering. The utmost any individual can attain is a certain character or personality, a distinct individuality whereby it differs in some respects from other similar units.

When Hume commenced his psychological studies by introspective study of himself, he discovered various processes of feeling, association and thought, but found it difficult, not to say impossible, to perceive anything like a soul. Kindly disposed critics have, however, managed to make out that there must be a synthetic spiritual activity answering to that of the body, a whole, an individuality. But this spiritual whole can only exist as long as the bodily and spiritual processes go on, it cannot be imagined as existing after they have ceased. It we care to call this whole by the name of soul, well and good, but it will be a soul in a very limited sense, widely different from the metaphysical Divine Spark which scholastic philosophers were wont to juggle with.

We must, then, agree with the much-abused McKerrow when he writes, in *The Appearance of Mind*:

" Life is not an attribute of us ; we are attributes of Life. We are not Something, Soul or Subject, Immortal, which puts on Mortality ; we are expressions of the continuing Life, the garments it puts on. Life is the whole, we the part ; Life the Reality, we the Appearance. We do not seek to preserve Life ; Life ' seeks ' to continue in us."

In the chapter on " The Creative Power " we explained why individuals differ, though it is one and the same force which permeates them all. The explanation is that individuals come into the world as a result, more or less successful, of the process of automatism. Individuals may be compared to electric accumulators, more or less perfect in construction, and thus able to bind and release more or less of the same electricity.

The soul of a human being does not exist when the personality is dead, any more than it existed before the individual was born. It is only the creative power that is immortal. To suppose that, after bodily death, we live on in a spiritual form unimpaired, with our little joys and sorrows, our good and bad qualities, is a primitive conception leading to the most irrational and grotesque consequences. Our separate individuralities are merely the ambassadors of the creative power on the spiritual plane, as separate bodies, whether of human beings, animals or plants, are ministers of the same power on the biological plane.

That we are ruled by automatism in a purely physical sense will surely be readily admitted by most. Mr. So-and-So does not decide for himself when he will be born and when he will die, he cannot alter the physical tendencies with which he came into the world, and when he is getting worn out by age and disease, he feels only too keenly how slight is his own importance compared with the forces which rule him. The body is an automaton; we can keep it decently oiled and in working order if we will; but the man was never born who could add a cubit to his physical stature.

In a spiritual sense, it is harder to recognise the same state of things, for we all of us feel the principle of immortality in ourselves, that is to say, we feel the creative power, and thus are apt to confuse this with ourselves, believing that it is *our* soul, whereas in reality we are its body, physically as well as spiritually. On self-analysis we are forced to admit that we are, spiritually, in the hands of higher powers; that love and fear, adventurous longing and perseverance, righteousness and charity are not things invented and patented by our own little soul, but are given us, like our bodies, by a higher principle. We see this same principle flowing through other individuals as well, who, like ourselves, are guardians of a lamp that burns eternally, but guardians appointed only for a time. Our sands run out, and others take our place.

That animal life is subject to automatism will hardly be doubted. We can get a very lively impression of this automatism from the discussions of agricultural experts, pig breeders for instance. So many pounds of foodstuff will produce so many pounds of meat in a certain time. But human bodies—and to some extent also the minds—are similarly subject to automatism. We have only to ask the actuaries of our insurance companies; they know to a decimal point how long we are to live, and a great deal more about our living; their tables and statistics are quite as accurate as those of the pig-breeder and very nearly as accurate as those of the astronomer. We can see records and statistics of disease and death, runaway horses, drunkenness, fires, births, illegitimate children, marriages, etc.—tables producing an almost cynical effect.

The greatest hindrance to a sober determination of our place in the universe lies in the doctrine of the soul taught us on religious grounds, which attributes to the private soul, the private individuality, an importance beyond its due.

Physically speaking, we have not created ourselves, nor have our father and mother; we are built up, like a mosaic pattern, of elements derived not only from father and mother but also from grandparents and great-grandparents and so on. The new-born infant does not owe 50 per cent of its body to its father and 50 per cent to its mother; it is a relatively small percentage that comes to us from our immediate parents. Our true progenitors go back for generations scattered about here and there, and we are merely a conglomerate of all, more inclined, perhaps, to "take after" a grandfather or a great-grandmother than after our father and mother. We are deeply fused with the race as a whole. An American authority, Professor John William Draper, draws attention to the fact that each human being owes its life to another and gives life to another in turn, each consequently losing its appearance of individuality when we consider its relation to the race. A section of life is not the whole. The mature individual cannot be dissociated from the multitude of forms it has passed through, and a human being, produced by others and producing others, cannot be dissociated from the race.

From the point of view of the soul, the position is even less favourable, since our spiritual equipment is composed not only of items from our parents and our ancestors, but from thousands of other fathers in all times and of all races. When an individual fancies he possesses an independent spiritual life, he overestimates himself as much as the sparrow sitting on the back of an eagle and boasting that it flies higher than all other birds. On taking stock of our spiritual assets, we are soon forced to admit that they are derived mainly from others. The greater part of our knowledge has been obtained through education at home and in schools or institutes, by reading and converse with others. If we do constitute a spiritual individuality, we must at any rate admit that it is in the highest degree based on and determined by the common stock of mind. Spiritually speaking, we are in a state of solidarity with other organisms, and we could not be imagined to exist as we are without them any more than we could be physically what we are without the various contributions from our physical ancestors.

That the individual who happens to have assumed our shape might just as well have assumed another may be illustrated rather comically by the following imaginary example:

Supposing Socrates had emptied his cup of poison but one hour later than he actually did, then neither you, reader, nor the present writer would ever have existed; in fact, not a single one of the persons at present inhabiting the globe would have existed, but an entirely different set of human beings. A paradox ? By no means. If the poison had been drunk at a different hour, then the gaoler and disciples would have left the prison at a different hour, and a whole series of juxtapositions in time would have been altered automatically. The disciples would have met people on their way home other than those they did, and altered the time arrangements of those people in turn. One might have missed meeting his sweetheart, another failed to get home to his wife in time, and so on, thus giving rise to a further series of alterations. The rings would expand with every minute, and the dislocations increase as time went on; even by next morning there would not be many of the citizens of Athens who had not been affected in some way by the original divergence of sixty minutes. A host of plans would have been overthrown, new combinations would have arisen, the young man would not have made the acquaintance of the sweetheart whom he chanced to meet, other marriages would have taken place, other children would have been born of existing marriages than in the actual state of things. By the following year there would have been children born in Athens other than those which actually were born, and this would in course of time have had its effect on other states and peoples; inevitably, the original difference of sixty minutes would make itself felt throughout the world until every race on earth was affected.

We have here chosen an instance of historical importance in itself for the starting-point ; but any little trivial alteration in the round of automatism would produce like results. A slave drops a sack of corn—if he had not dropped it similar dislocations would have ensued. The law of cause and effect is a far-reaching thing ; it rules the whole world of automatism, and this world embraces the physical world, whether the physical bodies be those of pigs or human beings.

But how about individuality, then, and the soul with which it is associated ? It will be seen from our example that individuality as such must be a matter of great indifference to Nature, since Nature would otherwise surely have taken steps to prevent the possibility of innumerable individualities having to give place to others on account of trivial accidents. The thing that persists and goes on unaffected by accidental mechanical causes is life, human life. Whether this life materialises in this or that or another way is a matter of indifference to Nature. It is surely hard to speak of an immortal soul at all, as associated with the single individual, when we look at this little example of how the tiniest alteration in the sequence of causes leads to one set of immortal souls numbering milliards uncounted being replaced by an entirely different set—and so *ad infinitum.*

If we try to get a philosophical view of the world we must habituate ourselves to the thought that our ego, the individual self, is not a finite system floating in air, to be explained from within its own limits. The individual is but a tiny leaf on the twig of humanity, which again forms part of a branch, the organic world, this again belonging to the tree or planet and solar system, whose roots go still deeper and farther back. To explain what a human being is we must begin with the cosmos itself.

Man, the individual, must be defined as a material, biological and spiritual expression of a greater power behind. Neither our body, our life nor our spirit belongs to us in this sense, as they would do if we were each of us an immortal soul or a monad in Leibniz' sense. *If* we possessed and were masters of ourselves, then our whole physical and spiritual constitution would be different. We should not be subject to toothache, senile decay, fear, pride, or lust; we should have a clearer insight into things. The struggle that goes on within us from birth to death, sometimes attaining such a degree of violence as to persuade people that they are possessed by God or by the Devil, would no longer exist. We should be truly masters of ourselves.

But it is not so. Nature has given us a power of attorney for a brief period, but that does not make us sole directors of the undertaking. We are servants, and nothing more; the stewards, not the possessors.

We must, then, agree with our determinist opponent McKerrow when he says that it is not ourselves who think and feel and will; it is something beyond, which uses us as a channel for expression, and these expressions we ourselves interpret as our thoughts and feelings and will. We are only justified in regarding ourselves as the subject in the sentence insofar as we identify ourselves with the creative power.

We sometimes see a prominent man described in flattering terms by journalists as "a single-minded personality." Unfortunately there is no such thing. One of the most remarkable things about humankind, spiritually, is that man is never single-minded. Each individual is a scene of constant warfare; lust and ambition, energy, idleness, high ideals, pride and faintheartedness alternate in our being; we have at times something of Tartuffe or Iago, Peer Gynt or Falstaff in ourselves, but fortunately also something of Plato or Newton. The so-called single-minded personality is only an individual who has attained a certain mastery, a certain harmony of the opposing principles within him; it is sufficient to call him a good steward of his inheritance.

We are still living to-day in the aftermath of the Victorian era, the age of individualism, when the single individual was set upon a pedestal socially, politically, and in the eye of the law. Individualism is a comparatively recent product of civilisation. In earlier times, individuals lived together in a community of interest so close that when a man committed a crime, not only he himself but his kinsmen and friends, or even the whole village, were punished, and all regarded this as right and reasonable.

But at the commencement of the past century there appeared in England a number of social economists, philanthropists and philosophers with hearts as expansive as their collars, preaching the sacred gospel of individualism. Free trade and free initiative generally were in the forefront of the programme; the individual criminal was not to be hanged unheeded, in hole and corner fashion, but with full music, trial by jury and the whole pageantry of legal institutions. " My house is my castle " was the motto of the age, and Scott's novels painted the glories of feudal times, when the knight lived in his stronghold with moat and drawbridge between him and the world. In the age of liberalism, everything centred round the individual. The philosophical exponent is Leibniz, whose system conceives the single human being as a monad, with the rest of the universe as its perspective. The rights of property in particular were regarded with a touching veneration in the Victorian era; a principle welcome to the good City merchant and the landed proprietor alike.

All this, however, led in practice rather to the fuller exploitation of the individual than his protection; and the system inevitably made for its own gradual dissolution. It was an age of transition. Modern limited companies and trusts, capitalism and industry on the grander scale, clubs, unions, friendly and co-operative societies and the rest, all forms of socialism, communism and collectivism point forward toward a new social form. Some have even suggested that a new type of individual is in process of formation, a new system of civilisation, based, not on individualism, but on co-operation and community of interest, with America and Germany as leaders of the movement, creating a new type of the white race, a type which, with its machinery and its highly differentiated social instinct, marks a new phase in the evolution of man. The sands of individualism are running out, and the future belongs to those who are able to work together without narrow egoism and misplaced ideals of liberty. Science, commerce and industry, militarism and socialism are as fingers on the same guiding and organising hand.

This social re-orientation was, as we have said, inevitable in the natural course of things, not only on practical but also on ideal grounds. For there was one thing which the liberal thinkers omitted from their calculations, to wit, the fact that from the first birth of mind here on earth, all men were thereby united in a community of mind; *and the magnificent progress and growth of the human race in later times is a product of this community of mind.* Even in ancient Egypt—and farther back, indeed, among earlier civilisations whose ways we hardly know, the mind of man was already laying the foundations of a common treasury of mind, since developed to an enormous degree thanks to the common effort. In this world of mind there is no such thing as the capitalist seeking to hoard up mind and guard his savings jealously against all others. On the contrary, the richest is here the most lavish, pouring out from his store on every side to the enrichment not only of others but of himself as well.

This Collective Mind is the greatest invention man has ever made, for it is by this alone that we are human beings at all—and this invention is a purely communistic one.

We may compare the Collective Mind to a great public library, in which we find our whole knowledge of the universe; here we can learn all there is to know of all there is to know of. We are all of us mainly readers, drawing knowledge from the common store, though we may occasionally contribute something ourselves. In any case, the contribution of any single individual is infinitesimal in proportion to what he receives. Individual mind is nothing compared with the Collective Mind.

Supposing, by way of experiment, we were to take a newborn infant and place it on a desert island, letting it grow up there without any instruction whatever, but merely seeing that it survived, we should then have an example of the individual mind. But a human being thus brought up would be little better than a beast of the field. It is only by drawing on the common store of mind that we are raised to the human level.

The difference between man and the monkeys is that the creative power has developed our spiritual receiving apparatus in such a manner as to enable it to profit not only by our own experiences but also by those of others, past and present. In the sphere of mind, man has realised the importance of solidarity and co-operation, and men have combined to form the most precious product of evolution, the Collective Mind, whose wealth—of laws and moral principles, literature, music, art, instruction and entertainment—is for the good of all.

In the biological phase, the dominant feature was the struggle of each against all, and mutual aid was a subordinate principle—rank liberalism in fact. In the world of mind the reverse is the case. Every contribution of importance offered by the individual will sooner or later be of value to all the rest. Without this communism, all spiritual life would stagnate and perish—indeed it could never have arisen.

Thanks to this communism, the evolution of mind has proceeded far more rapidly than evolution on the biological plane, for the line here lay through definite stages determined by the original form of the organism, and any errors made could hardly be corrected (thus we find, for instance, man with a skeletal structure suited to the needs of a fish). In the world of mind, on the other hand, it did not greatly matter if one happened to take a wrong turning; someone else would always discover it in time, and by corrective criticism lead the individual back to the right track; or at any rate prevent others from following the wrong one. This is due to the principle of co-operation. Errors of mind can in the long run only persist among peoples living aloof from the rest of the world, like the natives on Admiralty Islands or in the Congo, where mind is at an astonishingly low stage of development, compared, for instance, with that of the Mediterranean peoples, living in contact with the greater part of the world. The Collective Mind is the great instructor; it is this, and this alone, which has enabled man, in the course of a paltry hundred thousand years—a ridiculously short space of time from the point of view of evolution as a whole—to build up the wide ramifications of that civilisation which we now enjoy.

One is tempted to say that the creative power knew what it was about when it left the stranded ship of the biological phase and shifted over to the swifter and more seaworthy craft of the mind. Evolution could now be furthered on quite a different scale. Biologically, acquired characters could no longer be transmitted. Spiritually, however, the way was open, not directly, of course, but indirectly, inasmuch as one generation can learn from the one before it. The Collective Mind is our common spiritual inheritance, stored for the good of all; we now inherit the spiritual wealth acquired by our forbears. And this gave a mighty forward impetus to evolution.

A further advantage is that the Collective Spirit stimulates and encourages the power of mutation to a degree unparalleled on the biological plane. True, the cells on the biological plane could to a certain extent incite the creative power both by offering resistance and by providing material for a continuation of the creative process. But the material was here restricted to the organism already created. The creative power can juggle with the whole stock of spiritual values in the world and turn out new combinations *ad infinitum*. At the biological stage, however, it was confined to a far more restricted radius of action, having nothing but the lump of clay in which it dwelt to work on and transform; the potential combinations were far fewer; and were, moreover, constantly being further reduced as the process went on, until at last the whole had to come to a standstill when the individual attained perfection in its species, as a swallow or a cat. No more could then be done; further mutations would only be to the detriment of the species as such. On the biological plane there was not the same incitement to mutation as on the spiritual. The sum of all organic bodies on the earth could not exert a corresponding pressure on the creative power, or furnish aid and support for it in the individual. Each race had thus to shift for itself, as best it could, and the various races became hostile, one against all. All human beings are friends—in the sphere of mind at least. Wars notwithstanding, we still contribute each our mite to the common store of mind, which is the property of all mankind, and helps to fertilise the creative power wherever it is found, in whatsoever race or nation.

The Collective Mind started from small beginnings as a

common spiritual store, of practical importance more particularly to the individual. But in course of time it has grown to such strength and extent that it is beginning to develop a life of its own, independent of the individuals creating it. Just as national spirit, the spirit of an army, or that of a congregation, is something distinct from the individuals of which it is composed, so also the common store of knowledge has risen above the individual human being and is beginning to assume an independent existence, as a new factor acting on its own account : the Collective Mind. This incipient reality is evident *inter alia* from the fact that it is capable of acting on individuals through the medium of tradition, history, legal and moral obligations and customs, codes of honour, ideals of beauty, and the like. Mind, which began as an individual product, the property of the individual himself, is now beginning to reverse the position and take possession itself of the individual. It is like a bank in which we were at first depositors, now gradually by virtue of our loans becoming our master.

An American writer, Thomas W. Lawson, in *Frenzied Finance*, gives a graphic picture of how the Wall Street financiers built up the first great trust, the Amalgamated Copper. It began on a modest scale with the purchase of certain small copper mines and the amalgamation of a few existing companies ; but once formed, the trust rolled on its way, swallowing up one copper concern after another, buying up whole mountain ranges, cities and railways, spreading north and south, bribing politicians and newspapers, and growing by means of loans, issues of stock and an unparalleled system of inflation to a cyclopean undertaking, an omnivorous, plundering machine, and attaining at last the character rather of a natural force than of a human institution. The trust became a Juggernaut crushing all beneath its wheels ; nothing could check its progress, and those who had set it in motion stood by pale and terrified, helpless themselves to control the thing they had created.

Such a picture is apposite as an illustration of the human individual's relation to the Collective Mind. Originally, it started on a very modest scale, each individual contributing his own little scraps of wisdom and experience; ideas and thought categories arose, languages took form, rules were made, tradition and moral principles grew up; but all the time the individual reserved his own liberty in regard to the whole. In the stone age, man was perhaps still a race of individual minds, as the lions are to this day. Almost imperceptibly, however, the new creation was formed, the spiritual trust which aimed at gaining control of all. And one fine day man was confronted with the fact that this child of his was now an independent agent, and what was more, had come to be the guiding force. This creation of man was grown so strong that it could now dictate to the individual man what he should do and what he should believe; forcing its views upon him through the medium of public opinion, providing him with 99 per cent of his knowledge through schools, education and press, telling him, through traditions and moral principles, what was the proper thing, determining his legal rights and obligations through a system of laws, his æsthetic ideals through art, his national life through national and racial ideals, his religious life through the official or unofficial systems of religion. In face of this overwhelming, ever-increasing spiritual trust, individuals had to bow the knee.

The education of the schools is often a dubious advantage; we are taught what we ought to think about things before we become acquainted with the things themselves, and the habit of independent study is not only not encouraged, but rather the reverse. Some pyschologists, indeed, observing the growth of this outside influence on our minds, have gone so far as to assert that we do not think our own thoughts at all; they are simply forced upon us. Original thought, inventions and discoveries, art, are, according to their view, not a contribution of the individual at all, but merely a product of a certain power acting through the individual. A certain situation at a certain stage of world development called for the aid of certain thoughts; the mosaic of the new theory was complete but for a single piece, and this had at last to drop in here or there, as chance might have it. Often it came at several places together, as when several inventors claim the same invention, and endeavour to prove they have been working independently; which may be true in a superficial sense, but no more.

We can hardly find a better proof of the might and power attained by the common stock of mind in course of time than this fact, that some psychologists, and not the least among them, have been led to assert that thought, the most subjective thing there is, should really be something quite outside ourselves.

Actually, it is not as bad as this, though it may come to it some day. The creative power is still working through the individual, and as long as it is capable of throwing off fresh shoots, the units have their *raison d'être*, albeit only as purveyors to the common store.

Our position as individuals is, we have already mentioned, mainly that of recipients in relation to the common store of mind. What would the greatest thinkers among us be but for the common store they had to draw upon from the first? On the other hand, it must be admitted that this institution has not yet attained a stage where it can grow further without contributions from the individual; the common store of mind is not yet become the Collective Spirit.

We have already, by way of illustration, compared the world of mind to a gigantic trust, overwhelming all before it. It was, however, not a fair comparison, inasmuch as it may cast a certain odium upon this common spiritual property of ours, which, in contrast to so many other institutions, is not designed to serve the selfish aims of a few, but to enrich all shareholders alike. It is in recognition of this, and urged on by an overwhelming impulse, that man is ever striving to add something to the common store. The fact that recognition, fame, " immortality " is so eagerly sought, is certainly due, not merely to the material advantages it brings, which may often be rather negative, but rather to the assurance it affords the individual that his work has not been in vain; that he has really succeeded in contributing something of value to the common store of mind, something which will be appreciated and preserved.

Only think of the efforts we make to attain distinction in the sphere of mind. Rousseau touches the point with an effective comparison. What would a primitive savage think of the much-envied position of a European minister of state? He would infinitely rather die than endure the trials of such an existence. But the savage has no idea of what respect and power really mean to us. And here lies the essential difference between the two types: the savage lives in and for himself; the social individual lives outside himself; he does not know what it is to live without the opinion of others, and it is really in a way only by their judgment of him that he really feels his own existence.

It takes two elements to create a new thought, a scientific discovery or a work of art: the one which brings the new creation into the world, and the one which receives and acknowledges it—that is to say, the mind of the rest of humanity. We have all to get our examination certificate signed by the Collective Mind, and if our work is not appreciated there, we have simply failed.

Any one of our great museums shows us a representative collection of the work of all the individual minds that have "passed"—from the primitive Polynesian who made the first boat, to the learned physicists and atomists of our own day, whose mathematical formulæ are printed in books upon the shelves. Each one of these individual minds was recognised by the universal opinion, and thereby raised us to their level. The great poet, too, makes us a sharer in his mind. We all owe a debt to Shakespeare; he has, so to speak, shakespearised the world. Pasteur not only pasteurised a number of germs to death; he pasteurised the common stock of mind to further life. We are all marked in some degree by the great minds of the world, we are all ennobled by them; for, as Balzac puts it: *comprendre c'est égaler*.

The fact that man, from his first primitive beginnings, has tended towards a supra-individual principle as collective mind seems to prove that Nature's aim was not only to perfect man as a creature of mind, but more than this, to create a whole new world, a new stage of evolution, the world of the Collective Spirit.

Sociologists have long been aware of the supra-individual character of the common store of mind. Paul Giran, for instance, in *Les origines de la pensée*, recognises a supra-individual principle; he writes, that there is above and beyond the individual thought a collective thought, whose manifestations, language, creed, moral laws, etc., would be altogether incomprehensible if we reckoned only with the individual. The collective thought goes beyond the thought of the individual; it is of a different constitution. Durkheim has expressed a similar view.

The sociologists are undoubtedly right in maintaining that science, art and ethics would be unimaginable without the Collective Spirit as their aim. When we study or practise art or science, or act according to moral laws, this is not, as the utilitarians assumed, primarily in our own interest, but because we there find the main road to the land of the Collective Spirit. The force which urges us along this road is stronger than the instinct of self-preservation, as the martyrs of science, art and moral law have testified to the full.

If the Collective Spirit had no reality as the new world which is to supersede the old, it would be impossible to explain why we practise science, art, or moral conduct; art in particular would be an inexplicable phenomenon. In a world without any common store of mind, the individuals would become individualists to an extreme degree, as are some birds of prey not yet extinct. Even in certain animals we find the first steps towards a common stock of mind, especially among apes, deer, rodents, some species of birds, termites, ants and bees. All these creatures form communities, and it is the community that counts; the individual is but an insignificant piece of mosaic in the structure. It is as if Nature were here feeling about for the right touch; as if the instruments were being tuned up to the great concert of mind that was to begin in earnest with man.

It is the Collective Spirit that entices us and spurs us on to effort, as the magnetic pole makes the needle point towards the North. If a great painter and a poet were shut up in prison, condemned to spend the remainder of their lives there, with leave to produce as much work as they pleased, but with the proviso that it should be burnt at once and never shown to anyone, the two creative artists would soon lose their creative power. Why? If each practised his art for art's sake, it would not be so. But they work at their art for the sake of the Collective Spirit. If they cannot win their way to its forum, their energy will soon be exhausted. An artist will occasionally produce a work which is not to be made public until after his death. What pleasure can he find in doing such work? Simply the pleasure of knowing that his mind lives and bears fruit, and will, when he is gone, add something to the common store of mind.

The Collective Spirit is not a vague ideal; it is a thing that actually exists, though at present only in its earliest stage. We may compare the earth with the head of Jove, within which a new creation is gradually forming. And one fine day the new creation will spring forth, an Athena fully armed.

If we go back some hundred millions of years, we find life itself at a stage answering to that of the Collective Spirit to-day. Life existed, then, only in the form of microscopical bacilli, feeding on chemical products; it was hard to distinguish what was really life and what was merely dust. Life was hardly an independent reality as yet. These bacilli were nevertheless the first beginnings of that great, strong, richly-varied life that later spread abroad throughout the globe.

Man is a needle's eye, through which the creative power forces its way to reach the Collective Spirit. The creative power has always been working towards the achievement of mind—otherwise it would not have achieved its first great triumph, the creation of life from a material world. But many of its roads ended blindly; only a single narrow channel, that leading *via* the primates to man, offered a way through the barrier of matter and vital automatism to the wide fields where mind could expand in its full magnificence. At last, after inconceivable detours and conflicts, the goal was in sight. Is it strange, then, that mind should at times kick over the traces and behave like a young foal let loose in a luscious pasture? Mind is as yet so new to the world that its own existence turns it giddy. The envelope of mind, the body itself, is ages old; the young and fresh creation of the spirit is borne up by a venerable material structure with a host of winding ways and hidden chambers no longer serving any useful purpose. The body has done its part in bringing forth mind. And in the time to come it will be the business of mind to rid itself of this heavy and awkward prehistoric shell. Civilisation will, as time goes on, concentrate more and more upon this aim: the discarding of material values. It is the spiritual values we have now to consider.

The whole of evolution on earth must be regarded as a refining process towards the production of the Collective Spirit. Since its first appearance, we have seen it, in the form of a common stock of mind, gradually growing and ever increasing in wealth and power. One day, perhaps, it will break away from matter altogether, emancipate itself from individual forms and do away with all need of any planet. This will happen as soon as individuals are no longer able to contribute anything further to its development; when the creative power has reached its culmination in all spiritual respects.

In certain fields, our common knowledge seems already to have attained its utmost possibilities: in mathematics, logic; architecture, painting, sculpture and perhaps the art of the theatre; nothing can be produced in these spheres nearer perfection than what has already been done. Evolution has for the present concentrated its efforts upon other branches, such as natural science, sociology and philosophy, where there is still plenty of scope for further development. Here also, however, it is becoming more and more difficult for the individual to assert himself in face of the Collective Mind. The age of great individualities is past. A new Aristotle, whose thought should feed the world for two thousand years, is inconceivable. Aristotle was only possible at a period when the common stock of mind was still but a small estate, which could be administered by great individual minds. There are, perhaps, men born in our own day who are ten times greater than Aristotle, but their effect upon the world is not the same. The community of mind makes every one of us an Aristotle, a Plato, a Newton, a Shakespeare, a Goethe; but this very fact increases the demands made upon new independent thinkers who appear; and the requirements for such will in time become so great as to be beyond the power of any individual to meet; just as to-day no painter can surpass Raphael, no sculptor Phidias, no writer of comedies Molière.

The spiritual trust is like a commercial trust inasmuch as its increasing strength makes it ever more difficult for any single individual to compete with it.

There is still, however, ample scope for the individual in many fields. The common store of mind may be compared to a balloon half-filled with gas, and still receiving supplies from thousands of pipes, the individual contributors. In course of time, we may suppose, it will have received its full complement; then, the holding ropes are cut, and the balloon will soar up away from earth—the spiritualisation of our earth will be complete, collective mind will have passed through its final metamorphosis and become the Collective Spirit.

The history of civilisation gives us the progress of mind.

How it first began we do not exactly know, but one of the earliest steps was probably the development of human speech. The creative process in this field is still going on, though more slowly now than formerly. The more recent languages are, from practical and other points of view, undoubtedly better than the old; French, Spanish and Italian, for instance, must be considered improvements on the Latin. English is the richest, most practical and most living of all languages; we see a newer stage of it in the language of the United States of America, which will probably in course of time be simplified like Esperanto and become known to most people on earth. Speech was the first practical achievement of solidarity; for speech is something beyond the individual, not private property, but common to all who speak it.

The next advance was the invention of writing, which gave us the first firm bond between past and present. The ancient sages, Aristotle in particular, were especially active in procuring libraries of papyri. The Ptolemies collected some 700,000 scrolls in Alexandria, which were later destroyed by fire during the tumults and the invasion of Christian soldiery. Pliny relates of Asinius Pollio, the founder of the original papyrus library at Rome, that he was " the first who made the human mind a matter of state importance."

Then came the art of printing, and a means was thus found of reaching a wider circle. In this sphere of work also, the most rapid development took place. During the first century after the invention of printing, only 42,000 books were printed, but in the next, the figure exceeded half a million, and in the next again close on two millions. As to the number of books, periodicals and newspapers printed during the last hundred years, not even approximate figures are available, and it would be hopeless to attempt an estimate.

The establishment of academies, universities and the higher type of schools gave us the nurseries of solidarity in the sphere of mind. Museums were later added. One of the important cultural results of the French Revolution was the opening of art collections and other museums to the public in France, an example later followed in other countries. In former times, such collections had been the property of the Crown or of wealthy private citizens, and admission was only to be obtained by their special favour. Museums and the later public libraries founded on the understanding that humanity's common store of mind should be open and accessible to all humanity.

From earliest times, the theatre has been one of the most popular links between individual and collective mind, and the stage has preserved its attractions throughout the ages. The theatre is still a civilising element of importance, though scenic art, which began with moralising tragedy (Euripides, Sophocles) and scathing satire (Aristophanes) is now tending more and more in the direction of entertainment only; a development which is carried further by the cinematograph.

The Church, too, though often directly hostile to the advancement of culture, has been of great importance in its way as an aid to co-operation of mind, especially among primitive populations, where unity and advancement of mind could be better attained by setting up a supernatural divinity as the centre of worship.

Clubs and societies, press and politics, and economical, national and international unions and exhibitions are further expressions of the tendency to community of mind.

A triumph of importance in the solidarity of mind was achieved by the publication of the first encyclopædia. The appearance of this work created an enormous sensation and gave rise to discussion in all circles. Why should this be so? There were plenty of books already. The great point was, that a monument was here erected to the glorification, not of faith, but of knowledge; it was as if the Collective Mind held its first review, surveyed its own production, and cried aloud to the world at large that the future of mankind lay in the clear co-operation of mind, in the light of day, not in the dim religious gloom of the churches. Now, for the first time, it was possible to discern the Collective Spirit as the end in view.

In the previous chapters, we have referred to vegetation and the animal world as stages marked on the road behind, to indicate the forward march of the creative power. Flora and fauna have no further potential development, they are at a standstill. Similarly, great works of art, libraries, museums and academies are a series of monuments marking the advance of the creative power in the sphere of mind. As the human body derives its physical nourishment from the animal and vegetable kingdoms, so also we are nourished by the stores accumulated in libraries and academies of learning, art collections and museums, the sources whence we derive the strength for further production.

In the sphere of mind, the creative power has advanced tentatively by many roads.

In ancient Egypt, it was religion which was the growing-point of culture. Architecture, handicrafts and applied arts were all applied to the service of religion, and their manifestations exist to this day in the mighty temples, sphinxes, pyramids and tombs.

The culture of Greece was first of all religious. From the cult of religion as a centre the arts grew up and differentiated gradually, until we had an independent sculpture and painting; the art of the theatre arose, and music echoed over the isles of Greece. Culture blossomed out into sudden luxuriance and unprecedented wealth; mind was now master of the world, and as a final development came philosophy, marking the full emancipation from religion. A fresh harvest of the mind appeared with the Renaissance, when painting especially astonished the world.

THE COLLECTIVE SPIRIT

The method of art has always been to establish an interplay between the one and the many. The learned men of Egypt who made the pyramids and shaped the statues of the gods, established connection between past and present. The Greeks invented sculpture; and in street and market-place great artists spoke to the multitude through the medium of their works. In the Renaissance, imperishable works were produced on canvas, and a later period gave us the opera, through which the great composer speaks to the world.

It is a typical feature of the creative power that it tends to specialise. It will work for some time in one field, until it has attained perfection; then it passes on to another. And so it is we find artists of later periods unable to surpass the earlier masters. In painting and sculpture, music, architecture, poetry and perhaps the novel, art has already reached its culmination, and nothing more of permanent value can here be achieved. At the present time, the creative power centres round the study of natural science, sociology, hygienics and practical work; the leaders of our own time are Edison, Marconi, Karl Marx, Pasteur and Einstein, just as Wagner and Beethoven, Goethe and Schiller were the leaders of a former age, and Praxiteles and Phidias of an earlier still.

Thanks to modern means of communication, the telegraph, the telephone, radio, books and scientific journals, and not least the daily press with its increasing facilities for obtaining and circulating information, the entire population of the globe is gradually being fused into a community of mind. No new thought, invention or discovery can come into the world but it is communicated to all in an astonishingly short space of time. As soon as any individual has produced anything of importance to mankind, the news is spread throughout the globe, and the idea is at once assimilated by all. A voice in any quarter is immediately echoed in all the rest.

The process of evolution of the human mind, and the final results it comes to in the testing of all questions of the same kind is the same in all countries. It is an American writer, John W. Draper, who makes the assertion. And if we glance through the history of civilisation we find that there are only apparently different civilisations in the world. Even the most widely dissimilar types of culture fuse in course of time. The civilisation which probably originated in the East was adopted by the Babylonians, who passed it on to Egypt, whence it was again transferred *via* Crete and Mycene to Greece and Rome, who bequeathed it to us.

Even so mighty a power as Christianity was not able to transform the Græco-Roman culture. It was like the frog that swallowed the elephant; after the meal, the frog was nowhere to be seen, whereas the elephant stood there huge and mighty as before, only with a thin slimy film on its skin. When the Renaissance restored classical culture to eminence, it was simply because it formed the skeleton of all culture and was therefore indispensable. The Græco-Roman culture has again come to its own in modern times, but while in classical times it was the property of but a few millions, it is shared now by hundreds of millions throughout the greater part of the globe. We cannot but admit that Nietzsche is right in declaring this a complete victory of mind over the attempted undermining of culture by a few anæmic Christian mendicant monks.

But, it may be asked, are there no other forms of collective mind than the one which has come down to us *via* Greece and Rome? Are there not Asiatic forms of culture independent of ours which give the lie to any assertion as to the community of culture as a whole? Among the temples of Peking or in the crowded bazaars of India, do we not find a culture as distinct from our own as the Chinese pagoda with its writhing dragons is unlike the calm, clean-lined edifice of a Grecian temple?

That there is a conspicuous difference must be admitted. It is a strange experience for a white man to stand in Kioto or Nikko or one of the ancient temple cities of Japan, amid buildings so fantastic and alien in form as almost to make him shudder. But it is the past he there observes. But a few hundred yards away he no longer feels transported to a strange planet; the Græco-Roman civilisation appears again, but modernised, in the form of a railway station, with electric light and Pullman cars awaiting his pleasure and that of the yellow temple worshippers alike.

The culture of the East has, through isolation due chiefly

THE COLLECTIVE SPIRIT

to political considerations, developed along different lines from those of Græco-Roman Europe, but at the present time a fusion of the two forms is taking place in India and China, and more especially in Japan, showing that they are not so essentially dissimilar as to be beyond amalgamation. In less than a hundred years Japan has assimilated Western culture, and in the interior of China, where men still burn joss sticks to the spirits of their ancestors, we may already find electric light in the temples, while great steamers under the Chinese flag sail up and down the rivers and the Son of Heaven reigning in Peking has given place to a President in the modern style—another victory for Greece and Rome.

We still know but very little of Asiatic culture. Up to the present the process of development has been all on one side. It is the West that has forced its way into the East. But in one respect, we have also learned something : what the East needs is not Christianity ; it has mysticism and deities enough of its own, and our missionaries there make but poor headway. What the Oriental is interested in is our political, technical and mercantile progress, all that side of our civilisation which derives from Greece and Rome ; it is our science, not our faith, that these millions want.

But there is also another side to the question, namely, how far we can find anything of value to ourselves in the culture of the East. Schopenhauer was already aware of the wealth that lay hidden in the Upanishads and Vedic poems, and when the libraries of the East are once opened to us in earnest, we may believe they will afford important contributions to the common store of mind.

In a few centuries from now, or perhaps before, the East and the West will meet and unite ; for culture is of its nature a unity.

In ordinary every-day life we enjoy the benefits of community of mind with a kind of habitual nonchalance, as a matter of course. But in solitary confinement—one of the worst forms of punishment that can be found—we suddenly realise how indispensable they are. Camille Joset, the Belgian politician who was imprisoned by the Germans, states that physical starvation was nothing compared to the hunger of the mind which an educated person feels when shut up for years in a cell apart from his fellows. The years he spent in this manner, entirely devoid of all impressions from without, were an almost unbearable torture.

To travel in distant and sparsely inhabited regions face to face with soulless Nature reveals to us our loneliness as individual minds, and we feel a longing for civilisation. Nature can make an overwhelming and crushing impression on the human being who finds himself in utter solitude, debarred from all intercourse with minds of similar type. In the jungle, in the forests of Alaska, on the Pampas, where primitive life shoots up everywhere brutally, like a clenched fist, we feel a violent longing for culture; we think of clubs and universities, theatres, books and newspapers, lectures and museums and art galleries, recalling in mind the impressions of earlier days, seeking alliance with human culture past and present, to avoid being overcome by this mass of untamed, unspiritualised vitality that is at once impressive and stifling. Only the eccentric can endure the solitude of Nature. It is characteristic that one of the last things an Arctic explorer throws away when staggering under the weight of his load in the frozen waste is the little printed book with its problems to exercise the mind, a treasure brought from home and without which the solitude would be unendurable.

On the other hand, in places where the treasures of our common mind are stored, there is wealth at the disposal of the individual. A friend of the writer, studying as a young man at a commercial college in London, relates as follows:

"The working hours were long, from ten in the morning until nine at night, with only an hour's interval in the afternoon. This hour I spent every day for a year at the British Museum, which was close by.

"My experiences in this temple of the human mind made a far deeper and more ineradicable impression on me than the many hours spent at the school. In the midst of the sooty, noisy, busy city stood this temple, its portals always open, and from the moment one walked up the low steps under the Doric pillars into the twilight of the entrance hall, one felt a peace of mind, a sense of being lifted up, a feeling that eternity itself was speaking, and refreshing the mind.

"The place itself was like a monument to the mind of man. Treasures of all ages and from all quarters of the earth were gathered here, each with its own history, each whispering its own little word, and all seeming to combine in one full deep chord that rang through the lofty halls. Most impressive of all perhaps was the great reading-room, tier upon tier of knowledge lining the walls of one great arena ; the sum of human knowledge stored in a single room. There is a solemnity about the place such as one does not find in any church ; we are in one of the eternal mansions built by man as an abiding-place for mind."

The Danish high schools offer a striking example of the power of this community of mind. The founder's idea was to awaken the spiritual life of the people, and raise up a generation sunken in materialism to an idealised view of life. The lectures cover a wide range of subjects, from national history and general literature to the latest discoveries of modern science. The main thing is to unite all hearers in a common awakening of mind.

The secret of a speaker's power lies in his ability to unite his hearers in a feeling of community based on his ideas. One may call it mass suggestion, but this really explains nothing after all. What happens is, that the speaker brings all those present into a common harmony of mind, which each individual mind finds pleasurable.

Another instance of the effect of community of mind is afforded on a smaller scale by the theatre. It is a well-known fact that the most experienced managers cannot be sure of a play's success beforehand, even at the final rehearsal ; for the one-half of the whole is still lacking, to wit, the audience. Only on the first night does the piece receive its baptism of fire ; not until then can it be seen whether the dramatist has succeeded in his task, which is, to unite the thousands of individual spectators in one single organism, following with tense interest the action of the play and responding as one to its changing emotions. The feeling of an audience is something distinct from the feeling of individuals ; it is a collective factor which only arises here, but is nevertheless the decisive element.

A quaint and caricatured instance of this same power is shown in the domination of fashions in dress and similar matters. When certain mannequins appear at the races at Longchamps in tight skirts, we may be sure that ladies all the world over, from Montevideo to Helsingfors, will be wearing the same six months later. When a new kind of dance becomes the rage in America, we may be pretty certain it will find its way to Europe in similar wise. Nero is said to have been the first to wear a monocle; and even to this day it is a fashion in diplomatic circles. It is not ourselves, but fashion that decides what clothes we are to wear, what kinds of dance and music we are to affect for the season, what wines and what cigars we are to buy, what plays we are to see and how we are to do our hair. Fashion is the harlequinade of community of mind, but even in this form it is a power to be reckoned with.

The history of civilisation presents many different attempts at such community of mind in the form of caste, guilds, national, military and popular feeling, and even the spirit of art. The great invention of the ancient Church was the congregation, where all individual members were made one in the Holy Ghost—and it was this which gave the congregation its power. In our own day we may speak of the spirit of Prussianism, or the Junker spirit, the spirit of Bolshevism, the spirit of a true sportsman, and so on; all these are little preliminary steps towards the true Collective Spirit, its first experimental manifestations, its trial balloons.

History shows us a growing intimacy of spiritual co-operation. Scattered faculties have joined forces, influencing and encouraging one another, leading to a mighty increase in the total of the common store of mind combining towards universal effort. Individuals combine in the tribe, tribes form larger communities, and these again unite in nations; and in the fields of science and art all nations again combine.

Patriotism, which may or may not degenerate into Jingoism, is a first attempt at collective effort. We talk of the spirit of this or that nation, and it conveys a certain idea; it is a thing as real as the chair in which we sit. There is an almost Biblical forcefulness in the slogan : *My country right or wrong !* It is an idea for which we are ready to sacrifice our individual lives.

But there is something greater and loftier, nobler and more comprehensive than national feeling, namely, the feeling of humanity as a whole. We find it in the British Museum, the Louvre and the Vatican alike, in any great international scientific congress, in scientific publications, in international law and what we might call the public opinion of the world. Victor Hugo wrote not for the French alone but for all the world. The idea of internationalism is still in its initial stage, but it will grow stronger irresistibly, until the civilisations of the world are united into one. We are still living in the age of national culture, with its many illogical contradictions, but we are moving gradually towards something greater than this. Socialism, communism, international treaties, the court of arbitration at The Hague, the League of Nations—all point in the same direction. Goethe was not only a German, he was a citizen of the world ; and Kant looked forward to the time when the nations of the world should combine in common effort for the preservation of peace. It is the great fault of Christianity that it compromised with a narrow national feeling and thus became divided against itself; When the importance of the Collective Spirit as a philosophical principle is once generally realised, the adherents of that principle will be able to effect what the adherents of religion never could : to unite all individual human beings in one community. We have still some way to go before we reach that stage.

But it is a gratifying sign of the times that we have already to reckon with a popular feeling of the world as a whole ; a universal public opinion which even the greatest military power among the nations cannot defy with impunity. And this universal opinion speaks loudly in defence of human culture and its products, of mind and the treasures of the mind ; for these are the common property of all mankind.

The greatest disasters which have happened to the human race are not pestilences and famines, unsuccessful expeditions or defeats in war, but the destruction of its treasures of the mind. Whole armies have been swallowed up and history made no comment; but the destruction of the libraries at Alexandria, of the Moorish palaces in Spain and the burning of the Parthenon are rightly named as irreparable losses to mankind. During the late war, the world heard with something approaching apathy of the destruction of whole regiments, English, French or German; but the burning of the library at Louvain and the bombardment of the cathedral at Rheims were greeted with indignation everywhere; it was an offence against the Collective Spirit.

Mr. H. G. Wells, in one of his books, *The Dream*, speaks about " the great past of life," of the races of men and their slow growth in knowledge, of fears and dark superstitions and the dawning victories of truth, of the conquest and sublimation of human passions through the ages, of the divinity of research and discovery of the latent splendour of our bodies and senses, of possibilities amid which the continually more crowded masses of our race are blundering so tragically, yet with such bright gleams of hope and promise. Mr. Wells concludes with a reference to the human community with a common soul and an ultimate common destiny. In these words, he expresses in a lucid and convincing manner the ideas of the idealistic theory of evolution.

Practically, man has gained the greatest advantage from co-operation in the sphere of mind; the State itself is a product of this co-operation. On every side we see how the general development advances as soon as collective effort is introduced. There is something infectious, magnetic, about mind, which draws forth more power of mind to itself. We see how great writers and artists are constantly being influenced by one another; how one " school " after another arises, and whole nations, by intensive co-operation, have been able to make important contributions in the sphere of culture.

Two heads may be better than one; but that two hundred should be proportionately better still may be open to doubt; our modern parliaments, for instance, may be cited as typical talking-shops proving the contrary. But, after all, are not these legislative assemblies better than their reputation? It must be admitted that a parliament, in the discussion of a question, or its investigation in committee, often succeeds in throwing more light upon its various aspects than would be possible in any other way. The great defect of parliamentary work lies, not in the co-operation on which it should be based, but in the conflict of interests between different parties, leading to obstruction and compromise instead of rapid and firm decision. Where a whole assembly is at work unanimously on a question, when men of superior intellect unite, remarkable results can be attained in an astonishingly short space of time. We have only to think of such a document as the Rights of Man, or the Declaration of Independence. If parliaments were to be abolished, it would soon be found necessary to revive them.

J. W. Draper, whom we have quoted before, also considers that it is only where many are working together that we can be sure of arriving at right decisions. And he comes to the same conclusion as our idealistic theory of evolution, in regarding the unanimous judgment of humanity as a whole as the only criterion of truth. Man should cast away the restriction of his individuality, and remember that he has allies in race and kin enabling him to further indefinitely the degree of approximation towards absolute truth. He despises the views of his childhood, doubts those of a somewhat later stage; those of his race are less open to doubt. The successive stages gain in force and verisimilitude. How great, then, must be the strength and approximation of the view of humanity as a whole! Philosophically speaking, we have no absolute criterion of truth, but we can, step by step, attain ever-increasing degrees of certainty, our calculations grow more and more exact. Metaphysicians have erred in adopting an incomplete view of man's position, concentrating on a single section instead of taking a more comprehensive survey. In rejecting the oriental doctrine of the individual as centre of the universe, and adopting a wider and firmer view, we are doing as the astronomers who substituted the heliocentric for the geocentric view; and the exchange promises to bear fruit in more accurate results.

The experience of every-day life supports us here. When in doubt as to our own judgment, we seek the advice of a friend; we are mightily confirmed in our opinion when we find it backed by public opinion as a whole. Even the Church did not disdain the principle of councils and conclaves, as a surer means of getting at the truth. The degree of probability increases with the number of investigators; and the human criterion of truth must surely lie in the judgment of humanity as a whole, increasing further in accuracy with the spread of knowledge and enlightenment. And this being so, it would seem that the future of man may well be brighter than has hitherto been thought. Indeed, it seems hopeful in the extreme. Philosophy may find good omens in the great material and mechanical discoveries, improving means of communication and reducing distances. The intellectual contact resulting from this, the gradual disappearance of prejudice, and further investigation, will bring us ever nearer to the truth. Any falsehood, however powerfully backed, must be exposed. In a word, we have here a court of arbitration to which humanity can look with every confidence in the justice of its decrees. From the point of view of abstract philosophy it may still be far from infallible, but it is nevertheless the highest court to which we can refer as human beings, and there can be no appeal to any higher tribunal.

Draper here regards the Collective Mind of man as a supreme court, and in this view we can heartily concur. But the Collective Mind has also other tasks before it. One of them is to emancipate the individual from automatism; to awaken or at any rate to aid a sluggish creative power. We find instances of this in the effect of one man's talent and creative force on the work of another. Zola could not have written without Balzac, or Hegel without Schelling; and many similar instances might be found. The history of mind is a story of reciprocal influence.

And so the world of mind becomes a kind of perpetual motion; the accumulated store sets new creative power to work and thereby adds to its capital, increasing its own power of further increase.

When life was first born of matter and became an inner life, the creative power achieved its masterpiece. It moved from one sphere of action up to a higher, and introduced something entirely new into the world.

Recollecting this achievement, it need not seem impossible that a further leap in evolution might take place whereby this inner life hitherto associated with individual minds should combine its particles into a new organisation independent of the individual; a higher kind of world. Nietzsche's idea of the Superman that is to take the place of man was, if this supposition be correct, only a rather narrow prediction of what is to come. Nietzsche did not perceive the many indications of an evolution aiming, not at a Superman but rather at the production of an entirely new form of existence, a supermind, the Collective Mind, comprising in itself the best there is of mind on earth, a world emancipated from physical being, and purely spiritual in character, a phenomenon as distinct from our present life as our present life is from the purely material combinations which alone constituted the world before life came into being.

It seems to us that evolution is working toward this end, and that no rational interpretation of evolution is possible without it. If Nature had merely been aiming at the production of the Superman, it might have achieved this much more rapidly and easily, by making intellectual power and experience hereditary, so that human beings were born, not in their present state of deplorable blankness, but enriched from birth with all the knowledge and experience accumulated by their ancestors for thousands of generations, just as we inherit our bodily equipment.

Goethe has observed that, though the world as a whole advances, youth has still to begin at the beginning and experience for itself the main events in human life. And this is just the point. We cannot bring ourselves to believe that this serious defect in our mind as compared with the body should be merely a lapse on the part of Nature, an accidental error or omission. Assuming Nature to have an aim at all, we cannot suppose that it should fail in a decisive point. Seeing that we are as we are, we must believe that Nature

wants us as we are and not otherwise. But we are built as
channels for mind, as more or less adequately functioning
transformers of energy; and in the study of our evolution
to date there is nothing to suggest that we shall alter in
character in any essential degree. We do not look like
breeders either of future Supermen or of gods; everything
tends to show that our future will not be greatly different
from our present; we are servants, producers, in the employ
of a certain undertaking; our business is to supply it with
mind. And so it will remain. Man is plainly a means, not
an end, or more accurately, a transition stage leading to
something greater and more important. Nietzsche's Superman theory suffers from the same over-estimation of man
as we find in the revealed religions he so scornfully condemns.
The naked truth about us human beings is that we simply
have no independent spiritual life, and are not likely ever to
attain it. At the first stage of human life, in childhood, man
reveals his true character as an individual mind. Children
are altogether primitive, more like animals than anything
else, and only rise to better things as the common store of
mind gradually fills them with its own material. Luther
held that man was a child till his fortieth year; and soon
after that his power of mind declines. Our maturity lasts but
a very short time, and such maturity as we do attain is due
only in a very slight degree to our own efforts; most of it is the
work of the Collective Mind. Such beings no more contain the
material for Superman than for angels. Evolution shows us
nothing to suggest that the individual has advanced since
earliest times as far as culture is concerned. The thing that has
advanced is the Collective Mind. When we esteem ourselves so
mightily ahead of our forbears in the Stone Age, we are decking
ourselves in borrowed plumes. The essential difference between
us and them is that we went to a better school, that is all.

How is the transition from community of mind to the
Collective Spirit to be effected? How will the metamorphosis
take place? Let us first consider how it was that matter first
turned to life. If we look at an ant-hill, we see so many tiny
creatures each dragging a pine needle along, to be piled up

together for the good of all, but the individual worker has no idea of the end in view. It is the same with the formation of a coral reef. We ourselves are helping to build up a similar structure, a coral reef of mind. A new world is to be raised on our dead bodies.

This theory seems to us more in agreement with the facts of evolution than Nietzsche's Superman idea. And it is very characteristic that Nietzsche tells us so little as to how these god-like beings of his are to arise; he does not even tell us much as to their qualities. His conception is mainly that of an aristocratic product, a human being whose greatest virtue is a kind of hauteur, a being with steady eyes and calm, slow pace, dreading all change, and always disguised; for the loftier a human being's nature the more need of moving incognito (if there were a God, He would for sheer decency's sake have to appear in human guise!). According to Nietzsche, the Superman will be extremely courteous and polite in manner, suspicious of anything approaching *laissez-faire*, with a mild appreciation of women (those creatures whose heads are always full of dancing and foolishness and frippery), taciturn, loathing all scandal, capable of cherishing long enmity, *in eroticis* neither brutal, morbid nor prudent, hating all that savours of demagogic cheerfulness and proletarian intimacy, with a certain naïveté, like the eagle, which reveals its proud and magnificent stupidity in its mode of attack, always dashing down headlong, and with a power of shaping his surroundings and dispensing with the supports that lesser minds find needful.

All this is very fine and attractive, but it cannot be denied that the virtues Nietzsche here mentions are already developed among human beings of our own day, and were perhaps even more so in our aristocratic ancestors; such virtues, indeed, have always been admired in human society. That the trend of evolution in the future will be aristocratic we do not believe; it is more likely to be democratic. And Nietzsche concluded in the end that the Superman type had already manifested itself, especially in ancient Greece and during the Renaissance. Zarathustra, therefore, points rather backward than forward.

The imaginative H. G. Wells, too, goes astray when he tries to depict the human type of the future; his ideal is rather a race of men with "well ventilated brains," poring over mathematical and biological problems, a type which surely seems to exist among us at the present day.

Neither Nietzsche, Wells, Flammarion nor any other of those who have endeavoured to paint the future on our earth, with the exception of Fechner, has gone to the full extreme. They stop at the human type, instead of following evolution further to the next natural stage, the supra-human, where a new principle comes into force, and man is given his discharge because his task is done. Evolution hardly aims at producing individuals of gigantic dimensions. There were such already in ancient Greece and during the Renaissance. The human beings of the future will hardly be stronger individually than those of the present day; rather, indeed, weaker, with defective eyesight, poor digestions and "nerves." History seems to show us pretty clearly that any advance in culture is generally accompanied, in the long run, by physical deterioration. Races and nations which have attained a certain stage of refinement soon give way and are replaced by others more robust. Mind is developed at the expense of physical vitality; our contributions to the store of mind cost us life. And so it will be as long as intellectual qualities are not hereditarily transmissible; and there is nothing at present to suggest any intervention of the creative power to alter this state of things.

Men will become more alike; our common civilisation will mould the individuals more and more to the same type. Only by specialisation will the individual mind be able to achieve anything of importance, but what the individual gains in his special field of work he will lose in others. And in course of time, human activity in various fields will become superfluous, as one or another reaches its culmination of evolution. If, then, we would find the Superman, we must look back to earlier ages, not forward to the future; the greatest poets have already realised this, as is evident from their choice of subjects. If, on the other hand, we would study the evolution of mind, it is to the future we must turn our eyes. The sum of human mind will, thanks to the steady influx of fresh contributions, be ever increasing, and one day the Collective Spirit will shine out over the world in all its beauty and splendour; a light, compared with which the individual mind, even at its highest, will be but as a flickering candle.

The idealistic theory of evolution, then, offers us a hope of immortality very different from that of Christianity, for instance. It is more like the Nirvana of the Brahmins; most of all, perhaps, like Plato's ideal world. The Collective Spirit will be a world of ideas, freed from all earthly dross. But Plato regarded this world as having existed from all eternity, whereas the idealistic theory of evolution sees it as gradually arising through evolution.

The Christian doctrine of the soul, which postulates the persistence of personality after death, and even talks of a " resurrection of the body," leads to some very curious logical results. It ascribes to every human being an immortal soul, without regard to the nature of the human being, whether a personality of the highest culture, a savage from the wilds, a degenerate criminal type or a person partly or wholly insane. Nor does it matter whether the human being dies the moment it has come into the world, or lives to extreme old age; in either case, the soul is immortal! Distinction is, however, sharply drawn between man and beast. Only man is endowed with eternal life; all other animals are excluded (the dog cemeteries where one may read on tombstones pious hopes of meeting poor Fido again in a better world are not recognised by the Church as holy ground). In this respect, Christianity is less consistent than the religion of ancient Egypt, where animals were credited with immortality and embalmed accordingly. The Egyptian method was undoubtedly more rational; for how can we, in the light of evolution, make any such distinction between the lower animals and man? There exist to this day cannibal tribes whose rank in the scale of culture is hardly above that of penguins and beavers. And, looking back along the road of evolution, there must have been a time when beast and human merged one into the other, and man of the "immortal" soul, was hardly to be distinguished from the beasts that perish. The old-fashioned doctrine of the soul is inconsistent with the theory of evolution; and since the latter is based on facts, the doctrine of the soul must be discarded.

The hypothesis of a world of the Collective Spirit superseding the present world, and comprising, not all there ever was of mind, but all the quintessence of mind, obviates these difficulties. But another seems here to arise; it is hard for us to imagine a sum of mind without an individual form, a "soul" or repository holding it all together. It is easy enough to recognise mind as a reality of great importance to mankind; but when mankind is dead and gone, it would seem as if the mind must vanish with it. Is it not, one may ask, a little too much to suppose that a synthesis of soul-qualities should be capable of independent existence as a Collective Spirit when all bodies have perished? How can we postulate anything of the sort, when we do not even admit the existence of a personal soul save in conjunction with the body?

Our answer is as follows:

Even in the world as it is now, we can perceive that a synthesis of soul-qualities and manifestations, that is, the products of mind derived from a great number of human beings living in different ages, is a possibility, inasmuch as every civilised individual possesses, in his own mind, such a synthetic whole. There is, then, the possibility of a fusion of them all, though still presuming the existence of a repository, a living human brain, in which this can take place. A thousand impressions can merge into one idea in a single brain—it is in this way that scientific formulæ arise. Mind is a substance which enters easily into different combinations; it can always be refined and further distilled, and is always capable of assimilating further matter from the most widely different sources.

And further, it must be remembered that mind is not absolutely restricted to the living individual. A man possessed of mind in an exceptional degree can create a work of art which he endows with something of his own. When Leonardo da Vinci painted a picture, a spiritual process took

THE COLLECTIVE SPIRIT 153

place whereby he gave to a piece of canvas the power of speaking to others on his behalf. Similarly, a great singer can give a gramophone record the power of his song. Every artist is a Pygmalion. Thus we see that mind is not inseparably bound to the individual; but that the individual can at any rate transfer a portion of his mind to certain objects, which then act as his ambassadors, and speak in his name for centuries after his death. Mind can be transmitted, not only from man to man, but also from man to thing.

Very true, it may be argued, but we still require at least a thing, a physical object, as the vehicle of mind. We cannot imagine an artist whose mind lives on in its products after his death, unless in the consciousness of other human beings or directly associated with certain objects.

We perhaps cannot imagine such a state of things. Products of mind without living beings to perceive them may seem to us a contradiction in terms. It is hard for us also to imagine Plato's ideas floating at large as prototypes in space far removed from man's imperfect approaches. Our own experience can only conceive of mind as associated with some man or some object of man's creation. We know nothing of mind in itself, free of all association; and it is hard for us to conceive a thing we cannot observe.

So, then, when we cannot conceive what the world of the Collective Spirit will be like, it is because we naturally incline to an anthropomorphic view of the Collective Mind itself. But the world of the future will not by any means consist of soul qualities and manifestations as we know them. We cannot suppose the Collective Spirit to be a mere sum, the simple accumulation of a mass of facts, such as we find in a lexicon. The Collective Spirit will be itself a whole, as is an organism in which no part is a repetition of any other, but each portion indispensable to the whole.

At present, we have only fragments of mind, and can form no idea of what such a whole would be like. But we can, perhaps, through the most advanced sciences, gain some vague inkling of its form. Just as the science of mathematics is a whole from which every superfluous item has been discarded, so also the Collective Spirit will be a whole freed from all waste matter. Spiritually speaking we are still in an age of confusion, of endless repetitions, where worthy and worthless struggle for the mastery; we are in the midst of a battlefield filled with clamour and carnage. Out of this chaos the pure world of mind will gradually arise; a world of clean, essential lines, freed from all contradiction and defacement, a world as different from our present existence as this present world of life is from the glowing nebula of its original form.

To understand the character of the world now being formed we should study the results which modern science has attained by a particular application of logic. The aim here is to show that there exists a logical world independent of psychology. Professor Schelderup writes in this connection:

"Logically speaking, there exists but a single specimen of each idea, however many think it, and however often it may be thought. Thought is therefore not a purely subjective activity. The idea which my thought grasps is not numerically distinct from the idea that other people have.

"By such considerations, these writers endeavour to emancipate the logical content from thinking as an individual psychological act. The realm of truth is altogether independent of accidental human thought. The principles of logic and mathematics are apodictic, timeless and subjectless. Truth therefore by no means presupposes the existence of a thinking subject. A truth is valid even though it may never be discovered, never realised in any consciousness. It is a valid unit in the timeless realm of ideas."

We have quoted this passage to show that there are philosophers in our own day who assume the existence of a Platonic world of ideas, a world resting in itself, a supra-subjective kingdom. They are, however, guilty of the same error as Plato; they believe that this supra-individual world has always existed from eternity. They do not see that it is in process of formation, by the road of evolution. It has been said that we find in mathematics a consistency, a logical coherence, a certainty and inevitability seemingly far above all subjectivity and all conditional restrictions, bringing us face to face with an intellectual reality, a world of laws and relationships resting apparently in itself. And this is entirely correct; for the world so described is the world of the Collective Spirit, the world now gradually being formed. But it is erroneous to believe that such a world has always existed. It is, like everything else, a product of evolution. We see its fixed, unalterable laws in mathematics and logic, simply because it is this portion of the world of the Collective Spirit which first took shape. In other sciences, in art and ethics, there is not the same degree of firmness; the light of the spirit still flickers here. But in course of time, all the laws of science, art and ethics will become as firmly fixed as those of mathematics and logic are now. This will be accomplished when the Collective Spirit has attained independent existence, and the work of human kind as transformers of energy is at an end.

We cannot, at our present stage, attain to any real understanding of the Collective Spirit, for, practically speaking, we still know mind only in the rough, associated inseparably with individuals, subjective, and therefore relative. The ultimate essence of mind will be freed from all contradiction, without blemish or relative restriction, like the principles of logic and mathematics, but far more radiantly beautiful than these.

An eminent English writer, Bertrand Russell, has clearly realised the difference between the two worlds, the relative and the objective, though he again has failed to perceive that the latter arises out of the former by a process of evolution or refinement. He writes:

"We shall find it convenient only to speak of things *existing* when they are in time, that is to say, when we can point to some time *at* which they exist (not excluding the possibility of their existing at all times). Thus thoughts and feelings, minds and physical objects *exist*. But universals do not exist in this sense; we shall say that they *subsist* or *have being*, where 'being' is opposed to 'existence' as being timeless. The world of universals therefore may also be described as the world of being. . . . The world of being is unchangeable, rigid, exact, delightful to the mathematician, the logician, the builder of metaphysical systems, and all who love perfection more than life. The world of existence is fleeting, vague, without sharp boundaries, without any clear plan or arrangement, but it contains all thoughts and feelings, all the data of sense, and all physical objects, everything that can do either good or harm, everything that makes any difference to the value of life and the world.

"According to our temperaments, we shall prefer the contemplation of one or of the other. The one we do not prefer will probably seem to us a pale shadow of the one we prefer and hardly worthy to be regarded as in any sense real. But the truth is that both have the same claim on our impartial attention, both are real, and both are important to the metaphysician."

Metaphysicians in all ages have realised that the present world would be entirely incomprehensible, devoid of all meaning, indeed, if we did not reckon with some "other world" transcending this. Plato perceived with his inward eye the world of ideas. Even then it was in process of formation by man's contributions to the common store of mind. But it is only now that we are able to see it does not merely consist of ideas existing from eternity, but is a spiritual reality in the making now and here, to be completed and perfected at some future time as the result of the whole evolutionary process. In a word, the Collective Spirit will be a nobler, non-material successor to the present material world.

This Collective Mind is already, in its earliest stage of evolution, a practical reality of supreme importance, inasmuch as it is able to act upon us human beings not only through logic and mathematics, but through scientific, artistic and ethical laws and accepted rules. With the gradual advance of evolution, it will grow steadily firmer, and thus more powerful; and when at last it has attained completion, man may lie down and die, for he will have nothing more to do; we shall have accomplished the enormous task entrusted to us by Nature.

We are quite prepared to be questioned here as to the interesting point: how the Collective Spirit will emancipate itself from human beings and start on its own. We can only

THE COLLECTIVE SPIRIT

reply that it is no more possible to say anything definite here than it would be to say what will be the state of literature or politics in any country a thousand years hence. The creative power may have all manner of surprises up its sleeve. All we can do is to assemble a series of facts suggesting that evolution tends towards a metamorphosis of this sort.

And, after all, such an advance is not so fantastic as it may first appear. The transition of our earth from a ball of fire to the habitation of thinking beings is no less surprising. Many theories may be formed as to how the coming revolution will take place, and many ways may be indicated as the most likely. But we will not go into this here. All we can say with any degree of certainty at the present stage is, that an evolution in the direction we have stated is a natural consequence of evolution up to now. We should, therefore, do well to prepare ourselves for the same, on the very simple ground that it must surely be better for us to work with Nature than against it.

It is even more of a thankless task to guess at the sort of existence the Collective Spirit will come to lead when once it has emancipated itself from the material, biological and human planes. We can give but the vaguest fragmentary outline of what is likely. All that part of mind which is directly associated with material and biological functions will hardly play any part in the Collective Spirit. On the other hand, one of its great assets in addition to that of ideas, will be memory; the recollection of its own evolution. The Collective Spirit will comprise all the great and important happenings of earth, reflecting in idealised form all deep and beautiful feelings, comprising the greatest art and a science so comprehensive and clear that we human beings, who have no independent mind, can have no conception of it at all.

As to the purpose of this Being in the universe, we can hardly guess. But we may well imagine that similar forms of being will arise on other planets, and meet in conflict or co-operation to the further development of even higher forms. Why should evolution be limited to our earth? The entire universe is doomed to perish by the gradual dissipation of energy and it is to conquer this death of all material things that the Collective Spirit is born, as the natural consequence of evolution.

We have already mentioned that inorganic Nature, according to the law of entropy, presents a picture of decline, degradation, gradual exhaustion, all difference of intensity between the forces of Nature being effaced as time goes on. In contrast to this view, Auerbach has formulated a doctrine of ectropy, according to which the evolution of organic Nature proceeds in the opposite direction. This opposite process, however, will not avail to prevent the ultimate destruction of matter, but only to postpone it. The rise of organic Nature with its wealth of life is only a splendid sunset heralding the great night of the universe. Only the heir to all the culture of the world, the Collective Spirit, will be capable of absolute victory in the struggle. Though the whole universe perish, the Collective Spirit will exist unharmed. Once it has become a reality, the material world will give place to a spiritual world, no longer liable, as was to the lower form, to extinction.

This we shall never live to see; no human being will live to see it. Nevertheless, we are partakers in the process, helping on the work of Nature. And once we have realised this, we have, as it were, a firmer foothold upon earth. It is intolerable to think that we should live our lives in vain, without meaning or purpose. Hence the pretty fairy tale about the immortality of the soul, a faith in defiance of all likelihood and reason. It is surely better to realise our true aim in life, which is, to aid in the creation of a higher and more perfect life than our own. On the one hand, we have those who say: the individual counts for nothing, and is but a meaningless accident, a whim of Nature. On the other, those who say: the individual is all, the centre of the world, an immortal soul. The real truth lies midway between the two.

The reader may here object that we are dealing in mere fancies, which sensible people cannot stop to consider. We may point out in reply that one of the greatest of German philosophers, Gustav Theodor Fechner, the founder of the science of psycho-technics, which is now generally acknowledged as a reality, has given utterance to ideas closely allied to those of the idealistic theory of evolution. He asserts that the earth and the stars are beings with souls. The earth is a plant growing in the ether-bed of heaven, with inorganic soil, air and water for its root, and organic life as its leaf and flower. But in the great garden of the heavens there are, not one, but thousands and thousands of these higher plants, each in a higher sense supplementing the rest. When we are watching a game of chess, we do not seek the spirit of the game in the pieces themselves, but in the relative positions of the pieces and the squares. We have invented the game of chess, and we understand the position. But only earth knows the relations between her pieces, having the spirit of the whole in herself.

And Fechner concludes with a passage which might serve as the banner of the idealistic theory of evolution. Is the spirit of earth, he asks, only recipient? Has it not also activity? Has it a will? In so far as the will of all individuals aims at the same thing—and there is certainly a community in human will which seeks to order things to the simultaneous advantage of all—it coincides with the will of the superior spirit. Where there is conflict, this denotes divergent or conflicting motives in the superior consciousness. The individual human will is a weight in the scale of the higher freedom. We weight the scales as we will, and it weighs and balances our weights as it wills, altering their position according as they are found wanting here or there, or the reverse. Earth has a longer course of evolution to run than the individual human being, who needs but a short span of life to attain the end of his development. It is still comparable to a child at the state where individual impressions and wills are not combined, but isolated. The peoples of the earth are at war, and there is no common endeavour; but everything is working in that direction.

IDEALISING OR REFINING ACTIVITY

> Ideas are the active forces of history.
> *Hegel.*

> The great majority of people are greatly inferior to their ideals.
> *Rousseau.*

IT was Ludvig Feilberg who said that human beings were Nature's transformers of energy—a magnificent term, which, once we realise its meaning to the full, and appreciate its logical consequences, shows us as clearly as could be what it is that really takes place in the world, and what our business is in regard to it.

We have seen in the previous chapters that the aim of the creative power in Nature is to build up, in place of the perishable material universe, a higher, finer and richer spiritual replica of the same, which should at the same time be imperishable.

In order to attain this end, the creative power has made use of a process of distillation. In the material plane, it allowed the forces of Nature to meet in conflict, the struggle itself tending to combine and refine them in thousands of different ways. This process gave rise to a new world, that of the living organisms, which again are the first step towards a spiritual world. For we might well call life the first tentative form of mind, mind in the rough, an intermediate stage between matter on the one hand and the ultimate Collective Spirit on the other.

This organic epoch is evidently only a transition; it has not been able to effect any complete alteration in the conditions prevailing in the material world, to emancipate it from the law of entropy, for instance. Life in its first stage was content to materialise in a series of forms, plants and animals,

IDEALISING OR REFINING ACTIVITY 161

which continued, on a new plane, the struggle carried on by natural forces in the sphere of matter. The forms of life were the result of the struggle in the world of matter; and the struggle on the new plane led in turn to the creation and improvement of sensory and intellectual faculties, or more accurately, to the production of certain implements or forms of mechanism which gave rise to mind.

A violent competition now took place in the biological world between the various mind-producing machines, until at last one of them, the spiritual transformer which we call man, gained the decisive victory.

The human transformer of energy was found to be the most adequate and best constructed of all the various types (others relatively good but ultimately rejected as inferior were birds, apes and the higher insect forms); for only man was capable of doing what Nature demanded. This was: to effect a true idealisation or refinement of the coarser material, the transformation of matter into mind. The creative power then discarded all the other models by leaving them to look after themselves as best they could, which amounted in the long run to their extermination; and took up its dwelling thenceforth in the human system, concentrating there upon its higher aims.

The essential difference between man and the beasts is that man, in his brain and nervous system, possesses a good spiritual transformer of energy, a good machine for the production of mind, whereas those of the animals are less suited to the purpose. Even the animals, however, have this quality, this idealising or refining power, in some degree. When an animal makes use of its functions of sight, hearing or scent, an idealising or refining process really takes place, inasmuch as the organism here takes a material object and raises it to its own plane by making it a factor of sight, hearing or scent, as the case may be. Animals are therefore in a sense artists, creators of a form of mind, though but a primitive form; through the medium of their senses they are able to transpose matter to the perception of mind. When a dog sees a piece of meat through the window of a butcher's shop, it makes the dog's mouth water—because the dog has, by means of sense, idealised the meat, turned it into an idea and thus created an ideal replica of the object.

Human beings do the same thing, but our ideas are far richer and fuller, produced not only by the purely egoistic instinct of self-preservation, but by a longing to idealise and refine the things about us to the benefit of the common store of mind. The animal only idealises as far as this can benefit its belly and general welfare; the tendency to idealisation in man on the other hand, is so highly developed that it will carry us far beyond our own personal needs, to personal efforts in the cause of science, art or morality. And it is the higher development of this faculty in the human being that has enabled us to pass the examination of Nature and reap the reward of progress, while all the other forms are gradually being exterminated.

What we really do, then, is to create, by means of sense impressions and ideas, a new form of reality. We build up a spiritual world, rich in colour and sound, logical, abstract, intangible, the world of mind. In this respect we are all of us born artists. And art itself, as we understand it in our everyday speech, is merely a further stage of the same process, just as is science. Even primitive peoples have their art; for the tendency to artistic activity is as ancient as the mind of man; is indeed, identical with it.

If now it be objected that we are talking poetry and not science, we reply, that our good scientists themselves, working in study and laboratory, are no less poetic; for their work is an idealising process in itself. When a mathematician invents a new formula and associates it with a natural law, he, too, is a poet, since the formula is naturally not identical with the matter it refers to, but " only " a copy in mind, effected by a scientific transformation process. All the products of science, as well as those of art, are the results of an idealising process, and cannot be otherwise. But this does not by any means imply that to idealise a thing is always good art or sound science. The real value of any production here is determined by comparing it with what others have produced in the same sphere of work; and the final judgment is arrived at by the standard of the common store of mind.

IDEALISING OR REFINING ACTIVITY

The common store of mind is our great savings bank, where each individual human being deposits his own products of idealisation and refinement. The bank takes the product and examines it, and then, if it be found good enough, it is added to the common fund, in which all depositors have a share. But as we saw in the last chapter, the amount each individual receives from the bank is far greater than that he is able to contribute. Our individual minds are constantly at work, idealising and refining, but only a small percentage of our results will be of any value to the common fund; most of our results are of value only to ourselves.

Turning now to the question of the human understanding and its limitations, we must first of all remember that we are not creatures of mind alone, but only transformers, producers of mind. The limitations of our understanding are due most of all to the fact that we ourselves, as individual minds, are but implements in the hand of evolution, one of the channels through which it runs, not its ultimate aim. We are bound on all sides by our past, our history, the burden we have carried and still carry with us from our biological and material origins. In this respect, man is like a swimmer treading water, with his head up in the light and air of mind, while all the rest of his body is swayed by the inferior element, which hinders the movement of his thought as well.

Man is not sparing of criticism, but criticises all that comes his way. We may fairly say, however, that since the days of Locke, Hume and Kant, nothing on earth has been subjected to a fiercer critical examination than our understanding itself. Unfortunately, this critical keenness has led to the discouraging result that most writers on theory of knowledge assume that our understanding is more disposed to falsify reality than to represent it fairly. Here, however, the theorists go too far. The critics of the understanding have committed a fundamental error of assuming that there can be but one reality. Actually, from the point of view of understanding, there are three forms of reality, all equally valid, a material, a biological and a spiritual. The trouble, then, lies not in the nature of our understanding, but in the theorists' conception of reality. Reality, the world, is not a simple unit, as the mechanists assume (in supposing that all is derived from atomic vibrations) or as the idealists believe (assuming that the world ultimately consists only of monads, i.e. of mind). The world is, as the idealistic doctrine of evolution has shown, a trinity of matter, life, and mind derived from something unknown (the pre-material world) and moving towards something similarly unknown (the world of the Collective Spirit alone). It is this trinity our understanding has to measure, and the results must be different for the different sections. If the theorists cannot get our understanding to fit in with reality it is because they have not realised that its results must differ according as it is dealing with one or other of the three worlds. They try to crush the human understanding into their own preconceived idea of reality, a procrustean mangling process which the understanding naturally resists—whereupon they reproach poor understanding for being imperfect, or even positively false!

Our understanding has taken various measures of the three worlds we know.

Measurements applicable to the material world we call natural laws, on which we base a particular understanding, that of Nature.

Those applicable to the biological world we might call biological laws; they are concerned with such questions as growth, instinct, genetics, adaptation, cytology, propagation, disease, etc. We have here a biological understanding.

Those referring to the world of mind we call psychological laws, comprising psychology, ideology, logic, mathematics, theory of knowledge, history, religion, ethics, art and culture, etc. Here we require an understanding of mind.

If now we had a material, a biological and a spiritual instrument of understanding, the matter would be very simple; we should then presumably have a complete and perfect understanding. But we have only one, to wit, that of mind. And so we have to take all our measurements by the standard of the mind, which may well give rise to error when we have to employ it, not only for questions of the

IDEALISING OR REFINING ACTIVITY

mind, where it properly belongs, but also for questions of life and matter. Whichever world we view through our understanding, we can only get results in one sphere, that of mind, for the understanding is itself mind. We have to measure our pumpkins, sand and diamonds in the same bushel measure, for we have no other!

All our results, then, must be influenced by the nature of the instrument, our mind. It was the realisation of this fact which led Kant to a relativism in his theory of knowledge, and the cautious suggestion that we do not perceive the thing in itself, but only things as they appear to our forms of thought.

Kant shows unnecessary caution here. Even though we can only measure biological and material things by a standard of mind, we need not therefore regard our measurements as absolutely misleading or futile—always provided that the evolution which has taken place really is, as the idealistic theory of evolution holds, a refining process, that is, each world formed upon the one before it is merely a refinement, a richer and better copy of the earlier stage. It is not impossible that we might, by studying benzine and using benzine measurements, arrive at certain correct conclusions regarding petroleum and the crude oil from which benzine is produced.

There is no reason, then, to reject our understanding, as Bergson, like Kant, chooses to do, because it is an instrument of the mind. It may, for all that, be able to give us correct information even in matters outside the sphere of mind, though it will naturally be likely to give us the best and most reliable results in its own sphere.

It must be admitted, however, that the sceptics are right to a certain extent, in regarding our understanding as subject to the same disabilities as our intellectual apparatus as a whole; and this, unfortunately, has two serious failings. In the first place, the apparatus is so new and little tested, very much younger, for instance, than the body, from the point of view of evolution, and secondly, this apparatus is not designed for such perception as the theory of knowledge requires of it, but for practical ends in the first place, for the orientation and maintenance of the body, and further, and more especially, for the purpose of collecting material for the common store of mind. Our thought is young and inexperienced, and it was not primarily created for the purpose of studying itself!

Great artists have already appeared on earth; have attained, indeed, very near to perfection in their art. But we cannot claim any like degree of maturity for the work of man in metaphysics and the theory of understanding. Man's greatest achievements lie in the sphere of art. Here we can produce work with which the Collective Spirit itself could hardly find fault. But in the knowledge of things we have our limitations. A true understanding of the universe, embracing all phenomena, will probably only be attained by the Collective Spirit, and only then so far as it preserves the memory of all that the creative power has experienced in the earlier, biological and material phases.

This is one reason why we human beings have found it so hard to get a thorough intellectual grasp of the world itself, especially as regards those stages farthest from our own thought, the biological and material phenomena. It is characteristic of our intellectual powers that we can very well describe and analyse our own feelings and psychological development (e.g. in descriptive psychology, as in a novel or a play), but have still no really adequate knowledge or understanding of purely physiological processes, even those taking place in our own bodies, not to speak of those which take place in inorganic Nature. We have, it is true, a perception of Nature; we have formulated a whole series of natural laws, but even these reveal, again and again, some imperfection or positive error; we are constantly having to revise them, and that so drastically that if Nature were capable of laughter, it would many a time have had a good laugh at our expense. Biology, also, including the science of medicine, has repeatedly been guilty of the most glaring errors.

In considering the problem of our understanding we must never forget that, paradoxical as it may seem, thought was not given us primarily to think with, but to create with—Goethe has already said the same thing. Thought is so occupied with practical and ideal aims that it has little time or energy for other things. It is not of primary importance, for instance, to comprehend the physiological processes of our bodies. These processes have been instituted, once and for all, by the creative power at the biological stage, and are, properly speaking, no business of our understanding. Nor is it our business to investigate the development, composition and interplay of natural forces; these were determined by the creative power at an even earlier stage. From a purely practical point of view, of course, it is the duty of thought to consider these processes, but only in their relation to ourselves, in so far as we may thereby avoid irregularities prejudicial to our existence. But to identify ourselves with them so as to attain to an absolute understanding of their nature is beyond the scope of our practical task in life.

Thought can idealise—and this is its one great task, the purpose for which it is mainly intended. And by so doing it can, in the end, give us a richer and finer appreciation of concrete reality than we could ever attain by merely going through its evolution in ourselves. In place of a flat photographic reproduction of Nature, it gives us a splendid painting, with perspective and colour effects, with atmosphere, poetic feeling and a great deal more. No need then to look down on thought as inadequate. What it lacks in reality it gains a thousandfold in ideality.

The reader, we hope, will have understood from the foregoing why we consider human thought so inadequate for the study of existence and its problems. That there exists a problem of existence, a riddle of the universe, at all, is enough to make us humble at the outset. Why is there a sphinx? The mere fact that it is there should be enough to put us in our place, as labourers in the vineyard, nothing more. On the other hand, we must emphatically maintain that we have no reason to believe, as do the sceptics, that the vast problems of existence will remain for ever unsolved because we ourselves are cursed with an understanding so imperfect as never to be able to discern the true meaning of things. We are ourselves in process of evolution, in constant progress; our common store of mind is ever increasing; and this should give us hope. Even now, indeed, we are not so poorly equipped after all.

Nature has provided us, first of all, with a means of perception and adaptation in the form of our senses, which have, from a purely practical point of view, been of the greatest service to us, and supplement one another in such a way that one often corrects the errors of another.

These senses tell us, first of all, that we live in a real world, subject to constant change; and these changes our thought, aided by the common store of mind available, interprets as an evolution.

Evolution again, on further investigation, reveals itself as a refining process, in which we ourselves participate. We are ourselves capable of refining matter, namely, by lifting it up into the sphere of mind as a thought-replica of itself. This power is found more especially developed in artists and scientists, but we all possess it in some degree.

Once we have realised this, we can throw some further light on the nature of our understanding, since it is now plain that our senses and our thought do not subtract anything from the raw material of the objects dealt with, but rather add something thereto. We transform a material and biological world into a world of ideas. This is the world in which we move, and the world we know. And though we have as yet fashioned it but imperfectly, it is nevertheless possessed of further attributes, is richer and deeper and more beautiful than it would be if we were to "feel" it for ourselves—by Bergson's method of intuition, for instance, substituting for senses and mind another means of understanding of biological or material character. True, our mind does falsify the things it perceives, but it does so in the right direction, transforming baser metal into gold. The process involves a gain instead of a loss, and this might certainly be regarded as an extenuating circumstance.

The spectator in a theatre, watching a costly production from the stalls, gets a fuller and finer impression of the show than his friend who goes round to the wings and sees the various pieces of scenery so near that they appear only as chaotic blobs of colour. Mechanist investigators like Locke

IDEALISING OR REFINING ACTIVITY

may be compared to the man behind the scenes, intent on coming to close quarters, with the idea that he will get a truer picture of what is taking place than the man in the stalls, whose perception is illusory. He does not appreciate the importance of the fact that the whole aim of the production is to create an illusion; which means, that the more complete the illusion, the more completely "true" will be the spectator's perception. Certainly, he will be moving in an ideal world partly of his own creation; but since both he himself and the producer of the piece aimed at giving him this very thing, it is surely more sensible on his part to remain in his proper place than to assert a sudden and inconsistent passion for "reality," and upset the whole thing by reaching beyond it. He loses a great deal by so doing, and gets nothing worth mentioning by way of compensation.

The world of mind, then, is just as real as—indeed we may say far more real than—the world we reach by stripping the ideal world of its ideal elements and reducing it to a cold, dark, scentless, meaningless conglomeration of atoms in apparently futile movement.

Hegel has epigrammatically compared Kant's treatment of the problem of understanding to that of the scholastic theorist who declared he would never enter the water till he had learnt to swim. Hegel here brings forward the very natural objection to the severer critics: that we cannot criticise our understanding with anything but the same understanding; which involves admission of the understanding itself as valid. Lotze also wearied of his contemporaries' almost pathological preoccupation with the problem of understanding. "All this whetting of the knife," he writes, "becomes monotonous in the long run, when it is never to be used." We must first and foremost endeavour to get away from the fallacy prevailing in determinist circles, that a criticism of our understanding can lead to a kind of super-philosophy, based, not on "personal truth" but on "objective truth." We can no more attain anything of the kind than we can get out of our skins.

Our understanding, having its roots in the mind, is for that very reason keenest in its perception of the phenomena of mind. Descartes, in his *Discourse de la méthode*, already realised this. And what does the method consist in? Merely in setting one's thoughts in proper order, beginning with the simplest and easiest things and gradually advancing to things more difficult. And what are the "easiest" things to understand? Actually, the most abstract and therefore the most universal; the principles of geometry! Descartes realised to the full that the things most easily and naturally grasped by the human mind are the products of mind itself. This explains why, at a very early stage in the history of mind, we find such progress in the sphere of mathematics and logic. Here, it was a case of idealising products particularly well suited to the process, inasmuch as they were products of mind. From the point of view of mind, we can deal far more accurately, for instance, with figures than we can with laws of growth, magnetism, electricity or gravity, simply because figures are children of our mind, and more nearly akin to us than are the forces of Nature.

Otto Weininger, in his notes for a treatise on metaphysics, wrote as follows:

"If I may venture to make a personal observation, I was for a long time of opinion that the finest stroke of genius in Kant's theoretical philosophy was his idea that states of mind are only phenomena, like physical states. Later on, however, I had my doubts about this, owing partly to objections of moral theory. My work now is based on the view that states of mind have a greater reality than physical states, though I cannot offer any systematically and methodically perfect grounds for the assertion."

Weininger here touches the essential point in the problem of understanding. The principal difficulty arises from the failure to see that we must, from the point of view of understanding, set the phenomena of mind in a different category from those of matter; and that the former are more real, since they are nearer to the nature of our understanding. Actually, most investigators have, out of misplaced zeal for "realism" put matters the other way round. The English

IDEALISING OR REFINING ACTIVITY 171

empiricists began at the wrong end, namely, with Nature, and consequently soon stuck fast in barren scepticism.

The thing we know best and are most certain of is our own mind in its various states. From this we draw conclusions as to other people, and great poets and writers in particular can here operate with an astonishing degree of psychological accuracy.

We know ourselves best, and next our relatives, friends and those of our own race. Then we come to the animals as in the next degree of kinship, first and foremost domestic animals, and so on to the lowest forms, and then again to the plants. Last of all we come to inanimate Nature, which we understand least of all. In regard to mind, then, we are realists to a higher degree than in regard to Nature, for we know its processes better and do not need to idealise to the same extent. The ancient Greeks, animating Nature with deities, nymphs, naiads and the rest, idealised after their own fashion, and so do we when we attribute to Nature " natural laws " which we ourselves have formulated. The law of cause and effect, for instance, is a piece of our idealising work, not identical with reality, but a paraphrase. It is to the immortal credit of Hume that he demonstrated this.

Man is a transformer of energy, and our brain may be compared to a smelting oven or a refining works, in three departments.

One is the practical section, establishing contact between ourselves and the world about us, arranging and interpreting our sense impressions and placing them at the disposal of the body; this replaces the instinct which we find among the beasts.

The second is memory, which stores up our experience and the great mass of material derived from the common store of mind (through our education and upbringing, studies and so on).

The third is the finest of all, for it is here that the creative power is at work; here the material is melted down and new things born of it; here we find new ideas and ideals in process of formation; our scientific, artistic and ethical impulses keep the flame burning under the retort; this is the scene of all operations directed towards supra-individual aims.

Down beneath the whole extend the largely unexplored vaults of our subconscious mind.

On going through extant works on psychology, logic and theory of knowledge, we find that the psychologists have been occupied more particularly with the first two sections of the undertaking, the practical department and the department of memory, with some attention to the subconscious in recent times. But the one we have described as the most important, the creative section, has either been regarded as a negligible quantity or denied any existence at all.

This is easy to understand when we consider the determinist and mechanist views which have prevailed, for the practical and memory sections are under the control of automatism, whereas the creative section is controlled entirely by the creative power itself, and the mechanists prefer to close their eyes to this.

The senses are the observation-posts of the practical section. When the sense-impressions have arrived, they are put in order and arranged through the channels of mind which are usually termed the categories. The process takes place according to certain definitive principles.

The categories have a definite structure apparently not subject to any great alteration. This, however, is but an illusion, for our categories have naturally their origin like everything else; they have their evolution; they were born and formed in course of time, and new categories arise from time to time when the creative power finds it advisable.

The memory department is controlled by the association of ideas. As soon as an idea has been produced by the practical section, it is brought into contact with the memory department, where, by association, it is linked up with a number of previous ideas stored in the brain. And it is by practical co-operation between this department and the practical side that the work of thought from concept to inference and from inference to judgment is effected.

These two sections, which might be called the automatic sections, are closely connected and constantly interacting.

IDEALISING OR REFINING ACTIVITY 173

In the third section, the creative power is lodged, and this section might be called the mother section, for it is the oldest, and from it the others proceeded in course of time. Here the consciousness of the ego has its seat, the fundamental category superior to all the rest, the consciousness of the ego which is identical with the creative power. It is the creative power which has, for practical and ideal purposes, formed the categories or thought channels through which the material of ideas is passed to be refined in its passage and then transferred to the memory department.

What takes place in the brain is a constructive mutation process similar to that which took place on the biological plane when the creative power first constructed the body—we might say that the brain is engaged in the creation of a spiritual body. The process commenced on a small scale with the construction of sensation. Answering to the purely physical eye, we have the sensation of sight, to that of the ear, hearing, and so on. The memory department answers to the cell-body as a whole. Just as body and senses interact, so also do memory and sensation.

The categories or forms of thought are not a gift from heaven ; they have their natural history of evolution behind them, produced as they are by the same creative and idealising process, from which life arose on the biologial plane and natural forces on the material. The categories of mind arose one after another, like the organs of the senses and the organic and inorganic bodies ; they are merely a higher stage of the process which was already at work when the earth was still a globe of fire beginning to form its crust. Thus arises the otherwise inexplicable relation between material, biological and mental phenomena, each of them only a higher, finer and nobler edition of a corresponding phenomenon on a lower plane. If our thought forms and ideas then answer to reality, it is due, not, as Kant supposed, to the fact that categories are *a priori* forms, forcing reality into their own image, but to the fact that they are the refined results of a process which produced similar results in a coarser form on a lower plane. The whole is held together by the creative power, which twines up like a spiral throughout all evolution, forming at each turn an idealised image of the result of its work on the stage immediately preceding.

Evolution simply means that something repeats itself, but, be it noted, in a finer and nobler form with each repetition.

If we go through Höffding's categories, for instance, we soon find that they are not merely in the air, but rooted in existing realities on the biological and material plane. Take, for instance, the fundamental category of synthetic relation; the fact that we combine things and see them in relation to others. This power of mind does not arise of itself, but from the fact that evolution had already on the biological plane—and indeed on the material as well—worked synthetically, combining and separating material units as well as biological ones. We find again in Nature such things as continuity and discontinuity, equality and difference, analogy, negation, rationality, casuality, totality and so on, only in coarser forms. In the biological and material world, we find all thought categories again, only with the difference that they do not appear in the form of mind but as flesh and blood or material phenomena. If we were to believe the idealists, the idea of an elephant must have existed before the elephant itself. This is Plato's old misunderstanding, that ideas existed as complete prototypes before the realities, and that the present world is merely an endeavour to realise ideas which have existed from all eternity. Evolution teaches us otherwise. It shows that the creative power first gets to work on matter, then inspires it with life in different forms, including the form of an elephant, for instance; then at last comes mind, and creates the abstract idea: elephant, which includes the most elephantine qualities of all elephants. The idea thus comes last, and is merely the fruit of a tendency materialising first as matter, then as life, and ultimately as mind.

There is nothing in the sphere of mind which has not its counterpart, its ancestor, in the biological and material phases of evolution; for creation takes place, as we have seen, not by the sudden miraculous appearance of something out of nothing, but by the refinement of a given material, in

IDEALISING OR REFINING ACTIVITY 175

the same way as the artist effects a refinement of the model in his work. It is a fundamental principle of the creative power that it does not work at random.

All this has been but roughly put, and the reader will perhaps be rather startled. The philosophy of evolution is so new that we still lack a table of equivalents to show the derivative relation existing between material, biological and mental phenomena. Can any such table be drawn up at all? It is extremely difficult at the present moment, for it is only as a matter of judgment that we can as yet point out this or that as the model of any given mental phenomenon. If we were to draw up such a table we should be liable to the accusation that it was based on mere poetic analogy instead of scientific proof—an objection raised already against the work of the natural philosophers of the previous century, who made some attempts in this direction. Obviously, there would be considerable risk of error in drawing up such a table, for Nature is not a Botanical Garden, where every plant— every phenomenon—is labelled with its Latin name. We have to act on our own judgment throughout; and if our judgment be at fault, the critics will be down on us in a moment, and claim the error as proof that the whole theory is false. With all possible reserve, then, we would suggest that very possibly the force of gravity (attraction) on the material plane became sex-instinct on the biological and love on the spiritual. Cohesion on the material plane may have led to cell-structure in the biological plane, and solidarity in the plane of mind. But in drawing up a table of equivalents, we encounter the same difficulty as with the theory of knowledge, to wit, that our thought itself lies in the sphere of mind, and we can have no intuitive perception of biological and material activity. Our analogies will therefore be infected with mind, and we can hardly conceive the biological and material forms of mental phenomena, even though it be right in front of our eyes. There is an important task for future scientific study in this field.

When we do get so far, our table of equivalents will be found to contain a number of surprises; phenomena generally regarded as so dissimilar as to preclude any possibility of relationship will appear as closely akin, their apparent dissimilarity being due solely to a high degree of refinement. Even the fact that our ancestors swam about in the sea as fishes must prepare us for unexpected results when we follow the roads Nature has taken in the transition from matter to life and mind. We should probably be very disappointed if we could see the Florentine girls who served as models for those divine feminine creations of Botticelli ; and if we could take part in the Trojan War, or in Plato's Symposium as they actually were, meet Dante's Beatrice or see Cleopatra in her bath, or accompany Napoleon at manœuvres, we might perhaps discover that the idealising power is a force capable almost of turning black to white. As soon as refining activity commences, an inflation of values always takes place, and it may be painful enough to find ourselves confronted with the naked reality of previous conditions. Even in the biological world there is nothing but a sea of vague and often rather muddy instincts. Only in the sphere of mind is all made clear and clean ; we are transported, as it were, to the sunny heights of Olympus and a purer air. It is not strange that mind, first manifesting itself to the full as it did in ancient Greece, and seeing its unbounded possibilities, became itself intoxicated with existence, and played battledore and shuttlecock with ideas, giving little heed to critical objections or limitations. Every stream was made the home of a naiad, a satyr lurked behind every tree, æolian harps rang in the air, and sea and sky, sun and fire spoke with human voices. The idealistic impulse ran wild—and in the Iliad and Odyssey, in the magnificent monuments of Greece, we still feel the beat of wings in glorious flight. When a ray of sunlight touches a stone, a mechanical collision takes place between ether-waves and atoms. If the ray strikes an animal, the creature, with its power of sense, idealises the impression to sensations of light and heat. When a human being feels the ray, he gives it æsthetic attributes. Mind, then, is always a complete transposition of the material foundation, and it may be hard enough to discern the connection between the original cause and its ultimate effect.

But the idealised form is always, despite all inflation, the one that contains the profoundest reality.

Oscar Wilde says somewhere that it is a fallacy to say love is blind; on the contrary we cannot see properly without it. Only love can show us the inner, individual world, the joy and splendour that is in us all; we never see so truly as with the eyes of love.

And this love that gives us the finer sight is, after all, only the blind, brutal sex-instinct of the biological phase, idealised out of all knowledge in the sphere of mind. There is a greater difference between the two than between a pebble and a polished precious stone.

The pragmatists maintain that the world of ideas is merely a pale, vague world of shadows, incomparable with the wealth of luxuriant life. And they set life as higher than mind and action as higher than thought, accordingly. A strangely false conclusion! True, abstract ideas may be pale and vague, and consequently futile; but they can also be strong and splendid, with a halo of eternity about them, and then they count for something, they are true ideas. There have been many noble knights in history, but none that could equal the idea of a knight, which is the ideal, the quintessence of all that is knightly in all knights that ever were or ever could be. The love of any individual mother for her child may be open to doubt, but the idea of motherly love stands firm; properly regarded, it is greater and higher than any concrete instance. We sometimes hear it said that life is richer than literature. But the reverse is the case, for otherwise there would be no literature at all, at best a collection of biographies. It is because literature is abstract that it can give us the highly idealised figures it does. Think of the character in literature that we know. Don Quixote, Falstaff, Micawber and the rest, all mere abstractions, yet alive, alive! In literature and art we find a richer and stronger life than in the real world, for the idealising process is carried a step further.

Certain ideas are fixed and permanent, such as mathematical and logical terms, equality and difference, causality analogy, etc. But there are others which are a constant subject of discussion, as soul, immortality, eternity, infinity, time and space, artistic value, ethical value, the aim of Nature and of man, God.

We do not doubt that an effect can always be traced back to some cause, that a thing must either be continuous or discontinuous, that identity in a given case exists or does not exist, and so on. But as soon as we touch upon what are somewhat misleadingly called ideas of value, there is an end of the general unanimity.

What does the idealistic theory of evolution teach us about these things? According to our principle, all ideas are merely the reproduction in mind of phenomena in the biological and material phases of evolution. How then can such ideas as soul, immortality, infinity and the like, have arisen and give rise to controversy, when we cannot immediately point out their biological and material origins?

The answer is, that these ideas are prematurely born, provisional terms, which every now and then have to be passed on to the brain department of the creative power to be melted down again.

The refining section of the brain produces not only useful products, but also faulty ones, answering to the faults of which we find so many in the biological phase—the archæopteryx for instance; they have but a short lease of life and soon disappear.

The creative power often makes mistakes, even when working from a model; the very fact that it is creative implies that it must make experiments, and therefore it often produces ideas which are found to have no answering reality, and have accordingly to be rejected sooner or later.

In the sphere of mind, however, the creative power has a quick and effective auxiliary whose aid was lacking on the previous planes. This is the common store of knowledge, which acts as a sort of judge of new productions. The rapid advance of the creative power in the sphere of mind is due to the fact that it is supported by the common store of mind already created. This does not prevent the creative power from making mistakes, but it can reject a faulty product, either discarding it at once, or adopting it for a time and

IDEALISING OR REFINING ACTIVITY 179

then sending it back to be melted down again. In this manner, mankind has, in the course of ages, accepted and afterwards rejected a host of faulty products turned out by the creative power, such as nymphs and goblins, witches, purgatory, false codes of honour, metaphysical systems, supposed "laws of Nature," spirits, Darwinian selections and the like. All these products were turned out in haste, and as better ones were afterwards produced, the first faulty products had to be sent back for revision or discarded altogether. When an idea is not generally accepted, but subject to discussion, it means that the common store of mind is still in doubt, and has not yet arrived at a final decision.

Take, for instance, the idea of *God*. In this field, the creative power has been particularly fertile, which is not surprising, since a power which is itself creative would naturally find it easy to personify the idea of creative activity. Mankind has, in the course of ages, created a host of gods, from the Apis of the Egyptians, from Odin and Thor, to the gods of Greece and the deities of Druidical worship. All these have been rejected in course of time, but there still remains the idea of God, as the creator of the world, an idea still officially recognised but subject to discussion, and presumably, ere long, to be rejected in turn in favour of some new and loftier idea. The idea of God is one of those which the mind of man has repeatedly accepted in different forms, only to refuse it after a while and send it back for revision. The basis of this idea, according to the idealistic theory of evolution, is a reality, namely, the activity of the creative power itself. If ever we come to realise that the idea of God is identical with this activity, then the existing idea of God will be definitively deposed in favour of the creative power, and all strife and discussion on the subject will cease. Only a century hence, perhaps, our descendants will regard the Christian conception of God, still extant in the twentieth century, much as we now regard the ancient Greeks' ideas of their deities. It will appear as a delusion, understandable enough from the poetic and historical point of view, based on lack of insight, and not necessarily to the discredit of those who accepted it. And here it will doubtless be objected that we underestimate man's need of a personal God. The point is rather, to our mind, that others have overestimated it. The need of a God plays an ever-diminishing part in the life of man, and will be superseded by a scientific, artistic and ethical insight based on the principles of evolution.

Another term which is a fruitful subject of discussion is *Time*. Some philosophers maintain that time is almost the most important ingredient of existence; others deny its importance altogether. The idealistic theory of evolution holds that time is an idealisation, a common term for three things: astronomical time, which is identical with material movement, and is indicated in a purely external manner by the movement of a hand round a clock face, or the shifting of a shadow on a dial; biological time, or growth time, what we call the age of a man or an animal; and finally psychological time, which merely indicates that our thought is not fixed but is constantly moving, and therefore such time depends on the degree of activity in our thought life. In the material phase, motion and time are identical (a railway time-table is likewise merely a series of " times " denoting points of movement). In the biological phase, we have only growth time, the span experienced by an organism from birth through maturity and old age to death. And in the sphere of mind, we have psychological time, which is our perception of the changes in our thought, and as these processes may be more or less intensive, time appears to us longer or shorter accordingly.

That time is an ideal term, and not a thing existing in universal space independently of man's idealising power, is proved by the fact that we have little difficulty in contemplating the end of time. If all motion throughout the universe were stopped, all growth suspended, and all thought brought to a standstill, the whole being thereafter set in motion again, it would be impossible to determine whether a second or some millions of years had elapsed, for time would simply have ceased to exist during the interval. Time is an abstraction, and Newton and other great thinkers were wrong in attributing to it any physical reality. Einstein has also realised that time is relative, just as movement is relative. Where there is no

IDEALISING OR REFINING ACTIVITY 181

movement of anything relative to another thing, there can be no time. Time can begin, time can last for a longer or shorter period, and time can end; it is merely a quality of something, not eternal. Rosenkranz in his *Reform der Hegelschen Philosophie* has already pointed out that time would not exist if matter did not exist, and that it is the movement of ether that constitutes real time. It is the same with the idea of duration. Dead things can, under certain circumstances, move, but they have no duration. A living thing has duration, in so far as physiological processes take place in it, but duration is only an abstract expression of these processes. And it is much the same with psychological time. Here, also, time is an abstract expression of certain processes. The belief in the eternity of time is a scientific error answering to the religious error of assuming the immortality of the soul. It is for this reason that mankind has always raised objections to any theory of time as an objective term. Before the creative power began to operate in the pre-material dead world, time did not exist; and when the Collective Spirit has grown strong enough to emancipate itself from earth, and all processes come to an end, time also will cease. Time is merely an expression of the activity of the creative power at various stages (partly active, partly automatic). When automatism at last grows weary, and the creative power has finished its task, time will no longer exist. In the timeless human store of thought which we call memory we have perhaps a model on a small scale of what the Collective Spirit will become at last.

The idea of *space* is also an abstraction, which has given rise to much uncertainty. It has been said that we cannot imagine any cessation of space; we cannot conceive any place where space does not exist. But this simply means that we are making a false interpretation of the abstract term space. In the material and biological worlds, we have bodies with definite limits of extent; our own bodies, for instance. We know that such bodies have a certain magnitude; they may be large or small, and in order to obtain a standard of measurement applicable to them all, our mind constructs the idea of space, which is thus a purely imaginary standard.

This standard exists only in ourselves, not outside us; but we are inclined to forget this, and imagine that we and everything on earth, and all the stars in the sky, are tenants in a great house, an infinitely great house, which we call universal space. We further imagine, that when an object is moved away, it leaves a void in space which can then be filled by something else, just as a flat can become vacant in a big building. But universal space is a thought construction of our own, and has no more physical reality than the parallels and meridians of a school globe have on the actual earth. True, every object takes up a certain amount of space, that is to say, it is of certain dimensions, but space is an attribute of the object. Consequently, where there are no objects of any sort there is no space. If we were to set out from our earth on a journey through the universe, we should pass through the "space" of many objects, but we should never get out into universal space. It is for this reason that man finds it difficult to appreciate the idea of space, and the difficulty will not be removed until we realise the biological and material realities on which our idea of space is based.

The struggle of blind natural forces at the material stage was, as we have seen, succeeded by the struggle for life on the biological plane. In the sphere of mind, we find this struggle again in a finer form as a struggle between the abstractions of the creative power, artistic, scientific and ethical products, seeking inclusion in the common store of mind. It often happens that a mind product of slight value—in the eyes of posterity—attains recognition and usurps the place of others more valuable. Sooner or later, however, a revision takes place, or even a revolution, and a host of false ideas are rejected and replaced by others.

An idea which has been and still is a constant source of difficulty to human thought is the idea of the *Soul*. Answering to this on the biological plane we have the physical personality, the individual, and at the earlier, material stage the material unity, a certain combination of particular forces in certain proportions (a lump of gold, for instance). This is plain enough; the difficulty in understanding what a soul is lies in the fact that human imagination is not content to

IDEALISING OR REFINING ACTIVITY

regard the soul as analogous to the biological and material counterparts, a combination of certain qualities, but credits it with a false attribute of immortality. This is why there is always discussion about the soul. On the one hand, we cannot deny its existence—there is really something which sums up the spiritual forces in a human being, the total of all; there is a spiritual whole answering to the physical. But it is hard to understand that when this whole disappears in the biological phase with the death and dissolution of the body, the spiritual counterpart should continue its existence undisturbed. It is this invention of the Church which has so incensed certain philosophers that they have gone to the other extreme, and simply denied the existence of the soul. Mankind, after having naively assumed for a lengthy period that we must have an immortal soul, is now beginning to revise this view.

It will be seen from the foregoing that we define every product of mind as a refined product of Nature.

Science, art and philosophy (including religion) are the most important of the modes of this refining process.

In each of them it is a question of arriving at the most highly concentrated product of idealisation or refinement possible, care being taken only to work with the element which forms the object of the process, i.e. to avoid any introduction of foreign matter, which would adulterate the whole.

Truth, from the point of view of evolution, is a state of identity or equivalence between different stages of development. The terms: true science, true art, true philosophy, simply mean that in the course of the work in each field, no irrelevant minor elements have been introduced, no deviation has been made, no foreign matter of any sort has been allowed to creep in; in a word, that the subject has simply been lifted from the material or biological plane up to that of mind.

The craving for truth is something we instinctively feel as the base of our whole intellectual life. Our mind's principal task is to give us a true image of reality, for without this, the creative power would have no ground to work on, and its constructions would be simply in the clouds. Hence our longing for truth; a longing which increases as our mind advances. The lower orders of beings do not recognise the importance of truth, but it is recognised in science, art and philosophy. If a scientist puts forward an assertion based on a mathematical calculation, and an error can be demonstrated in his working of the sum, then his assertion is rejected. Similarly, the work of a painter is rejected if it shows faulty perception of the object, looseness of composition or the like.

When we say that mathematics, logic, natural science, etc., contain *truth*, this simply means that we have, in these sciences, found incontrovertible equivalents in the sphere of mind answering to realities on a lower plane. This is how it is that formulæ work out correctly. When we are told that water boils at 212 degrees Fahrenheit, this means that there is a material reality behind the formula, which can be tested.

The truth of mathematics lies in the fact that it contains a series of idealisations, made with such critical severity that the original basis can be discerned through all its constructions. Euclid began with a single principle based on reality, and from this he built up the rest of his system, taking care never to go beyond the limits of his original foundation. All the principles of mathematics really say the same thing, only in different,—more condensed and refined—forms.

The same applies to logic. Here, too, we operate with certain principles, which are constantly varied and extended. And a similar mode of procedure is followed in natural science.

Astronomers have, by means of calculations, succeeded in demonstrating the existence of certain heavenly bodies not discernible through the best telescopes of their day; the improved instruments of a later period have rendered those bodies visible to the eye. This shows that the basis on which the astronomer worked was correct, and that he kept within its limits in his calculations, without regard to the fact, irrelevant to his calculations, that the bodies themselves were not visible.

Book-keeping by double entry gives us a little example of the idealising or refining process of mind in close corre-

IDEALISING OR REFINING ACTIVITY 185

spondence with reality. If it be desired to investigate the work of a great business concern, we can examine its offices, ships, factories, branches, look into the safes and talk to its employés or its customers. But much may also be learnt by simply looking into the books. We find here a concentrated image of the whole undertaking, an idealised image, but for that very reason clearer and deeper, less obscured by irrelevant details than the impression afforded by personal inspection of the work.

We have seen that our understanding becomes clearer and more comprehensive the higher the stage of evolution reached by the phenomenon to be considered. By analogy with ourselves, we are better able to judge of what takes place in animals than of how blind natural forces operate. This is due to the fact that the animal, thanks to the work of the creative power, has been raised to a higher stage of idealisation than the forces of Nature, and the task before us is thus easier, since the object has already been idealised to some extent, and there is less remaining for us to do. It is precisely as if we were trying to form an image of two houses, one fully built, the other as yet only carried up to the first floor. We can form an image of either, but the process in the former case will be easier, and probably more correct in its results than in the latter, where it will largely depend on our power of idealisation, that is to say, the power of drawing conclusions from a part as to the whole.

The idealists maintain that it is we ourselves who with our senses and ideas create the whole world. But this is not correct. It is the creative or idealising power that has created and is still creating the world, first biologically (plastically) in the form of plants and animals, the process being then repeated in the mind of man, which is thus only carrying on the work already begun.

Science is one of the forms in which we know this process of refinement. It gives us laws and formulæ, and shows us the relation between numbers of different phenomena. Art is the other form. It gives us the external image, but in such a manner that innumerable individuals fuse together and become a type, containing the most characteristic features.

186   THE COLLECTIVE SPIRIT

Science gives us a true picture of details and their relations; art gives us a true picture of the whole.

The fact that we have no complete understanding, but can only understand the different phenomena more or less completely according as they are higher or lower products in the scale of evolution, throws some light on ourselves and our importance in the economy of Nature. We are only transformers of energy, a stage of a process, and those other stages nearest to ourselves are the ones we can best understand. We have, therefore, as already mentioned, only a relative and restricted life of mind. Nature presents her objects more or less veiled to our view, and if we would lift the veil, it can only be done by taking the main roads that lead to the Collective Spirit, that is, by utilising science and art.

Regarded as individual minds, we are like ants living in a great community. The ant knows its comrades and feels instinctively that its own task is to gather building materials and food for the good of all. So, also, individual minds know their fellow-creatures and instinctively gather supplies for the Collective Spirit. But as the ant is restricted to the neighbourhood of its particular colony, so also we have to stay where we are unless we obtain aid from the common store of knowledge. Science, art and ethics can raise us up above the whole and give us a view of the whole such as the ant can never have.

It is, however, not only in these loftier activities that we discern the idealising process. We know it well from what we call the great moments of life. Everyone knows how our whole view of life can be altered under the influence of serious happenings or strong emotion. The same world looks very different to us in joy and sorrow, in fear and love; it is, as it were, coloured by them, lifted out of its everyday appearance. When anything unusual happens, on days of great rejoicing or solemnity, the idealising process is most keenly felt. Our activity of mind must have somewhere an accumulated store of will and power to idealise, that is, to present objects in a finer and more poetic light. In the solemn moments of life we often have recourse to music, which seems to further the idealising process; it "thrills" us.

It is worth noting that idealisation always accompanies everything of great importance in our life, and especially all that tends to the maintenance of the species, as in the attraction between the sexes. The process is here seen at its height. A young man in love sees not only the object of his affections, but the whole world, in a new light; all is transformed, he is in the power of something beyond himself, he is under a spell.

And it is a well-known fact that the farther an event recedes in time, the more we beautify it in memory. The people we met in our childhood under particular circumstances are surrounded by a halo—or totally forgotten. To say that a thing remains in our memory is simply another way of saying that we take from surrounding reality certain phenomena, idealise the raw material and store it up, afterwards taking it out and letting it shine.

Children have a high power of idealisation; or more correctly, we can in children study this power as a pure culture. A piece of linen hung out to dry near the cemetery wall becomes at night a ghost; the heroes and heroines of inferior novels are invested with a glory beyond their deserts; bad marks at school can overwhelm our whole little world with misery. Children live in an ideal world, at once more beautiful and more terrible than that of adults.

It is only when we grow up and gain experience that we learn to be cautious with these constructions of the mind, and see that they often do not answer to the concrete world; that the collision between imagination and reality may lead to unpleasant consequences for ourselves. We thus discover a weakness in our own mind, that of idealising too loosely, giving the imagination too few realities to work with. Afterthought, mature consideration, which is the necessary corrective to the idealising power, then comes to our aid. But this is after all a part of automatism, and thus of secondary importance. Thought proper operates in the creative department of the brain.

The creative power is found most keenly active in the child

and the gènius; this is why a man of genius often has something of the child about him. Human beings of the average type are more or less representatives of common sense and considerations of practical advantage (automatism); the struggle for life has impaired their idealising tendencies in course of time, and they have to be content with the idealising products of others, that is, in the form of art. There will always be more Philistines than men of genius in the world, and it is just as well, for a world composed of men of genius alone would be in a state of constant disturbance.

Genius is altogether indeterminable and indeterminate, distinguished from the respectable citizen by lack of respect for ordinary conventions. A genius may often be quite incapable of doing a simple sum in arithmetic; he appears as a confusing whirlpool in the steady stream of automatism, and may at times be so difficult for other people to get on with that his fellows do their best to get rid of him, only to regret it afterwards and raise a monument to his honour.

The man of genius seems to look out beyond the bounds of humanity into the future. In practical matters he often comes off badly; the common herd will be irritated by the very fact of his evidently seeing something they cannot discern. And a torrent of vicious envy rises about him. But the genius is only a transformer of energy of a particularly fine quality, he serves the same master as the rest of us, and if he be not acknowledged at his true value while living, he may be sure of recognition after death.

We mentioned before that it was a good thing to have imagination, for without it, mind could make no progress. But imagination must be kept within bounds, or the result may be disastrous. And the supreme court which decides whether imagination has gone too far, or has created a valuable product of refinement, is our common store of knowledge.

This brings us to the most debatable of all terms, that of value, in the sense of value to the common store of mind. Anything here accepted as of value *is* of value; all else is valueless.

By looking into the common store of mind at its present

IDEALISING OR REFINING ACTIVITY

stage, we can ascertain what has been the aim of the creative power up to date. But another point of no less interest to us is the question as to its aims for the future.

We might perhaps suppose that since we have the creative or idealising power at work in us, and in the conscious part of ourselves, to wit, our mind, it would not be difficult to ascertain what it is aiming at.

But we find a difficulty here all the same, for the creative power, even when working in the sphere of mind, is blind at its furthest point; it is not identical with our mind, and does not move along the roads of our consciousness, but works only as a tendency. It only coagulates, only develops vision and reflection after its work is done, that is to say, after it has handed over the work to automatism. The creative power is like an electric drill boring in rock; all is chaos and disorder while it is actually at work, and it is only when the current is switched off that we can get a proper view of the result.

In considering the future aims of the creative power then, we have nothing to go by but a tendency. This tendency appears in our ideals, which answers to instincts on the biological plane, and which we may define as the highest form of instinct; they may often be vague, but they are nevertheless the only lines of sight and direction for our development.

Ideals! What astonished Kant was not only the starry sky above him, but equally so the moral law within himself. The great thinker realised that mathematics and logic and criticism are not alone supreme in the world, there are such things as ideals. It is ideals of art, science, morals, which urge us on; we sacrifice all else for these, and when we are false to them, we act as suicidally as does the bird which fails to obey its own nesting instinct.

A strange and remarkable thing about our life on earth, the most characteristic feature of existence, is that ideals have, quite instinctively, always been formulated and to some extent fulfilled. The whole process of evolution seems to be a realisation of ideals. Without ideals, mankind would inevitably collapse and perish. Ideals are the higher instincts which guide us, it is they which urge us forward and keep the whole idealising process in motion.

A thorough pessimist was Voltaire, who declared that we leave the world as wicked and foolish as we found it. If all mankind shared this view, evolution would end at once, and the whole machinery come to a standstill.

But the hopeless philosophy of Voltaire has no adherents.

An error in the opposite direction was that of Leibniz, who declared this to be the best of all possible worlds.

And this philosophy likewise has been rejected by mankind.

The truth is, that this world is not the best possible, but has a chance of becoming so one day; for there is already present in it a striving towards ever higher spiritual values and a strong conviction that these are to be attained. This conviction manifests itself psychologically as *Hope*; and the word is set as an invisible motto above the creative department of the mind.

Recognition of the fact that we are all, through this idealising process, on the way to a higher and nobler reality will sooner or later put an end to the pessimists, who, in the present transition stage between religious and scientific views of life, have been suffered too long to wave their black flags of despair above our heads.

This gloomy view of life is gradually being shaken off. It is from America—of course, one might almost say—that the new spirit comes. There is growing up in that country a literature and a philosophy which show us the bright sides of life, though without omitting the shadows, in such a manner as to make us understand that life is not a curse, but a great rich gift; and that we can each of us help in the construction of a better world, spiritually as well as socially, for all mankind. In America, and in Europe also, a new humanism is being born.

Why take such a dark view of life? For, after all, despite all grumbling and groaning in literature and the theatre, we human beings are born incorrigible optimists. There is in humanity an astonishing amount of invincible courage and joy in life, a spirit that will go on and make itself felt, despite all opposition, a fighting spirit.

On a gloomy, wet November day in one of our great cities,

one may feel that life is not worth living. And then, maybe, there comes a workman on a bicycle, ploughing through the drizzle and the mud, and whistling the while as cheerily as a starling on a fine spring morning. "Why be downhearted?" Man's motto seems to be: Never give in! When an aeroplane crashes, the answer is not: stick to the ground, but: up again! Better luck next time. An earthquake lays a whole city in ashes; but the work of reconstruction is commenced at once among the smoking ruins. There was never a hazardous expedition announced but volunteers were at once forthcoming. The greater the risk, the better. Any movement involving hard work and struggle, unpopularity and little reward beyond the honour of victory in some distant and problematical future will always find adherents. Great financiers, who have long since made as much money as they care about, will still go on speculating, working to build up this or that until they are involved in a final crash. What is it that urges them on? In all fields of art we find an incessant conflict between cliques and schools, critics buzzing round like infuriated wasps every time anything new appears, using their stings viciously, though it may be to their own destruction. Scientists sacrifice health and life in their laboratories, teachers wear themselves to death in social service; people of all classes will suffer any hardship and ignominy for the sake of a cause they can serve. Politics, science, art, philosophy and religion all have their martyrs; the anarchist flings his bomb and perishes with his victim; the airman rushes to death like a seabird crashing against a lighthouse, a poor old woman shares her crust with the birds; everywhere we find an endless, unbounded love of sacrifice.

Surely all this varied human life with its spiritual struggles and competition, its smiling courage and patience and trust, in spite of all, cannot but fill us with admiration for humanity. And it would all be incomprehensible if there were not somewhere behind us a driving force, a spiritual magnetism drawing us ever toward the pole of high ideals. The ideals may be still vague, apparently conflicting, but they are nevertheless the deepest reality of life. We are all of us—every one of us—fighting for some ideal, whether our field of action be great or small.

And our strongest ally in the struggle is *Hope*. Without hope, our planet would be like Dante's hell. No higher life would be conceivable, evolution itself would end. Hope! The word is not found in any handbook of philosophy. And yet, philosophically speaking, it is the most interesting of all ideas, and the most indispensable.

Hope is the general term for our idealising and refining power, the inherent tendency of man to formulate ideals and strive toward their attainment, the deepest motive in the universe, and one without which all talk of evolution would be meaningless.

ETHICS, ART AND SCIENCE

Virtue is Knowledge.—*Socrates.*

THE work of the creative power in the sphere of mind has been defined in the previous chapter as an idealising and refining process.

The individual can direct this activity in two ways, inward or outward.

When it is directed outward, to the world about us, we raise and transform our surroundings into an ideal world, by means, *inter alia*, of science and art.

If the idealising power be turned inward toward the individual himself, it serves to transform, refine and idealise his own self. This process is felt as a conquest of self, and leads to the development of what we call morality or ethics.

Ludvig Feilberg has noted this conquest of self as one of the most remarkable phenomena of mind. A curious contradiction this: to conquer oneself! Why are we so oddly constituted, having not one, but two natures, one at feud with the other, leading to what we feel as a conquest of self?

The riddle is solved when we realise that this conflict between the flesh and the spirit is but a natural expression of evolution, the evolution of Nature, from the biological to the spiritual plane. The struggle which we feel within us is the meeting of the two planes. Two worlds are ever fighting for the mastery in man, matter and the automatic world of life on the one hand, and, on the other, the world of the Collective Spirit. Hence arise collisions. Man is not a self-contained, harmonious compartment of Nature, but an intermediate stage between matter and spirit, a stage on the road of evolution. Only from this point of view can we explain the fundamental contradictions of human life—and explain them optimistically. The pessimistic attempts at explanation (Buddhism, Christianity, Schopenhauer) are merely a substitute, a dummy teat to quiet us, as is the theory of the immortality of the soul.

Biologically speaking, in the flesh, we are individualists caring only for ourselves and acting throughout from egoistic motives ; we are still beasts of prey. Spiritually, we are a part of the Collective Spirit, which is something beyond the individual.

There can be no doubt, then, but that the stage of discord at which man at present stands will sooner or later be passed. In course of time, as the conquest of self becomes an art and then a habit, it will efface itself, that is to say, it will no longer be felt as an effort. By that time, the spirit will have finally and definitely conquered the body, and the individual spirit can pass over into the greater and more comprehensive Collective Spirit. An evolutionary process will have reached its conclusion.

At present the process is still going on, and it is by no means painless to ourselves. This struggle between the biological and the spiritual gives rise to all the discords that harass our earth, the impulse to kill or steal, cruelty, hatred, envy and so on, waste products of the struggle for ideals. The struggle between material and biological, at an earlier stage of evolution, led to similar phenomena, only in a biological manifestation ; hence, perhaps, all the strangely vicious and misshapen animal forms that now exist, creatures of cruelty and venom, to all seeming the incarnation of evil. The creative power has had a hard struggle to raise the harsh forces of Nature to the higher stage of life, and often it has come off second best, has been checked, caught up in automatism and been forced to compromise. And the result is seen in the many more or less unsuccessful species, which have attained but little higher in evolution than the blind and brutal forces of Nature which prevailed at the earlier stage. Something of the same sort takes place now in the higher plane of evolution, where the issue lies between biological and spiritual. Here, too, we find a host of faulty products, in the form of individuals possessed by vicious instincts, hatred, jealous persecution, cruelty, hypocrisy. But there are, fortunately, other individuals who feel that there is no progress to be achieved by letting the animal instincts have their way. Our business is to combat and subdue these instincts, to improve ourselves, and even among quite primitive peoples we find a recognition of this principle. Emile Durkheim has formulated it as our first duty: to establish a moral code.

Feilberg defines good as that which furthers natural development, and evil as that which is only very slightly developed and condensed. In one sense, we may say that the whole world is evil, inasmuch as all evolution is a struggle towards its ethical improvement. Evil is the *status quo*—this is Nature's answer when we ask. But it must be a consolation to us that the world was formerly even more evil. Evolution is a process which gradually refines and improves what is evil—or exterminates it.

Nietzsche maintains that it is futile to call a thunderstorm ethically wrong because its lightning strikes us, or a fly because it stings. But here he is in error. Both actions are ethically wrong inasmuch as each in its way offers a hindrance to the refining process of Nature. The thunderstorm and the fly, then, must either be controlled or exterminated; and this is just what man does by the invention of lightning conductor and insect powder.

But we do not, in ordinary everyday speech, call a thunderstorm or a fly ethically wrong; though we do say that the acts of a malicious or evil disposed person are wrong. The difference is that a person, a conscious human being possessed of mind, has a responsibility which we cannot attribute to the thunderstorm or the fly. And in what does this responsibility consist?

We have seen that man is divided into two Egos: an automatic Ego comprising the greater part of him, his whole body and most of his spiritual life, and a creative Ego which is the creative power itself operating through his mind. Neither of these belongs absolutely to the man, in the sense of being attributes of a soul gifted with freedom of action, responsibility and immortality, as religion would have us believe. It is rather the man who belongs to these two powers jointly; he is the channel through which they operate. The automatic Ego is not free; its action is determined by the past. The creative Ego, on the other hand, is determined by the future and must be termed free *in relation to the other*.

The question now is: when a man acts ethically, is it his automatic Ego that acts, or his free and creative self? The answer is: it can be both, but when the action demands an effort, a subjugation of self, it's the creative Ego which is functioning for the time being, acting in despite of the automatic self.

The conquest of self would be a contradiction in terms if we had not this explanation. Ethical action is one of the roads by which the creative or refining power moves forward; there is in each of us a tendency to moral action, an instinct, which occasionally conquers in the struggle against our automatic self.

But can we, when it comes to the point, determine for ourselves whether the creative Ego shall take the lead, or the automatic be suffered to take its own way? This is the crucial point, for on this it depends whether man is a free agent or not.

In answer, we must say that we cannot ourselves determine the relative proportions of creative power and automatism in ourselves. And we are thus, to a certain extent, born unfree. But we should not therefore fold our hands resignedly and submit ourselves to fatalism, for there is, after all, a way in which the creative (in this case the ethical) power can be stimulated to an increase of power. Socrates has formulated the principle in his definition: Knowledge is virtue; which may be reversed to mean Virtue is Knowledge. Through knowledge, afforded us by the common store mind, the creative power in each individual obtains valuable assistance, the sum of all individuals' creative power here coming to its aid. Thus we can, and should, improve ourselves; and even the criminal has a prospect of rising to something better, through the aid of enlightenment, as has fortunately been proved often enough. Just as the creative power in the sphere of art can draw inspiration from the common store of mind with its accumulation of imperishable art, so also it can, in the domain of ethics, gain strength by drawing upon the ethical achievements similarly stored.

The common mind of humanity is a magnet which draws the individual minds to itself, and as the force of the magnet is increased by constant addition, its work becomes easier. Thus the world advances in morality with an ever-increasing velocity, until the time will come when the term morality itself will be obsolete, since its opposite will have ceased to exist. When that time comes, the Collective Spirit will have gained one of its greatest victories, comparable to these gained in the sphere of art when painting and sculpture reached their culmination.

Immoral individuals are unsuccessful products of Nature, akin to the misshapen creatures produced during the period of biological mutations, the waste products of biological evolution, which are now extinct or in process of extinction.

There is this fundamental difference between the thunderstorm and the fly, on one hand, and a human being on the other, that the former cannot act otherwise than they do, for the activity of the creative power in them has ceased, and they can merely go round and round in a state of automatism at a low stage of evolution, until they disappear.

Man, on the other hand, still has the creative power at work within him, it is active and living in ourselves and can lead us on to higher goals. We, unlike the fly and the thunderstorm, are born into the world with inherent possibilities of further development.

But this is not all. Man has, in the common store of knowledge, a moral auxiliary. The common store of mind is a moral magnetic pole, and the ethical compass needle oscillating in the individual is drawn towards it. When we do not act according to ethical principles, we suffer for it in two ways; our own conscience accuses us, and the spirit of society condemns us through the medium of public censure or ill repute.

In face of the determinists' pessimism, then, we can maintain that we have a chance of leaving the world better than we found it, since part of our Ego has a tendency to moral progress, that is, to the furtherance of natural evolution ; and because we can, by acquiring knowledge, increase our moral capital on the way. If this were not so, then, all education, all good example would be to no purpose.

Animals have no such possibilities of development. We can, by starving and beating an animal, teach it to perform certain automatic actions within narrow limits. But by showing a child what is right, and punishing it when it does wrong, we can increase the child's ethical capital, and raise it to a higher sphere.

This is what Schopenhauer failed to understand. Like the ancient astrologers, he held that our character is given us once for all at the moment of birth ; in the course of our life, it could unfold and exhibit various sides, but it could not be improved. This view naturally rendered him a pessimist. He would not admit that our character can, under favourable circumstances, be altered just as our artistic sense can be developed with proper cultivation. But this is what evolution teaches us, when rightly interpreted.

The worst fault of the determinists is that they preach a gospel of hopelessness in this respect. By denying the existence of free forces in us, they only help to weaken those forces. All ethical education should aim at opening man's eyes to the possibilities of development inherent in himself, and encourage him to assist the ethical processes of Nature. This the individual can do by opening his mind to all that is good and beautiful, and hoping that the defeats suffered in the fight between automatism and the spirit may become fewer and fewer. By seeking to extinguish this hope in us, the determinists are working directly in opposition to the process of Nature itself.

How is man to know what is moral and what is not ? We have not all, like Socrates, a dæmon at our ear, to whisper a warning when we are inclined to act wrongly.

But, after all, have we not ? We know pretty well, every one of us, when we are doing wrong, when we let ourselves drift idly on the stream of automatism (that is, at a low degree of condensation) and shirk our duty of self-conquest.

The child knows it, the criminal knows it. Our mind is so cleverly contrived that it rings an alarm when we take a wrong turning; conscience tells us what we are doing, though it may perhaps only tell us after, in the form of remorse. Just as animals have an instinctive sense of what is wholesome or harmful, so also our spiritual equipment includes a warning element. And if we do not hear it ourselves, those about us will be pretty sure to do so, and to let us know.

The difficulty in formulating a moral code lies in the fact that in the transition period mankind is now going through, all types of humanity are represented, from the most altruistic to individuals so ill-equipped from birth that they may be said to be still at an almost bestial stage. There must, then, be different moral laws at the different stages of development in the human mind. More will be asked of the greater spirits of society, who have had access to more enlightenment and education, than of the savage on the Solomon Islands or human beings brought up in ignorance or false doctrine.

Lombroso has already pointed out that criminals are either mentally deficient or abnormal; and this is the standpoint adopted by modern criminologists. The criminal should be treated as a patient. If incurable, he should be permanently isolated; otherwise he should be cured. A prison should not be a penal institution but a mental sanatorium. We must remember that the criminal is punished by Nature itself in the very fact of his being a criminal. Dostoyevsky, who was himself perhaps the greatest psychologist that ever existed, arrived at this result after having lived for years in Siberia in the House of the Dead, with the vilest scum of Russian society. His great idea is that crime and punishment are one and the same, both being symptoms of an internal suffering or irregularity. In other words, evil exists only as a disease, as a lack of enlightenment, and brings down its own immediate punishment on the unfortunate sufferer. Wicked men do not go to hell, they are punished already on earth. The tyrants who oppress us suffer the more, the more they oppress. It was therefore that Jesus had pity on those who crucified Him, and prayed: " Father, forgive them, for they know not what they do."

It has been said that man is the cruellest of all animal forms on earth; and this is true if we alter it to: man *can* be so. This is due to the fact that man is able to use his mental powers not only for the furtherance of natural development, but also in the cause of bestial lust and vice. He can, moreover, go so far as to surround his own egoistic actions with a halo of spiritual splendour, so as to dazzle others. Hence arise the great hypocrites of the world, the inquisitors, whom the champions of morality themselves are hardly able to reach.

Human cruelty, meanness, artfulness, malice, greed, envy, jealousy, thieving and murderous tendencies, can all be traced back to the biological stage of evolution, when the earth was inhabited only by the beasts, and the only law obtaining was that of each against all. Life then was a bitter and cruel thing, and in almost every case ended with an unnatural death.

The development of the spiritual element, especially the spirit of society, aimed at rescuing life from this state of things, and it has already succeeded to a certain extent. But the bestial element found in the spirit a new weapon which it could use itself, and the social spirit has not yet grown strong enough to exterminate the instincts which have had free play for millions of years of struggle for existence and propagation; nor has it been able to prevent these lower instincts from assuming a spiritual camouflage.

With the advance of spiritual development, man has understood and accepted the ethical law formulated by Kant: that we should act in such a way that our action may serve as a rule to be followed by all. It has cost a hard struggle to get so far. But it is encouraging to note that in our own day, despite atheism and other forms of godlessness, our morals are better than at any previous period in the history of man. There is a greater security in society, a higher sense of law and order, less cruelty, harshness and unfairness than in earlier times. Slavery, a blot on the culture of the ancients, has been abolished, the inquisition is at an end, the last witch has been burned; and public opinion, the best guardian of morals, is grown strong enough to rule as the supreme law throughout the world. Considering the enormous increase in the human population of the globe, and the consequently keener competition, and the fact that old religious ideas which formerly helped in some degree to keep the baser instincts in check have now lost their power, with no positive substitute from science, we cannot but say that our morals have done very well.

The Church has been a moral edifying factor of great importance, but owing to its own limitations, is so no longer. It is the fault of the Church that it cultivates only that one part of the creative or refining power which turns inward and aims at elevating the individual morally, without realising that there is also another aspect of this creative power, namely, its tendency to create a spiritual world of a higher type through science and art, and without understanding that moral progress is only designed to serve as a basis for the development of power in this respect. In the view of the Church, a high morality expressed by the principle of charity is the final aim, whereas from the point of view of Nature's evolution, this is a precautionary measure, a principle of spiritual hygiene. This is naturally partly due to the fundamental error of the Church, the assumption that man possesses an immortal soul, which can be purified and led up to eternal bliss. The Church regards moral doctrine as identical with the doctrine of the soul; any progress to be attained by man in other ways is of no interest to the Church.

But morality may be exaggerated—as we see from the example of monks and nuns and pillared saints. We smile at them in our enlightened age, even though we may admire them. And why? Because they made such a narrow-minded use of the moral idealising power in themselves. They forgot that morality was but a means to higher development for the common good. An artist, whose morals in a general sense may be indifferent, but who devotes himself intensely to his art at the greatest cost to himself, giving lavishly of his artistic power, is serving the Collective Spirit far more than himself. And we admire and honour him accordingly, despite his frailties. The criterion of a man's greatness lies, not in his value from the point of view of morality, but in his value to the cause of the Collective Spirit.

The Church has never been able to realise this, and for this reason alone the Church is doomed to lose its place sooner or later. Its task in the service of solidarity is historically limited, its chief importance in society lies at the initial stages of social development, when animal instincts are still highly prevalent and disturb existence generally, so that moral improvement is a necessary condition of further progress. The great field for the Church lay among the barbarous pagan people, the worshippers of Thor and Odin with their bloody sacrifices. Here the teaching of a gentle Christ had a true mission to fulfil, that of taming these wild beasts and raising them to a higher stage of culture. The conquest of northern Europe by Christianity thus represented an advance in culture; whereas its conquest of the countries possessing an ancient civilisation of their own was in many respects a retrogression.

The Church and its doctrines are only a scaffolding for the world of the spirit which man is now building. And in most societies to-day, the scaffolding has served its turn and would be better done away with. In course of time it will disappear, as all such temporary aids must do.

There remains, then, as the foundation of the new spiritual world, a morality based not on the doctrine of the immortal soul, but on the recognition of the solidarity of mankind; that mankind have a common origin and are moving towards a common end, that anything to the detriment of one is to the detriment of all, while the progress and welfare of the individual contribute to the welfare and progress of all. We are all, so to speak, in the same boat.

The idealistic theory of evolution holds that morality is social in its nature; but this does not mean that it comes to us as a message from without, from Society, for instance, and that the principle is established on purely practical grounds. Morality springs from an instinct, an ethical law within ourselves which is itself the final court of appeal. And this law demands of us an attitude which Christianity somewhat sentimentally describes as loving our neighbour as ourselves, but which we should prefer to call the sense of solidarity. Loving our neighbour is simply another way of saying that our interests are identical; and this feeling of solidarity is an indispensable foundation for the Collective Spirit, the next stage of evolution.

When once it is understood that morality is spiritual hygiene, that evolution calls for a definite standard, and that it is an evolutionary advantage for the individual as for the whole to submit to moral laws, to be truthful, honest, upright, reliable and persevering, to keep one's eyes fixed on the ideals ahead, to hold envy in check and subjugate mere animal desires, to be guided by considerations of the general good in the widest possible sense, instead of by egoistic interests— then the true evolution of morality will be assured. And no Church will be needed. The doctrine of evolution itself will suffice; for we can read these truths from the story of evolution itself.

When people are taught that there is only one life for us, the life we live on this earth, and that this life becomes richer the more we serve and merge ourselves in the Collective Spirit, we shall attain a degree of solidarity hardly conceivable as yet, and a sounder foundation for further development than any religious myth, however beautiful, or promise of eternal bliss acting like a drug to the sense of life.

Maupassant, himself a pessimist, makes one of his characters compare life to the climbing of a hill; during the ascent, one is cheered by the view of the summit ahead, but on reaching it, the downward road begins, and the end of it is death. A toilsome climb, and a rapid descent, with nothing but death at the end.

But the idealistic doctrine of evolution maintains that man's road leads ever upward; there is no descent upon the farther side. As long as we live, we can contribute something to the economy of Nature, and after our death, what we have so given is preserved. We die, but our work goes on. The appreciation of this fact gives life a positive value, and we have then no need to fear what comes after. It lies with us to determine whether death is to make an end of us and all that we were. From a purely physical point of view, there is no need to cherish any fear of death. As a Danish poet puts it : " I should be a fool to fear you, Death ! For as long as I exist, you are not there ; and as soon as you arrive, I cease to exist." It will be one of the tasks of the doctrine of evolution to wean humanity from the doctrine of immortality as preached by the Christian Church ; and the task will not be an easy one. All such developments take time. Keener minds will first realise the truth, and after a while it will become more generally received.

But there is no reason to be discouraged by the fact that evolution is a slow process, as long as we can feel that it is tending in the right direction. The day will come when morality will be a thing of the past, a stage on the road behind us ; for it will have entered into the spirit of man as a part of that spirit, a function acting as involuntarily as the circulation of the blood in our bodies.

The danger that threatens mind is not only that its products, and itself, may be devoted to the service of brutal instincts. There is another peril, inherent in the very constitution of mind, to wit, that of vanity, conceit, the megalomania that may lead us to overestimate ourselves. Mind, as a factor of evolution, is still but a newcomer, a self-made man, a gold-digger who has made his pile and is apt to confuse his own value with the value of the gold he has found.

There is a great expansive power in mind ; the individual is apt to feel himself as a god, because he feels the divine creative principle at work within him. In a way he is right, but only in a way, for this expansive feeling may easily lead him astray and cast him over a precipice instead of aiding him upward. He fancies he can solve all problems in the twinkling of an eye. And he grows impatient of delay and leaps too soon. Instead of using his mind to learn from Nature and from the common store of knowledge, he is inclined to give his own theories and imagination free play. He shirks the task of sober investigation and considered judgment, having recourse instead to an " opinion " of his own which is not amenable to objective criticism. Every human being is inclined to overestimate his power of mind, to be vain about it; and in nearly all of us the germ of megalomania lies awaiting its chance. Nero and Caligula, Xerxes, Napoleon, Wilhelm II are examples showing that high position may lead to madness. Philip of Macedon was aware of the danger, and charged a slave to wake him every morning with the reminder that he was mortal.

Nature herself, however, guards us against this danger by the special form of idealisation which we call the sense of humour, one of the greatest aids to the development of mind.

Humour has a double task, to warn us when the animal instinct in ourselves or others is growing too strong, and to counteract the conceit which is apt to arise in the best of us when we confuse our own little personality with the majestic creative power that makes use of us.

The madly fantastic combinations our mind can produce may be seen in our dreams and imaginings, where we gambol to our heart's content heedless of the stern reality of the world —and never appear ridiculous. In our imagination, we can say just what we like. And when we build castles in the air there is no limit to their height and grandeur.

If it were not for the saving influence of humour, we should lose our foothold upon earth.

Humour makes us blush, so to speak. And that is a wholesome corrective. When we look around at life, we cannot deny that Balzac was right in calling it *la comédie humaine*. The people inhabiting the earth are a strange mixture of mind and beast. The pessimists call us smiling beasts. But it is just the smile that carries us beyond the individual, and enables us to rise to a higher world. The thing that makes human beings so like clowns is the fact that they are always being drawn two ways at once. On the one hand we have impulses of egoism and desire, our inheritance from the period of our animal existence. On the other, we have the Collective Spirit, and the ideals we feel ourselves impelled to follow. When we stumble, or make an error that is to say, when we are false to our ideals and give way to lower instincts, we have recourse to smiles as an aid or corrective. The fact that we can laugh heartily at ourselves and our fellow men shows that we are conscious of higher aims. That is why great poets, moralists and prophets have always used humour as a means of pointing out our weaknesses. Swift, Cervantes, Shakespeare, Molière, Hans Andersen, Dickens and Thackeray, to name but a few, have all striven to combat the lower animal instincts of mankind, and all have used laughter as a weapon wherewith to pierce our armour of conceit, and correct us when we confused ourselves with the higher forces whose servants we are.

Tragedy has one weakness when it seeks to point a moral, namely, that it is apt to become stilted and take too lofty a view. The humorist avoids this peril. He speaks in simple fashion, showing us the disproportion between our aims and the means we employ, the difference between truth and exaggeration; he confronts us with a picture of ourselves which may at times be high caricature, but has nevertheless a depth of truth in its presentment. And we may laugh at ourselves, but not infrequently we may feel more inclined to weep. Such figures as Don Quixote, Harpagon, Malvolio are at once comic and tragic.

But there are still further tasks awaiting the humorist. The creative power has, on the biological and spiritual planes, personified itself in a series of individuals, not in order to give each personality a special metaphysical importance (as the envelope of an immortal soul, for instance) but in order to set them fighting among themselves, and thus get them sorted out, obtaining ultimately a natural product of higher value, the Collective Spirit. The individual has therefore only a temporary existence—as we may indeed observe in the life around us, where individuals are constantly being born, to live for a while and perish. That such an individual should lay claim to immortality is one of the most flagrant examples of megalomania in humanity; the individual confuses itself with the creative power.

The Church, with its thousand year old tradition and the weight of its consequent authority, has instilled this precept into mankind with such vehemence that it is now almost ineradicable. Philosophers and poets must be called in to aid in solving this tangle of human thought. And here is a task for the humorist, the humorist above all. He might, for instance, depict the great meeting in heaven after the Day of Judgment, when all the souls awake to new life in celestial garments, and the struggles that would arise as a result. No poet has ventured to imagine anything of the sort, far less to write it ; it would almost inevitably be stamped as blasphemous, and render him amenable to penalties at law. Even apart from this, there is still the force of public opinion to reckon with, and behind that again, perhaps, the doubt in his own mind, a last vestige of the faith of his childhood. But some day there must come a satirist who shall follow up the Christian principle of immortality to its logical consequences, and show the abysmal difference between the little Christian soul and the great Collective Spirit : here in very truth we should have a Divine Comedy.

Religion has, thanks to its favoured position in regard to the law, too long escaped the refreshing cold bath of satire. The fact itself reveals a weakness. All that is of the spirit should be capable of enduring the test of satire and laughter, even of the coarsest caricature, thereby proving its inherent health and strength. There is a subtle danger in breathing for too long an atmosphere entirely free from germs ; the organism becomes delicate and less able to resist a normal air. The Church has, by arbitrary legislation, protected itself against satire, and as a result, it breathes only artificial air. But the microbes will pour in upon it one day, and its reign will speedily be at an end, for it has already lost its power of resistance. Humour has achieved great things in the world already ; its greatest task of all perhaps lies here.

Schopenhauer quoted the temples and churches, pagodas and mosques of all countries in all ages as a magnificent testimony to the deep-rooted tendency to metaphysical speculation in mankind, closely following the purely physical needs.

But if we look at our world of to-day, we find that the temples of science and art have grown up close about the old churches, and that human beings congregate ever more and more in theatres and lecture halls, in libraries and museums and art-exhibitions, concert rooms and sports grounds, clubs and dance halls. With the spread of enlightenment, people turn their backs upon the Church, and frequent instead the places where art and the joy of life are to be found. Art appeals to us in many different forms, and we are the more ready to listen, since art is now, at our present stage of evolution, one of the few really voluntary forms of personal work that remain to us.

Art offers scope not only for the artist, but for every one of us; the Collective Spirit needs the services not only of the creative talents among us, but also of those who receive and assimilate the products of art in their minds, and thus act as its supports and preservers.

In every civilised community, artists have always occupied an honourable position, and have always been judged by other standards than the rank and file. An artist's greatness and importance is not estimated by the measure of his personal behaviour. Numerous great thinkers and artists have committed more or less serious offences against current ethical tradition; we need only mention such names as those of Ovid, Bacon, Voltaire, Victor Hugo, Byron, Edgar Allan Poe, Dostoyevsky and Oscar Wilde. Judged by the common standards of everyday morality, all these would inevitably be condemned. But they have all furnished imperishable contributions to the common store of mind, and are honoured accordingly. The production of good work in this field seems to carry with it a general absolution, for men recognise instinctively that a great artist is worth more than a score of highly respectable citizens with no particular creative power.

That a high sense of art can be developed side by side with a coarse and barbarous moral code is seen to the full in the examples furnished by classical times and in the Renaissance. The Florentine nobles of the fourteenth century were great connoisseurs of art, and at the same time thoroughly familiar with the use of the stiletto. The Vatican itself was at one time a meeting place for the greatest artists and the bloodiest assassins of the world.

What is the use of being respectable citizens if we are insignificant in all else? Artistic sense seems indeed to be at least as important as ethical propriety. There is nothing to surpass, nothing to equal, the creative faculty in man; and we are ready and willing to forgive those who possess it.

Art has from the earliest times played an important part in human life, and its importance will increase as we go on. But art is not the privilege of the few; the many must be admitted to its circle. Art must become democratic; and this need not be a matter of any difficulty, seeing that we are all born artists by nature.

Our theory in this respect is the direct opposite of Nietzsche's. His idea was that the mass of the people is simply Nature's roundabout way of creating a few great minds. This is not the case. The aim of great artists is to raise the masses to their own level; and when their work is appreciated, they succeed in so doing. Without this reciprocity between artist and public, art itself would simply be incomprehensible. And we find in fact that art, like all else of value in the world, is more and more becoming common property; our culture is becoming universal.

We cannot here enter into further consideration of the different branches of art, but will merely note that we find in each of them interesting and characteristic manifestations of the creative power.

That art idealises will hardly be disputed. We do not call a photograph or a wax figure art, because it is too exact a copy of the reality, leaving no scope for further idealisation. We feel that it is not enough for a work of art to resemble Nature, it must contain something more, something added by the personality of the artist, showing us the model, the natural object, on a higher and more refined plane. It is the business of the artist to continue where the creative power, as seen in the model itself, came to a stop.

The poet's preference for freedom in treatment of his subject is in accordance with his calling. But what is his calling? It is what we all of us feel when we perceive and think; that is, when we transform a product of Nature coming to us from without into a something of higher value, a refining process. The poet, for instance, refines upon the ordinary prose of normal speech. He writes in verse. It would have been easier to say what he had to say in prose, but he is a poet, and his task is to elevate our minds; he uses the language of the gods. From the point of view of mere common sense, there is no point in expressing a sentiment in a form at once more difficult to write and perhaps not quite so easy to read as the ordinary. But the form of verse is as old as literature itself. The Iliad and Odyssey are written in hexameters, and even as late as Shakespeare's day, verse was the natural vehicle of the poet. Nowadays, prose is often substituted for verse, but it is as a rule a camouflaged prose, a prose distinguished from the ordinary language of everyday use by the quality known as style.

In all branches of art, painting, sculpture, the novel, drama, music, the artist idealises, lifting up the concrete to the world of the abstract, and giving it an added splendour. The struggle and progress, or the defeats, of the creative power form the ever varied theme, presented by the artist in all possible combinations, on the canvas, on the screen, in plastic form, in the novel and on the stage.

In the drama, the dramatist shows us the creative power in its essence, freed from all disturbing minor incidents. He takes the common drama of everyday life and cuts out all that is trivial, all details irrelevant to the main idea, and gives us the clear outline of his theme.

Take any evening at the theatre. The curtain rises, and we see an ordinary drawing-room, with people moving in and out. They are dressed in the fashion of the day, like the spectators; they speak quietly, without extravagant gesture. All savours of the reality we have just left behind in our own homes; it is like a section of everyday life cut out and served up on the stage before us. Strange, that people should come from a distance to see this. There is no music, no dancing, no magnificent oriental pageantry; to all appearance, we are watching nothing but the scenes we can observe for ourselves at home, the life we know well enough already. But there is a difference. The play is the work of an artist, a dramatic master. And what we now see taking place before us, reality to all appearance, is yet reality with a difference, reality foreshortened, so ingeniously arranged that the spectator retains the illusion of something natural and ordinary, while at the same time he is carried far beyond it by the movement of the action and the signiffcance of the dialogue. Ibsen gives us a play consisting, apparently, of two hours' conversation between the actors on the stage ; yet he manages at the same time to reveal not one but several whole human characters with such intensity that they remain alive and present in our minds for years after. This effect is produced by idealising reality in such a manner that we are not aware of it to such a degree as to affect our appreciation. In art, as in life, the great thing is to be "natural"; yet natural in such a way that we give, not a dull flat copy of reality, but a truly idealised presentment of the same. Otherwise, the result will merely be stilted and unnatural. All good art is natural. But at the same time it leads us up to a higher plane, to an ideal world, where the objects considered are transformed into transcendent types. The Greek sculptors used women for their models, and from these, they created goddesses to the admiration of posterity.

Music shows us the idealising power with great distinctness. For what is music but a form of utterance invented by the mind, by that section of the mind in which the emotions predominate? Kant rightly pointed out that primitive music answers rhythmically to the human emotions. The state of emotion in ourselves is transformed into corresponding rhythm and melody. Music affords a channel for shades of feeling so fine that not language nor any other art could compass their expression. On all the great occasions of life, man invokes the aid of music ; only with its aid can we feel ourselves lifted up above the life of everyday, emancipated from automatism.

Many people use music—and indeed the enjoyment of other forms of art—as a substitute for the exercise of creative power by themselves ; they take it as a drug, and lose themselves in visions of greatness and beauty, to the neglect of action and effort. Music can also, as Tolstoi has so forcibly shown, act as a spell, a morbid fascination, drawing us down into a world of unwholesome fancies. But more often by far it acts as a stimulant, sets the creative power to work, and lifts us out of our natural dulness; it inspires us. Those in whom the creative power is most active have no need of music. But they are very few. Such natures are often so charged with the creative force that music actually produces a kind of spiritual explosion in them, they are carried beyond all self-control. Most of us, however, need music as a form of comfort and encouragement; it acts as a salve to the wounds received in the battle of life, gives us fresh courage and endurance, may even act as an aid to thought.

We all feel music as something uplifting, and this feeling answers to something fundamental in our natures, the need of idealising. Music is a thing all can understand, a common form of utterance and expression; we are all at home in it, and sharers in its kingdom.

It is a well-known fact that beautiful music does not lose by repetition. This is indeed a criterion of all good art. We do not tire of looking at Grecian statuary, or the work of the Dutch and Italian masters, or of listening to the symphonies of Beethoven. The greatest works of art are assimilated in our common store of mind, as perfect products of the idealising power; they live their own unending life while generation after generation perishes.

In this common human thirst for art, in the sacrifices laid upon its altar, we have the strongest confirmation of the idealistic theory of evolution.

We mentioned in the previous chapter that not only the artist, but also the scientist, is constantly idealising, albeit in a different fashion. The artist gives us an idealised image of the external appearance, of the phenomenon as a whole; the scientist on the other hand, is interested chiefly in the details, their relations and interactions, which he endeavours to determine by laws and formulæ. In his idealisation, he often moves farther from the model than does the artist, and it is therefore often more difficult, requires greater insight, to estimate the value of a scientific work than that of a work of art. We can each of us form our own opinion of a drama or a piece of music, but a work on mathematics or atomic processes calls for special knowledge of the subject. The idealisations of science are farther from Nature; and those of the abstract sciences, such as higher mathematics, for instance, farthest of all. Nevertheless, true science, like all true art, can be traced back to Nature ; the connection must exist, otherwise it is neither science nor art.

In this connection it may be asked : is philosophy to be reckoned as science or as art ? Philosophy is higher than either. Science concerns itself with details, and art with the whole ; but philosophy aims at giving us an idealised view of the world, and this must include details and their relations as well as the whole.

We have said that art and science are the two roads by which we can idealise in externals ; but this does not mean that there are no other ways. There are undoubtedly other ways. All manifestations of the human mind involving personal risk, surprise, joy and sorrow, strong emotion, and not least affection, love and sexual attraction can lift the individual to higher ideal worlds.

The creative power, in its forward progress, has not only created a number of species, but has further divided these into sexes, male and female, and these unite to produce fresh individuals. The object of this, as regards the race, is evidently to mix the characters of individuals to the greatest possible extent. Where propagation takes place by the single individual throwing off spores or splitting up into new individuals, the offspring will be uniform with the parent-form, often, indeed, indistinguishable from it. Propagation by sex affords abundant opportunity for the power of mutation to effect new fusions and combinations. In sexual selection it has been found, as Schopenhauer has pointed out, that the individual is impelled by an instinct favouring the race rather than itself, each seeking what it lacks in itself.

It is characteristic of evolution that the farther we progress along the scale, the less accidental will these combinations be. Among human beings, we often find individuals preferring to refrain from propagation rather than propagate through the medium of another individual for whom no sympathy is felt. Animals as a rule are not particular in their choice of partners, as long as they keep within their own species ; man is more critical in his choice, and selects the one particular individual who alone can satisfy his desire. Where great love is felt, we are lifted up into an ideal world which we had not perceived before. All seems more brilliant and more splendid.

Schopenhauer writes :—

"The delusive ecstasy which seizes a man at the sight of a woman whose beauty is suited to him, and exhibits union with her as her highest good, is just the sense of the species which, recognising the distinctly expressed stamp of the same, desires to perpetuate it with this individual. Upon this decided inclination to beauty depends the maintenance of the type of the species : hence it acts with such great power.

"Thus what guides man here is really an instinct which is directed to doing the best for the species, while the man himself imagines that he only seeks the heightening of his own pleasure.

"In fact, we have in this an instructive lesson concerning the higher nature of all instinct, which, as here, almost always sets the individual in motion for the good of the species. For clearly the pains with which an insect seeks out a particular flower, or fruit, or dung, or flesh, or, as in the case of the ichneumonidæ, the larva of another insect, in order to deposit its eggs there, and there only, and to attain this end shrinks neither from trouble nor danger, is thoroughly analogous to the pains with which for his sexual satisfaction, a man carefully chooses a woman with definite qualities which appeal to him individually, and strives so eagerly after her that in order to attain this end he often sacrifices his own happiness in life, contrary to all reason, by a foolish marriage, by love affairs which cost him wealth, honour and life, even by crimes such as adultery or rape, all merely in order to serve the species in the most efficient way, although at the cost of the individual, in accordance with the will of Nature which is everywhere sovereign.

"Instinct, in fact, is always an act which seems to be in accordance with the conception of an end, and yet is entirely without such a conception. Nature implants it wherever the acting individual is incapable of understanding the end, or would be unwilling to pursue it. . . .

"The longing of love which the poets of all ages are unceasingly occupied with expressing in innumerable forms, and do not exhaust the subject, nay, cannot do it justice, this longing which attaches the idea of endless happiness to the possession of a particular woman, and unutterable pain to the thought that this possession cannot be attained—this longing and this pain cannot arise from the wants of an ephemeral individual; they are the sighs of the spirit of the species, which sees here, to be won or lost, a means for the attainment of its ends which cannòt be replaced."

The high degree of idealisation which takes place when a man or a woman is possessed by great love, is, as we see, regarded by Schopenhauer as a mere illusion, the spell cast by Nature upon Man in order to attain its ends in the propagation of the species. That love is important to the race is evident, just as its private importance to the individual is beyond question. But has it not also an importance which Schopenhauer overlooked, to wit, importance from the point of view of the Collective Spirit?

Obviously, we cannot all, like Dante or Petrarch, transpose our love into immortal verse and thus hand over our happiness and pain to posterity for ever. But even though love be, among ordinary mortals, a private affair, or at the utmost an affair of the race, it may at any rate be indirectly of importance to the Collective Spirit in awakening the individual to the fact that higher worlds exist. It is not only the scientist, artist or philosopher who can ascend Olympus; we can all rise to those heights, for we all have the idealising power within us, only awaiting the opportunity to make itself manifest.

Love is, strange as it may seem, a one-sided thing . . . when I love, the loving proceeds from myself; and so unrequited love is often the strongest; for the whole thing depends on *my* idealisation. We are often surprised to see a handsome and accomplished man infatuated by an apparently insignificant girl or *vice versa*. But we are apt to forget that the object of our affections does not create the passion in us, but only calls it forth. The lover is a Narcissus, in love with his own reflection. Each of us has his own ideal of beauty; and when we fall in love, it is this ideal that attracts us, rather than the individual who personifies it.

As regards the distribution of the idealising power between the two sexes, it is evident that woman is specially gifted with that part which expresses itself as love, whereas the artistic and scientific form of idealising power are less developed in her. Her work in the cause of the Collective Spirit is thus more indirect than man's, though by no means altogether insignificant, as Otto Weininger would have us believe.

Love gives us proof that morality is not the highest thing on earth; ordinary morality *may* be suspended for a time and replaced by another code. Great love bursts all bounds of morality, and makes, as Schopenhauer says, an otherwise honest man unscrupulous, the once loyal man a traitor. " All's fair in love and war."—In love at least a particular code of morals obtains, that of sex, which is often in direct opposition to the general.

Hence arise many conflicts and collisions, in regard to which the Church reveals a complete lack of understanding. According to the laws of the Church, any breach of the marriage bond, any form of free love, adultery, etc., should be regarded as a mortal sin. This merciless code, however, is fortunately not accepted by the majority of mankind.

In H. G. Wells' novel, *The Dream*, there is a wife who has committed adultery—she has been unfaithful to her husband while he was on active service, and she is about to have a child. The husband acts as he is expected to do according to the ordinary code of morals. Though he loves his wife and realises that she loves him in spite of all, he taunts her with her shame and leaves his home, to marry another woman whom he does not really love. Too late he sees that he has acted in a manner as barbarous as it was foolish; he has followed the line laid down by a social code and thereby destroyed the happiness of two individuals. But the Church would approve his action, because he followed the accepted code; the Church would say he was right.

The stubborn attitude of the Church on this question arises from the view that all sexual intercourse is in reality a fall from grace, a sin that smirches the immortal soul; and as a logical consequence of this view, the Church of Rome, and many others, have imposed celibacy on their priests and priestesses. In this connection also we may mention the embittered opposition of the Church toward all forms of birth control, artificial prevention of motherhood, artificial fertilisation and the like. The Church has had to sanction the institution of marriage, but it will go no farther; any other form of sexual intercourse is banned; and marriage itself is required to be permanent and indissoluble. All this is really due to the fact that the Church is solely concerned with the future welfare of the *individual* in another world, and leaves us to get on as best we can in this.

Humaner public opinion has risen in protest against this narrow view. Love between man and woman is regarded as the highest law. Love must have its way, even though it be in opposition to the laws of Church and State; and it may still be ethically right.

Here, it seems to us, there is a weakness in our ethics. There is not one morality, there are two; a code of Church and State, and a code of sex. The latter shows that life here on earth is the main consideration, all other laws must give way to the principle of love. The Church has also had to give way a little here, in admitting divorce, and even aiding in the union of divorced persons. The claims of life have here conquered those of the Church. The code of the Church has had to give way to the code of sex, and the purely worldly character, the relativity, of morality is emphasised thereby. Morality is not a divine but a human institution, a form of spiritual hygiene, designed, not to secure immortality for the individual and eternal bliss for the individual, but to provide a foundation on earth whereby the individual can exert his creative powers in the service of the Collective Spirit. Morality is a means, not an end, and if the means gets in our way, we make short work of it without scruple.

What we have said above may perhaps be formulated briefly as follows: Ethically speaking, we are possessed by two different instincts. One is that of the accepted moral code, which says: a promise once given must never be broken; happen what may, a man must keep his word. The other is the code of sex, which says: A promise may be broken under certain circumstances; to wit, when the happiness of lovers is in question.

This latter code, earthly as it may seem, is, nevertheless,

the higher of the two. A Chinese proverb expresses the supremacy of the sex code by saying : The smile of a beautiful woman destroys cities and realms. And so indeed it is, and this shows us as plainly as could be wished that social morality is not the ultimate aim of evolution. It may be useful, it may be predominant, but it may, and must, at times be suspended in favour of a higher.—It need hardly be added that any appeal to the code of sex as a cloak for looseness and licentiousness is an abuse, and as such to be condemned, not least by the code of sex itself.

We have seen that when great Eros enters on the scene, there is always a very high degree of idealisation, which, as it were, lifts the individual to a higher and more splendid world. But such idealisation may also occur on other occasions when something great is at stake. In cases of personal danger, great joy or sorrow, strong emotion, in the enjoyment of great art, in all unselfish action, in our memories of childhood, in the solving of difficult problems, in all supreme effort, we feel this idealising power. We are carried away by the powerful current of Nature and uplifted by it.

Ludvig Feilberg has given numerous fine and striking examples of this fact. In one case, on revisiting his former home, he tells how the growth of trees newly planted in his childhood gave him a sudden appreciation of Nature's development. The same process at work in the neighbouring village was less directly apparent. But if a geologist showed him the strata on the spot, he would again perceive something of the marvellous course of evolution, a glimpse of something great and splendid passing by.

The one thing that makes life so rich and wonderful in itself, helping us through all adversity, is this feeling that we live in an ideal world, a world of constant progress.

When we go out into the country on a fine summer's day, and rejoice in all the beauty we find there, our pleasure is due to the fact that we recognise in Nature a series of examples of Nature's idealising power, instances of the same process we can feel at work within ourselves. When we enjoy a good book, or feel the spell of quiet halls where the great art of the world is preserved, looking down on us from every side, or when we are engaged in the laboratory on some contribution to the solution of great scientific problems, we feel the same thing ; a glimpse of the spirit, transporting us to the world of ideals. And when, despite former disillusions, we follow the impulse to help some poor fellow-creature at some cost to ourselves, though we may be convinced the other does not deserve it, we cannot but feel a little of the same uplifting ; be it ever so little, we are lifted some way above the level of the ordinary.

We are creatures of little magnitude by the standard of the universe, but from our insignificant outlook we can yet discern the stars. Science, art and morality offer us three ways which we can safely follow if we would share in the evolution that is taking place around us.

The ultimate aim of it all, the crystal world of the Collective Spirit, in which all the noblest, most beautiful and most concentrated products of evolution are comprised, is something we ourselves shall never see. But we can, in the great moments of life, have some inkling of what is to come ; we can feel the processes of Nature in which we partake, and if we strive to aid them, instead of hindering, we feel within ourselves a calm and content, a confidence and hope, that are our reward as faithful servants.

CRITICAL OBSERVATIONS ON THE IDEALISTIC THEORY OF EVOLUTION

It is impossible to prove anything.—Pyrrho.

IT was a principle of etiquette in Corea that persons admitted to the presence of the Emperor were required to tremble all over throughout the duration of the audience, by way of showing their respect for imperial majesty. It will, we fear, be only too plainly evident that we have exhibited similar tremors in our exposition of the idealistic theory of Evolution.

When confronted with the Emperor—or in the present instance, with the whole army of science, which has attained such imposing results on a mechanistic and deterministic basis, it is not to be wondered at that a mere indeterminist should feel his insignificance, having nothing himself to offer beyond philosophy, that philosophy of which it has been said that it could never prove anything, since nothing could ever be proved by anything at all.

The Emperor sees through it all at once and lays a kindly, condescending hand on our shoulder, saying with an indulgent smile:

"My dear young friend, consider the experience of others, and be wise! Have we not had proof enough that the days of speculative philosophy are numbered? Why dig up old bones? Even inductive metaphysics will still be metaphysics. Think of the rapid strides made in the field of natural science, due to the fact that we have put aside all philosophical speculation and keep resolutely to the *terra firma* of experience, more prosaic, it may be, but for that very reason all the surer! Look at science, young man. Science can point to the most marvellous results already; and it is well on the way to making us—well, if not gods at any rate supermen, lordly beings who have but to press a button and the elements obey their lightest wish, who can defy the limitations of time and space with wonders out-doing the Arabian Nights. The scientist of to-day is the true representative of the will to power; it is the principle of his creed; he lives in a world beyond good and evil—*jenseits von Gut und Böse*. Aim and purpose? He cares for none of these things. The meaning and relation of things are all his care; he alone is endowed with true superiority, for he sees through life's illusion; he knows that this world of ours is only a piece of clockwork going round according to regular laws, and that individuals acting, as they fondly believe, of their own free will, are no more free than the iron filings moving toward the magnet; that evolution is only a semblance of development, that all is predetermined, and evolution itself, having expanded to the full, must contract again; he can reduce all phenomena to atoms and motion, he knows that truth is relative, and all talk of positive progress mere foolishness. Learn of him, young man; for only so can you gain admission to a privileged society, the circle of the truly wise, the exclusively initiate, who can utter the shibboleth of scepticism. Nobody cares to be laughed at; and laughed at you will be if you declare your faith in some vague creative principle of existence. A form of energy creating from within, yet not physical energy, but only a creative impulse, not even conscious of itself, but only following a general tendency, with aims that seem to shift as it goes on, an unconscious artistic and moral idealising power—but with conscious expression—from the point of view of science, this is sheer insanity! A creative power can find no place in the laws of Nature; and there is no room for it in the world of matter. Once we begin to compromise with occult principles of this sort, we shall simply be mingling faith and reason, a sure sign either of religious mania or of softening of the brain. Let the masses believe what they please; we scientists have our noble scepticism, and we are prouder of it than of the imperial purple. Science has fought for centuries against theology; and you offer us a new theology, camouflaged in the guise of science."

Certainly, the Idealistic Theory of Evolution is open to criticism on many sides, and from many different points of view.

It is immediately apparent as a weak point in the new doctrine that it seeks to replace the Darwinian theory of evolution (even granting this to be incorrect) by another which, to say the least, is still more complicated. It is unfortunate that the prime mover of the new doctrine should be a hardly definable creative power, a power indicated by turns as creative, mutative, idealising and refining, which, despite its many names, is hardly amenable to experimental investigation in any laboratory. It is not easy to get hold of this mystic power, which appears everywhere as anonymous, but has nevertheless exerted enormous influence, a power first apparent in the world of matter, then shifting up to a higher plane and manifesting itself as life, to reappear finally in the world of mind; situate in the brain of the individual, yet not so much for the benefit of the individual as for the creation of a new and highly problematical world: The Collective Spirit.

Must not this appear to many, and especially to men of science, as a mere figment of the brain? Can we ever conceive mind pure and simple, mind having no connection with individuals of flesh and blood, dissociated from all feeling and desire, from joy and pain, from questioning and action? We cannot imagine a being of mind alone; or at best, such a being will be so far removed from all likeness to ourselves that we can only set it down as a religious speculation. Each one of us has, if not a soul, at least something we call a soul, a synthesis of perceptions and consciousness, a centre where all mind-impressions meet. But where is the soul that can gather up in itself all the infinite store of knowledge and art, emotion and morality which are to be united in the Collective Spirit? We can only imagine such things in connection with the individual mind.

There has been a tendency among philosophers of recent times to make philosophy a special science, employing the same exact, critical and inductive methods as the other sciences. Men are still seeking to establish a scientific psychology, a science of ethics and a science of æsthetics; though with little success hitherto. These endeavours are based upon a love of truth, a distaste of all that savours of guesswork, postulates and assertions beyond proof—and this in itself is all to the good. But an error lies in the method; for the customary scientific mode of procedure cannot be employed when dealing with the creative power. Scientists here have committed the fundamental error of closing their eyes to the existence of the creative power and regarding the world as *determined solely by automatism.* This may be justifiable enough in ordinary sciences, or at any rate desirable where it is required to ascertain the relations between phenomena which can be predetermined and checked. Technical science must base its researches on experiments which can be tested, that is to say, repeated; but the creative power never repeats itself, and is thus not amenable to the usual methods of testing. Evolution, creative evolution, means the constant creation of something new, that is, the production of a result amounting to more than the sum of the factors which produce it. Evolution cannot be reversed, cannot be repeated, and thus cannot be proved, in the ordinary scientific sense of the word. And this is why the ordinary methods of technical science are inadequate for the consideration of evolution as a whole, and especially of its latest and greatest results, the phenomena of mind.

Several of the exact philosophers have been forced to admit that the customary method could not be applied in the case of all phenomena, as those of ethics, æsthetics and evolution could not be placed under the microscope. But instead of abolishing the method and finding another, they endeavoured to solve the difficulty by declaring that there must be two sorts of truth. Astounding as it may seem, it has, since the days of Kant, become the custom to assert that truth is not one, but two; there is a scientific truth, based on pure reason, and another, that of practical common sense, which concerns itself with ideas of value, especially ethical values. That the two forms of truth are constantly coming in conflict with each other apparently does not matter! Pure reason says one thing, practical reason another. By way of example we may mention, that pure reason, according to Kant, teaches us that there is no aim in existence, whereas practical reason admits the doctrine of teleology.

One would think that honest seekers after truth would rebel against such Jesuitical dualism and demand one truth valid for all ideas. But this is by no means the case. On the contrary, we repeatedly find this dualism in philosophical works. Only that part of the world which can be comprehended by pure reason is recognised as scientific. The field of science is subjected to limitations. This may be permissible in science, which can be tested in laboratories, but as regards philosophy it is indefensible. The very aim of philosophy must be to give us an interpretation of the universe based, not on *some* facts, but on *all*, comprising all phenomena, theoretical as well as practical, real and ideal.

It is, we cannot but think, first and foremost the duty of philosophy to show us the relation between ourselves and the apparently chaotic world about us. To do so was the aim of the great natural philosophers. But they did not succeed, because they had no knowledge of evolution. The doctrine of evolution is the line which links up all phenomena, and the greatest asset philosophy has ever had; only now that we possess it can we hope for a true interpretation of the universe.

The theory of evolution has placed the so-called scientific philosophers in a serious quandary. The mechanists tried to get out of it by transposing, or rather reducing, all phenomena to states of motion. The vitalists have endeavoured to give us an interpretation of evolution, and thus of the universe, by postulating a vital force aiming only at the maintenance and continuance of life to infinity, without distinguishing between purely primary, temporary forms of life and the most highly developed forms as found in the human mind. But the mechanistic and vitalistic theories of evolution reckon only with part of the facts, not with all, inasmuch as both neglect the spiritual or ideal.

It is these last which the idealistic theory of evolution especially considers. If we take all the stages and factors of

IDEALISTIC THEORY OF EVOLUTION

evolution: material, biological and spiritual, from the lowest to the highest, then the idealistic theory of evolution must be the result. If we investigate the idea of evolution, we are inevitably led to the idea of value. Here for the first time we have the irrefutable proof that pure reason and practical reason are united. The bond of union between them is—evolution.

Briefly, the theory of evolution says that an imperishable world of mind, the Collective Spirit, is in process of formation, by refinement, to take the place of the perishable physical world. Or, in other words, the physical world is giving birth to a spiritual world, which is a copy of itself but in a finer, and imperishable form.

Such a process naturally cannot take place purely mechanically, there must be some non-mechanical ferment to explain it, an element which, for lack of a better term, we have called the creative power. We are obliged to reckon with this element, for, as Dr. Richard Eriksen writes, we cannot explain life and mind by mechanism and matter alone. Dr. Eriksen writes:

"Inertia can only explain its own continued existence; it cannot explain its origin or alteration. In other words, mechanical matter cannot explain itself to the full, far less life or spirit. All attempts to derive life or mind from mechanical matter have proved fruitless, save when life or mind is somehow smuggled into matter beforehand. The mechanical processes can thus only represent one side—the external side—of existence. Even chemical processes cannot be wholly explained mechanically. We may formulate the position by saying that chemical processes comprise mechanical processes but cannot be reduced to these alone. Similarly, we may say that biological processes comprise mechanical and chemical processes but cannot be reduced to these alone. And finally, the psychological processes introduce a further element, which cannot be derived from mechanical, chemical and biological processes alone. In this connection, mechanism appears as a far more subordinate factor in existence than we should have imagined. . . .

"Furthermore, we can see all along how the vital and psychological processes become mechanised; but we never find purely mechanical processes becoming organic or conscious."

And this is just the point. Through all the stages of evolution we find a new element coming in, something which was not there before, and thus must have been created on the way. There must be a non-mechanical, non-vital, non-spiritual Something, which intervenes and carries the process further. This unknown quantity we call the creative power. We use the word power in preference to the word force, for force is a purely physical term, and power better expresses the idea.

It is characteristic of exact philosophy that its exponents are forced to ignore all artistic, ethical and ideal manifestations, that is to say, all aspects in which the creative power has not given place to automatism. Creation is simply denied, and the term creative power must be an empty phrase, an unscientific postulate. We can expect nothing else from this point of view.

But the point of view is itself erroneous. Exact philosophy maintains to begin with, as Huxley did, that all phenomena have existed from the beginning. And when we bring forward the theory of evolution, and argue that evolution can only be explained as a continued series of creative processes, the answer is that only automatism can be scientifically proved, and if anything does exist beyond automatism, it is no concern of science. The philosopher here ignores the fact that he is thus declaring all evolution, indeed, the universe itself, unscientific, for if a part of it be so, then the whole must be, since all parts are inter-related. Unscientific! It is unscientific when a poet writes a poem, that is to say, brings into the world something which was not there before. It is unscientific, but it is a fact. And to deny creation here is to deny facts. The determinist philosopher here speaks with unction of the resignation to be cultivated by devotees of the exact sciences—a resignation, alas, which but too often serves as a comfortable excuse for the little philosophical mind that lacks all wider outlook, lacks the power of combination and interpretation which Plato and Aristotle regarded as the most important qualifications of a philosopher.

The exact philosophers shirk their work. Fearing to encounter difficulties, they shut their eyes to them, and instead of grappling with problems, they leave them in the hands of the technical experts. Philosophy is thus reduced to a mere catalogue, a list of the data communicated by the special sciences, indexed as they come in, without comment. The philosophers may be right in asserting that the special sciences will in course of time attain such a degree of perfection that philosophical problems will be solved automatically, and the interpretation of the universe will be afforded by a mere reading of the scientific results. But is it consistent with the dignity of a philosopher to await this consummation and meanwhile do nothing but look on? Should not philosophy be active, should it not seek to further the process of interpretation by assisting science not only as an amanuensis, but as itself an interpreter? We think it should be so. It is a well-known fact that the results of research in one branch of science may bear fruit in their influence upon scientists working in quite different fields. And similarly, the far-seeing philosopher, considering phenomena together, may be able to discern certain lines of direction invisible to the specialist operating only in his own limited field. Philosophy may thus be a real aid to science. It is a centre which should not only collect but also sum up and interpret results, co-operate with the special sciences. Philosophy can render little service to science by too modestly declaring itself of no value.

The criterion of any philosophical system is its agreement with reality, its inner logic, its extent and power of development. All systems hitherto have failed in one or other of these points. We offer here a new system. There are many gaps in it, and in its newness it may well be subject to infantile diseases. But mind itself is comparatively new to earth, and subject to the same.

We are well aware that our interpretation will have difficulties to encounter, for it is fighting on two fronts, against the scepticism of science on the one hand and the opposition of the Church on the other.

The scientist will doubtless object that our system is

anthropomorphic; that we have attributed human qualities to nature and evolution. We admit quite frankly that this is the case. But is not all our science more or less anthropomorphic? What science offers us as objective is always found, on critical examination, to be a more or less successful attempt at disguising our own thoughts so that they seem to come from without, from above or from below, as long as it be not from man. All this is illusion. Science cannot get out of its anthropomorphic skin, however it may try. The idealistic theory of evolution does not partake in this comedy. We comfort ourselves with the thought that in judging of things from the point of view of humanity, we cannot go very far wrong, since we ourselves are a part of Nature, and it cannot be altogether alien to our mind. Anthropomorphism is a thing to be proud of. At any rate, we are likely to get farther when we begin from the basis of the human mind, than when we try, as science, for fear of anthropomorphism, often does, to adopt a biological or mechanical point of view; that is, to argue from what we imagine such a point of view would be. Even a double somersault of this sort cannot do away with the subjective element. The would-be objective scientist goes on describing a footprint in the sand, arguing about it and about, without discovering that it is his own. It is more honest to admit that we cannot go anywhere without leaving a mark.

From the religious point of view, objections will be raised more particularly against our idea of the Ego, which will also be liable to misinterpretation. Does the idealistic theory of evolution really mean to suggest that the Ego is simply a grammatical invention? It is all very well to talk ironically of man as the centre of the universe; but could we live our lives at all if it were otherwise? Is it not ridiculous to set, as Lichtenberg does, in place of " I think " the form " It thinks "? Or to maintain, with Mach, that the only realities are our perceptions, whose closer connection in one individual than another is the only reason for distinguishing between individuals?

We answer, that we do not deny the existence of an Ego in man, any more than in an animal—an Ego developed to a higher or lower degree. The spiritual Ego is, as the bearer

IDEALISTIC THEORY OF EVOLUTION

of spiritual qualities, a practical unity, and without this unity, man could not live as man. The Ego is therefore a reality, but only as long as the body, to which the mind is linked, continues to exist.

As regards the interaction of mind and body, the idealistic theory of evolution does not venture to offer an account; it must be left to the scientist to throw light on this subject by experiment, as indeed on the activity of the creative spirit individually and as a whole. The Ego is not a grammatical invention, but an invention of the creative power, a practical arrangement; it is not, however, in itself the aim of evolution, but only a means to attain the end. Lichtenberg and Mach go too far in substituting " It thinks " for " I think." There is certainly an Ego, a spiritual individuality, though it may not be so firmly and clearly defined as that of the body. There is no complete parallelism between the physical and the spiritual Ego. If such were the case, then the Ego as a whole would be subject to automatism, leaving no scope for the action of the creative power. When a human child is born, it is already a physical whole, but its spiritual personality is present only potentially; it has yet to grow. And from the point of view of mind we are always growing. At what point the spiritual Ego reaches its culmination of development it is not easy to determine; often it is not until late in life, and the Ego then is an amalgam, containing a small percentage of the individual, and a high percentage of the common mind.

This Ego is designed to serve two ends; quite practically, to look after the body, to maintain and preserve it; and spiritually, to raise the individual to an ideal world. It is characteristic of great men that their activity amounts to an escape from the individual to the supra-individual, through the medium of science, art or morality. The greater the Ego in itself, the less it will be concerned with itself and the more it will be interested in all others. The Ego tends to efface itself, a tendency which culminates in complete self-sacrifice, as we find it in the case of martyrs to any cause. This shows plainly enough that the Ego is in the service of higher powers. Every human being is born and brought up in the belief that he is a general commanding. Actually, he is only a private in the ranks. Our place in the economy of Nature has been defined once and for all by Feilberg; we are transformers of energy.

The scientist may object to the speculative nature of our work, and point out that we merely bring forward hypotheses, instead of letting facts speak for themselves. But it is a mistake to believe that speculation is not resorted to in scientific work. Speculation, in this connection, simply means constructing some hypothesis on the basis of conclusions from a series of facts. Such hypothesis may on consideration prove to be insecurely founded; it may prove to be wrong because it has been wrongly constructed. But it may also prove correct, and bear fruit in the impulse to further investigation. All great scientists have worked from hypotheses. Modern atomic research is based on hypothesis, and so is the study of light, and so is the invention of wireless telegraphy. Edison's inventions were not the result of accident, but of a speculation which proved correct.

And we now put forward our conception of the creative power and the Collective Spirit as a hypothesis, in the belief that science cannot dispense with its aid in the interpretation of evolution.

Philosophy has received from science the theory of evolution, and has found in it a key to all the problems of philosophy, including that of existence. So important is this material, that we have no hesitation in asserting that philosophers of the future will have to devote their attention principally to the study and interpretation of the doctrine of evolution.

The idealistic theory of evolution is an attempt in this direction. It is concerned with evolution and nothing else. Our theory does not aim at any profound metaphysical explanation of existence. It describes a process of Nature, sets out a series of facts in their order, and interprets the whole as a refining process. It says, in effect: The course of evolution up to date has, as the data shows, tended in the direction of mind. And since we can still observe this tendency continuing, through millions of different channels, with increasing force, we are led to postulate the Collective Spirit as the next stage of evolution in the future. But as to the ultimate meaning of this process and its resultant Collective Spirit, we do not venture to offer any suggestion. Our purpose is only to sum up and interpret, not to give reasons why. The reader must then decide for himself how far the results we have arrived at are suitable for the foundation of a view of life.

The idealistic theory of evolution does not deal with metaphysics in the stricter sense of the word; but we think it may nevertheless be of some importance in a general sense as a substitute for metaphysics. As we noted in the introductory chapter, there are two kinds of metaphysics nowadays. On the one hand, there is the scientific and entirely negative view which holds that we know nothing whatever as to the aims of evolution, and that scepticism is the only permissible attitude of mind towards the riddle of the universe. On the other hand, we have a religious feeling supported by the so-called revealed religions, promising its adherents eternal life in a better world if they will but fulfil certain requisite conditions in this. These two points of view, however, cannot in the long run satisfy those who, unprejudiced either by scientific scepticism or Church dogma, seek for unity in the universe. It is not a sign of spiritual sanity to assert that we must crucify reason in order to attain to faith; and that the harder we find it to do so, the greater will be our gain. This is merely a paradox.

The task of the future will be, not to widen the gulf between knowledge and faith, but on the contrary, to bridge it. Our endeavours should tend in the direction of finding a connection between the phenomena of the external world and the ideal forces which we perceive at work within ourselves, the powers which urge us on. Once we have understood this relation between external and internal, we have no need of more profound metaphysics. And it is an explanation of this relation which the idealistic theory of evolution offers, vague and imperfect though it may be as yet. We realise then that we are evolutionary products of a process tending toward higher aims, and that it is to our own interest to work with, and not against that process, that is, to contribute what we can in the way of help.

Every spiritually conscious human being has certain duties towards himself; he must first of all *live* his life, learn to know it practically by taking part in it as actively as possible; but he has also some theoretical duties as well. He must familiarise himself to the best of his ability with the history of mankind, especially the development of culture and science, he must learn something of the language and views of other nations, visit other countries if he can, and emancipate himself from national prejudices, as befits a citizen of the world; and, finally, he has to *formulate for himself his own view of life.* It is this last point in particular which offers serious difficulties, even to well-informed and accomplished people. Many of the best among us consider it hopeless to find a definite personal attitude towards life, and simply accept one or other of the two generally acknowledged authorities, science or religion. They may feel that both these are only provisional, but they do not attempt to work out for themselves a personal view from the data given.

It is this which the idealistic theory of evolution endeavours to do. We start from the fundamental consideration that though the world may be divided into many worlds this way and that, though there may be many scientific and technical truths, though evolution has proceeded through numerous stages, and two prime forces such as creative power and automatism are constantly interacting, there must yet be one single truth comprehending all, a line of purpose linking all phenomena. There must be some bridge between ourselves and Nature. Natural philosophy provides this bridge. Here science and religion meet in a higher unity.

From the University chair and the pulpit of the Church protests may be raised against the idealistic theory of evolution. It will, perhaps, be urged from both sides that it is entirely superfluous; science will condemn it as unscientific, and the Church will say: We asked for bread, and you give us a stone. More especially, the Collective Spirit will be regarded as a product of mysticism, now equivalent to a sort of glorified public opinion, now to a kind of spectral figure floating at large in the universe. But what is our earth itself at the moment, but such a spectral figure? The difficulty

IDEALISTIC THEORY OF EVOLUTION

in assimilating the idea of the Collective Spirit lies in the fact that we human beings still persist in regarding existence from our own little point of view, and can only slowly rise to a higher outlook. It will still, perhaps, be long before the feeling of human solidarity has grown to such a degree that our common endeavours can unite in building the temple of mind for layman and learned, the central edifice whose pillars rise high above university and Church alike. But we are not discouraged; for we know that when a new truth is being brought into the world, the world, according to the law of automatism, offers resistance to the utmost of its power.

We are firmly convinced that sooner or later, the idea of the Collective Spirit will be triumphant. Neither barren scepticism nor anæmic religious dreamings will be able to hold the field in the long run; for both these make for pessimism in the end, both are inimical to life. The future belongs to those of brighter view and higher courage, who in the midst of all adversity hold fast by their faith in *this life;* who realise that their task lies here, on earth.

If there really were, as religion asserts, an all-wise God, a beneficent Providence, guiding the steps of man and of the universe, then all would be easy and simple enough and very different from what it is. Such a God would not tolerate all the injustice, suffering and waste attendant on the struggle for life. If there be any God behind it all, concealed in the creative power or in Nature, then it must be any rate be a God of quite a different type from the Father-God which the Church would thrust upon us; for there is certainly nothing fatherly, in the human sense, about it.

The difficulties which mankind, in common with all living things, has to encounter, are plainly due to the fact that we are not Nature's aim, but only an instrument of Nature's purpose. Each individual human being desires happiness for himself; peace, health, pleasure in life, a comfortable existence, various enjoyments—but Nature has designed us for quite other things. It does not wish us to settle down in comfortable content; on the contrary it lashes us to effort and struggle, subjects us to the utmost pressure in order to extract the last degree of energy for its own purpose, to wit, the creation of mind; mind condensed through the struggle against matter and against ourselves. If we do not voluntarily obey, it tortures us with remorse, pains of conscience, dulness and boredom and weariness of life. Just as our body is punished by sickness and debility if we do not keep it in proper training, so also our mind is subject to countless ills if we do not follow the rule of Nature and exert ourselves to pay tribute to Nature's store of mind.

In one way, we may say that our development takes place against our will—for our own little inclination is rather towards creature comforts and ease, whereas that of Nature urges us on to work and sacrifice. We have in ourselves different natures constantly at strife—a thing which would be inconceivable if a beneficent Father had created us and were ever at hand to guide us.

It is not to be wondered at that in this "Age of Confusion" there should arise pessimists seeing only the darker side of life. Our business is to enter the lists with them, on the ground of evolution; we must strive towards a higher view. By a right interpretation of evolution, and by this alone can we formulate a philosophy of happiness. A nice sort of happiness! some may exclaim. But, after all, is it so little? A doctrine based on evolution, on development, demonstrating progress achieved, slow and painful though it be, from chaos to our own ordered world, and pointing forward to an inconceivably great and beautiful future for the spirit of man, ever seeking to realise ideals, and setting up Hope as humanity's most precious possession—may we not call this a philosophy of happiness after all? Let sceptics and bigots and doubting spirits and pessimists oppose it, grant it is as yet a mere hypothesis, frail in construction, imperfectly formed and expounded, strange and incomprehensible, positively displeasing even to many, it will nevertheless appeal to some at the present time, and to ever-increasing numbers in the future.

The idealistic theory of evolution, as a contribution to philosophy, may be summed up as follows:

It points to the probability that evolution is a process of Nature due to an activity which we have called the creative power. This activity, which science will have to investigate and elucidate further, created first the forces of Nature, then life, and finally mind; and it is at present operating through the medium of individual human beings for the production of a common store of mind.

Every time the creative power produces a material, this is at once handed over to automatism, which maintains it for a time, but is incapable of doing so indefinitely. It is, therefore, not only the forces of Nature which are doomed ultimately to perish by dissipation of energy, but the whole earth and all its creatures : plants, animals and man.

The only thing that seems imperishable is the common store of mind, the noblest of Nature's products ; for this is non-material and non-individual. It must therefore be assumed that when all else perishes, this will live on as mind alone ; the common store of mind will become the Collective Spirit.

Evolution on this earth is seen to be an idealising or refining process, the material once given being subjected to a degree of refinement at each successive stage.

The problem of understanding arises from the fact that we, as beings endowed with mind, can only view phenomena through the medium of mind, though the majority of phenomena are not of the nature of mind, but only approximating to it, products of refinement checked at a lower stage. Our power of understanding phenomena is, therefore, more or less perfect according as they are nearer or farther removed from our own stage, that of mind.

The creative and idealising power in the individual condenses in the form of art and science when it is directed outward, and in the form of morality when directed inward. Thus science, art and morality are naturally connected as forms of the same activity.

The idealistic theory of evolution points out that man is not an immortal soul but merely a transformer of energy, an instrument utilised by the creative power. Man is an intermediate stage leading not to superman on earth or angels in heaven, but to the Collective Spirit. Man is not an end but a means to an end, and for this very reason he has certain obligations. We are the servants of a process of Nature, and when we do not obey its behests, but hinder its operations, we are punished as disobedient servants. If, on the other hand, we aid the process, we have our reward in spiritual health and growth, and consequent content and joy in life.

The foregoing is based on ideas first put forward by the Danish philosopher Ludvig Feilberg, and it is fitting, therefore, to acknowledge our debt to him as the true founder of the idealistic theory of evolution.

In one of the galleries at the Vatican, the walls are painted with a series of maps showing how the geographers of the Renaissance imagined the outlines of sea and land. Compared with modern maps they look oddly misshapen and awry, almost childishly drawn. These maps nevertheless formed the foundation of our own, and an imperfect map is better than none at all.

The idealistic theory of evolution may be compared to one of these preliminary attempts. It will be improved as philosophy and science discover new data.

And now we have put forward all our arguments. Will they prove convincing?

The confirmation which comes from the reader's heart is the most important in the long run. Many will perhaps, at first, find it difficult to relinquish the last frail thread that holds us to a faith in personal immortality; to offer up, as it were, personality itself on the altar of the Collective Spirit. It will need nothing less than a revolution in the sphere of mind before this view can be generally established.

We are of opinion that such a revolution has long been preparing, and that it is inevitable. Evolution itself speaks plainly enough, and the truth of its doctrine finds an echo in ourselves.

What the present age lacks in the sphere of metaphysics is spiritual unity. A member of the French Academy once exclaimed: "Where, O Soul, canst thou find a place between brutal materialism and unintelligent religion?" Mankind

IDEALISTIC THEORY OF EVOLUTION

is divided into two camps: that of the agnostics, who have given up all hope of finding a meaning in existence, and the steadily decreasing company of the orthodox believers. There is a space here waiting to be filled. The world is at last ripe for a creed as far removed from the chill and barren scepticism of the determinists as from the childish myths and dogmas of the Church.

For Product Safety Concerns and Information please contact our EU
representative GPSR@taylorandfrancis.com
Taylor & Francis Verlag GmbH, Kaufingerstraße 24, 80331 München, Germany

www.ingramcontent.com/pod-product-compliance
Lightning Source LLC
Chambersburg PA
CBHW061440300426
44114CB00014B/1776